The Cultural Literacy Trivia Guide

Written by:
Steven J. Ferrill

Edited by:
Bill Moushéy
and
Jeannie Gibbons

With special thanks to:
Connie Ferrill, Kathy Brumbaugh and Mike Nolan

ISBN Number 1-893937-03-8

Printed in the United States by
Independent Publishing Corporation
St. Louis, Missouri 63011

For Sara Jean
And Seth Joseph
The great joys in my life

TABLE OF CONTENTS

Preface

1. Abbreviations 8
2. Also Known As 13
3. Ancient History 16
4. The Animal Kingdom 18
5. Anniversary Gifts 26
6. Architecture 27
7. Art and Artists 28
8. Astronomy and Space 32
9. Awards 35
10. The Bible 36
11. Black History 39
12. Business and Industry 41
13. Celebrity Relatives 44
14. Cinema 46
15. Cities 61
16. Civil War 65
17. Colleges and Universities 67
18. Composers 70
19. Countries 75
20. Dance 110
21. Explorers, Inventors, Discoverers 112
22. Famous Names 116
23. Familiar Quotes 120
24. Fashion 125
25. Food 127
26. Geology 130
27. Holidays and Observances 132
28. Human Body 134
29. Languages 138
30. Latin Phrases 139
31. Literature 141

32. Music 164

33. Mythology 171

34. Native Americans 175

35. Newspapers and Magazines 177

36. Notorious People 180

37. Organizations 182

38. The Plant Kingdom 184

39. Plays and Playwrights 187

40. Poets and Poetry 190

41. Potent Potables 193

42. Presidents, Vice Presidents and First Ladies 195

43. Religion 210

44. Revolutionary War 213

45. The Roman Empire 214

46. Royalty 216

47. Saints 221

48. Science 222

49. The Seven Wonders of the World 226

50. Shakespeare 227

51. Ships 232

52. Sickness and Health 234

53. Sports 237

54. Television 246

55. U.S. Government 251

56. U.S. History 256

57. U.S. States and Territories 262

58. United Nations 281

59. Women 282

60. World Geography 285

61. World War I 293

62. World War II 294

63. Zodiac 296

PREFACE

Cultural literacy is a very important part of the trivia craze that came into prominence with the Trivial Pursuit phenomenon of the early 1980s. One advantage of increasing your cultural literacy is that you will be armed with the knowledge you will need to compete in any one of the cerebral contests that have become so much a part of American culture. *Who Wants to be a Millionaire?, Jeopardy!, Win Ben Stein's Money, History IQ,* College Bowl and Trivial Pursuit are just a few of the many quiz shows and games in which one may compete with a high degree of success if one is culturally literate. If you are a person who finds these contests intellectually stimulating, fun, and/or profitable, this book is for you. By studying the categories listed herein, you will greatly enhance your chances of ending up in the winner's circle.

I walked a very fine line while compiling the information in this book. If I had included both information commonly known by the typical high school graduate, and information known only by individuals with expertise in specific fields, the book would have become unmanageably large and difficult to study. What I have decided to include in this book is what I term "information on the periphery of common knowledge." For example, under the heading of World War II, the names of Franklin Delano Roosevelt, Joseph Stalin and Winston Churchill are not listed as leaders of their respective countries because this is common knowledge. On the other hand, military leaders whose ranks are below those of the generals and admirals have not been included because the information is too trivial to be included in most of the competitions listed above. I drew upon personal experience when considering which information to include and which to leave out. I have competed in hundreds of trivia night competitions, local and regional college bowls, and I seldom miss a quiz show on the radio or television. I have spent years paying close attention to the categories and the types of questions most commonly asked.

Another consideration when writing this book was how to make the information accessible to any individual who wishes to learn the greatest amount of information in the shortest period of time. The solution is a format that I call "the most obvious answer." For example, look under the Countries chapter in this book, and find Norway. For the clue, "Composer", you will see only one answer. There have been many composers from Norway, but Edvard Grieg is the only one renowned enough to warrant a question in a typical trivia competition. Now look under the chapter, U.S. States and Territories. Find Georgia, Swamp, and The Okefenokee. There may be dozens of swamps in the state of Georgia, but only one about which you are likely to be asked in any competition. I eliminated hundreds of pages of nonessential data by using this format, in the hope that it will prepare you, the reader, by the most efficient means possible for any upcoming intellectual challenge.

I hope this book will spark your intellectual curiosity and that it will provide the resource materials you need to broaden your cultural literacy. Take it with you on the way to your trivia event. Have someone present the material to you in the manner in which you are likely to hear it in competition. If you are playing on a team, have each team member read a few questions to the other members. This will provide a fun, semi-competitive environment in which to cover material that will likely be included in your upcoming match.
Best of luck!

Steven J. Ferrill
© Trivia Productions, 2001

1 *Abbreviations*

AA .... Alcoholics Anonymous
AAA .... American Auto Association
AARP .... American Association of Retired People
ABC .... American Broadcasting Company
ABC .... Islands: Aruba, Bonaire, and Curaçao
ABC .... Powers: Argentina, Brazil, and Chile
ABM .... Anti-ballistic missile
AC .... Alternating current
ACLU .... American Civil Liberties Union
AD .... Anno Domini (in the year of our Lord)
AFI .... American Film Institute
AFL .... American Federation of Labor
AFT .... American Federation of Teachers
AI .... Amnesty International
AI .... Artificial intelligence
AIDS .... Acquired immune deficiency syndrome
AKC .... American Kennel Club
AM .... Amplitude modulation
AMA .... American Medical Association
ANC............. African National Congress
ANZUS .... Australia, New Zealand, United States
AP .... Associated Press
ASCAP .... American Society of Composers, Authors and Publishers
ASCII .... American Standard Code for Information Interchange
ASPCA .... American Society for the Prevention of Cruelty to Animals
AU .... Astronomical unit
AWACS .... Airborne warning and control systems
AWOL .... Absent without leave
BASIC .... Beginner's all-purpose symbolic instruction code
BATA .... Bouquet, Aroma, Taste, Aftertaste
BC .... Before Christ
BLM............. Bureau of Land Management
BPOE .... Benevolent and Protective Order of Elks
BTU .... British thermal unit
c. .... Circa (on or about)
CAD .... Computer aided design
CAM .... Computer aided manufacture
CARE .... Cooperative for American Relief Everywhere
CBC .... Complete blood count
CBS .... Columbia Broadcasting System
CCC............. Civilian Conservation Corps
CDC .... Centers for Disease Control

CEO .... Chief Executive Officer
CFC .... Chlorofluorocarbon
CFS .... Chronic fatigue syndrome
CIA .... Central Intelligence Agency
CIO .... Congress of Industrial Organizations
CIS .... Commonwealth of Independent States
CNA............ Certified Nurse's Assistant
COBOL .... Common business oriented language
COLA.......... Cost of living allowence (or adjustment)
COO .... Chief Operating Officer
CORE .... Congress of Racial Equality
CPR .... Cardiopulmonary resuscitation
CPU .... Central processing unit
CRT .... Cathode ray tube
CSA .... Confederate States of America
CTW .... Children's Television Workshop
DAR .... Daughters of the American Revolution
DAV .... Disabled American Veterans
DC .... Direct current
DDS .... Doctor of Dental Surgery
DEA .... Drug Enforcement Agency
DFC .... Distinguished Flying Cross
DNA .... Deoxyribonucleic acid
DSC .... Distinguished Service Cross
DTP .... Diphtheria, tetanus, pertussis
DVD .... Digital video disc
EEC............. European Economic Community
EEG .... Electroencephalogram
EKG .... Electrocardiogram
EMT .... Emergency medical technician
EOEC .... Equal Opportunity Employment Commission
EPA .... Environmental Protection Agency
ERA............. Equal Rights Amendment
ESOP .... Employee stock ownership plan
ESP .... Extrasensory perception
FAA .... Federal Aviation Administration
FCC .... Federal Communications Commission
FDA .... Food and Drug Administration
FDIC........... Federal Deposit Insurance Corporation
FEMA .... Federal Emergency Management Agency
FHA .... Federal Housing Administration
FICA .... Federal Insurance Contribution Act
FM .... Frequency modulation
FTC............. Federal Trade Commission
FTD .... Florist Transworld Delivery
GAO .... General Accounting Office

1   *Abbreviations*

GAR .... Grand Army of the Republic
GATT .... General Agreement on Tariffs and Trade
GI .... Government issue
GMT .... Greenwich mean time
GNP .... Gross National Product
GOP .... Grand Old Party
GPS .... Global positioning system
GSA.............. General Services Administration
HBO .... Home Box Office
HIV .... Human immunodeficiency virus
HMO .... Health Maintenance Organization
HMS .... His/Her Majesty's Ship
HRE .... Holy Roman Empire
HRH .... His/Her Royal Highness
HTML .... Hyper text markup language
HTTP .... Hyper text transfer protocol
HUAC.......... House Un-American Activities Committee
IBM .... International Business Machines
ICBM .... Inter-continental ballistic missile
ICC .... Interstate Commerce Commission
IMF .... International Monetary Fund
IOC.............. International Olympic Committee
IPO .... Initial public offering
IRA............... Individual retirement account
IRA............... Irish Republican Army
ISBN .... International standard book number
ITT .... International Telephone and Telegraph
JAG.............. Judge Advocate General
LASER .... Light amplification by stimulated emission of radiation
LCD .... Liquid crystal display
LED .... Light emitting diode
LNG .... Liquified natural gas
LOX............. Liquid oxygen
LPN .... Licensed Practical Nurse
LSD .... Lysergic acid diethylamide
M*A*S*H* ... Mobile Army Surgical Hospital
MFN .... Most Favored Nation
MGM .... Metro-Goldwyn-Mayer
MOCA .... Museum of Contemporary Art (Los Angeles)
MODEM ..... Modulate/demodulate
MOMA .... Museum of Modern Art (NYC)
MRI .... Magnetic resonance imaging
MSG .... Monosodium glutamate
NAACP .... National Association for the Advancement of Colored People
NAFTA .... North America Free Trade Agreement
NASA .... National Aeronautics and Space Administration

NASCAR ...... National Association for Stock Car Automobile Racing
NASDAQ ..... National Association of Securities Dealers Automated Quotations
NATO .... North Atlantic Treaty Orginazation
NBC .... National Broadcasting Company
NEA .... National Education Association
NEA .... National Endowment for the Arts
NIMBY .... Not in my back yard
NLRB .... National Labor Relations Board
NOW .... National Organization for Women
NPR .... National Public Radio
NRA .... National Recovery Administration
NRA .... National Rifle Association
NSA .... National Security Administration
NTSB .... National Transportation Safety Board
NYSE .... New York Stock Exchange
OAS .... Organization of American States
OAU .... Organization of African Unity
OED .... Oxford English Dictionary
OEM .... Original equipment manufacturer
OEOB .... Old Executive Office building
OPEC .... Organization of Petroleum Exporting Countries
OSHA .... Occupational Safety and Health Association
OSS .... Office of Strategic Services
OTC .... Over the counter
P & L .... Profit and loss
PAC .... Political action committee
PBS .... Public Broadcasting System
PETA .... People for the Ethical Treatment of Animals
PIN .... Personal identification number
PLO .... Palestine Liberation Organization
PMI .... Private mortgage insurance
pp .... Page
PTA .... Parent-Teacher Association
PVC .... Polyvinyl chloride
P's & Q's ...... Pints and quarts
QVC .... Quality, value, convenience
RADAR .... Radio ranging and detecting
RAF .... Royal Air Force
RAM .... Random access memory
RCA .... Radio Corporation of America
RCMP .... Royal Canadian Mounted Police
REM .... Rapid eye movement
RKO .... Radio Keith Orpheum
RNA .... Ribonucleic acid
ROI .... Return on investment
ROM .... Read only memory

1 *Abbreviations*

RSVP .... Repondez, s'il vous plait (Please respond)
SALT .... Strategic Arms Limitations Talks
SAM .... Surface-to-air missile
SAR .... Sons of the American Revolution
SAT .... Scholastic aptitude test
SBA .... Small Business Administration
SCUBA .... Self-contained underwater breathing apparatus
SDI .... Strategic Defense Initiative
SEATO .... Southeast Asia Treaty Organization
SEC .... Securities and Exchange Commission
SETI .... Search for Extraterrestrial Intelligence
SONAR .... Sound navagation and ranging
SPF............... Sun protection factor
SSR.............. Soviet Socialist Republic
START .... Strategic Arms Reductions Talks
SUV .... Sport utility vehicle
TKO .... Technical knockout
TNT .... Trinitrotoluene
TVA .... Tennessee Valley Authority
UAE .... United Arab Emirates
UAR .... United Arab Republic
UHF............. Ultra high frequency
UL .... Underwriters Laboratory
UNCLE........ United Network Command for Law and Enforcement
UPI.............. United Press International
URL .... Uniform resource locator
USO .... United Service Organization
USSR........... Union of Soviet Socialist Republics
UV .... Ultra-violet
VAT .... Value added tax
VHF .... Very high frequency
VHS .... Video home system
VOA .... Voice of America
WAAC .... Women's Auxiliary Army Corps
WAAF .... Women's Auxiliary Air Force
WAC .... Women's Army Corps
WASP .... White Anglo-Saxon Protestant
WCTU .... Women's Christian Temperance Union
WHO .... World Health Organization
WTO .... World Trade Organization
WWF .... World Wildlife Fund
WWW .... World Wide Web
WYSIWYG .. What you see is what you get
YUPPIE........ Young upwardly mobile professional
ZIP .... (in zip code) Zone inprovement plan

Also Known As 2

Arouet, François-Marie	Voltaire
Arquette, Cliff	Charlie Weaver
Austerlitz, Frederick	Fred Astaire
Baker, Norma Jean	Marilyn Monroe
Baline, Israel	Irving Berlin
Beedle, William	William Holden
Bell, Acton	Anne Brontë
Bell, Currer	Charlotte Brontë
Bell, Ellis	Emily Brontë
Bernard, Rosine	Sarah Bernhardt
Beyle, Marie Henri	Stendahl
Birnbaum, Nathan	George Burns
Blair, Eric Arthur	George Orwell
Blixen, Karen	Isak Dinesen
Bojaxhui, Agnes Gonxha.	Mother Teresa
Bonny, William	Billy the Kid
Boyd, William	Hopalong Cassidy
Boz	Charles Dickens
Bratsburg, Harry	Harry Morgan
Buchinsky, Charles	Charles Bronson
Bullock, Annie May	Tina Turner
Cannon, Sarah Ophelia	Minnie Pearl
Cansino, Margarita	Rita Hayworth
Carpentier, Harlean	Jean Harlow
Chapman, John	Johnny Appleseed
Chwatt, Aaron	Red Buttons
Clemens, Samuel Langhorne	Mark Twain
Cohen, Jacob	Rodney Dangerfield
Cohen, William	Howard Cosell
Cornwell, David John Moore	John LeCarré
Crocetti, Dino	Dean Martin
Crosby, Harry Lillis	Bing Crosby
Danielovitch, Issur	Kirk Douglas
DeSalvo, Albert	The Boston Strangler
Dodgson, Rev. Charles Lutwidge	Lewis Carroll
Dorsey, Arnold	Engelbert Humperdink
Dukenfield, William Claude	W. C. Fields
Dupan, Amandine Aurore Lucie	George Sand
Dwight, Reginald	Elton John
d'Aquino, Iva	Tokyo Rose
Einstein, Albert.	Albert Brooks
Estevez, Ramon	Martin Sheen
Evans, Mary Ann	George Eliot

2 *Also Known As*

Fernier, Vincent	Alice Cooper
Finklea, Tula Ellice	Cyd Charisse
Fitzgerald, Roy	Rock Hudson
Friedman, Esther Pauline	Ann Landers
Friedman, Pauline Esther	Abigail van Buren
Geisel, Theodore	Dr. Seuss
Gillars, Mildred	Axis Sally
Goldenberg, Emanuel	Edward G. Robinson
Gow, Eleanore	Elle McPherson
Gumm, Frances	Judy Garland
Gurdin, Natasha	Natalie Wood
Gustafsson, Greta	Greta Garbo
Guynes, Demetrea	Demi Moore
Hines, Milton	Soupy Sales
Horowitz, Jerome	Curly (Howard)
Hovick, Louise	Gypsy Rose Lee
Hyra, Margaret	Meg Ryan
Jackson, O'Shea	Ice Cube
Jacobs, Amos	Danny Thomas
Jefferson, Arthur Stanley	Stan Laurel
Jenkins, Richard Walker	Richard Burton
Johnson, Caryn	Whoopie Goldberg
Johnson, Claudia Alta Taylor	Lady Bird Johnson
Kaminski, David Daniel	Danny Kaye
Kaminsky, Melvin	Mel Brooks
Kappelhoff, Doris	Doris Day
King, Leslie Lynch, Jr.	Gerald Ford
King, Riley E.	B.B. King
Kittle, Frederick	August Wilson
Knickerbocker, Dietrich	Washington Irving
Korzeniowski, Teodor Josef Konrad	Joseph Conrad
Kubelsky, Benjamin	Jack Benny
Lamb, Charles	Ilia
LaCock, Pierre	Peter Marchall
Leach, Archie	Cary Grant
le Seuer, Lucille	Joan Crawford
Longbaugh, Harry.	Sundance Kid
Levitch, Joseph	Jerry Lewis
Little, Malcolm	Malcolm X
Mallon, Mary	"Typhoid Mary"
Mary Westmacott	Agatha Christie
Micklewhite, Maurice	Michael Caine
Morrison, Marion	John Wayne
Morrison, Jeanette	Janet Leigh
Munro, Hector Hugh	Saki
Old Possum	T. S. Eliot

Owens, Diana	Queen Latifah
Palmer, Vera Jane	Jayne Mansfield
Parker, Robert Leroy.	Butch Cassidy
Perske, Betty Jean	Lauren Bacall
Peters, Jane Alice	Carole Lombard
Pratt, William Henry	Boris Karloff
Poquelin, Jean-Baptiste	Molière
Robertson, Anna May	Grandma Moses
Porter, William Sydney	O. Henry
Sanford, John	Redd Foxx
Sang, Chan Kwong	Jackie Chan
Schwartz, Jeremiah	Andy Devine
Schwartz, Bernard	Tony Curtis
Silberman, Jerome	Gene Wilder
Slye, Leonard	Roy Rogers
Smith, Walker, Jr.	Sugar Ray Robinson
Smith, Lula Carson	Carson McCullers
Smith, Francis	Dale Evans
Stephens, Ruby	Barbara Stanwyck
Stewart, James	Stewart Granger
Sukilovich, Malden	Karl Malden
Sumner, Gordon	Sting
Tracy, Woodrow	Woody Harrelson
Weiss, Erich	Harry Houdini
Williams, Thomas Lanier	Tennessee Williams
Wofford, Chloe Anthony	Toni Morrison
Young, Andre	Dr. Dre
Yule Jr., Joe	Mickey Rooney
Zelle, Margaretta	Mata Hari
Zeiger, Lawrence Harvey	Larry King
Zimmerman, Robert	Bob Dylan
Zuck, Alexandra	Sandra Dee

Fictional Also Known as:

The Shadow	Lamont Cranston
Spiderman	Peter Parker
The Incredible Hulk	Dr. David or Bruce Banner
The Lone Ranger	John Reid
The Green Hornet	Brett Reid (John's Grandnephew)
Wonder Woman	Diana Prince
Tarzan	The Earl of Graystoke
Captain Marvel	Billy Batson
Superman	Clark Kent
Batman	Bruce Wayne
Robin	Dick Grayson
Batgirl	Barbara Gordon

3 *Ancient History*

Ages of prehistory:

3,000,000 to 8,000 B.C.	Paleolithic (Early Stone Age)
8,000 to 2,700 B.C.	Mesolithic (Middle Stone Age)
2,700 to 1,900 B.C.	Neolithic (Late Stone Age)
1,900 to 500 B.C.	Bronze Age
500 to 51 B.C.	Iron Age

Four earliest centers of civilization:
Nile River valley
Indus River valley
Yellow River valley
Tigris and Euphrates Rivers Region

Human relative, extinct for 30,000 years .... Neanderthal

Earliest known walled city, c. 9,000 B.C. .... Jericho

Ancient Sumerian city .... Ur

Ancient North African city .... Carthage

Ancient Sicilian city .... Syracuse

Ancient empire of the Tigris River Valley .... Assyrian Empire

Capital of the Assyrian Empire .... Nineveh

Ancient city of Crete .... Knossos

Ancient city in Asia Minor .... Troy

Ancient Mesopotamian city .... Babylon (on Euphrates River)

Construction project in Egypt, c. 2600 B.C. .... The Great Pyramid of Cheops

Indo-European people of Turkey, c. 1900 B.C. .... Hittites

Astronomical site in Britain, c. 1800 B.C. .... Stonehenge

He created Hanging Gardens of Babylon .... Nebuchadnezzer II

Legal code giver of Babylon, c. 1780 B.C. .... Hammurabi

Ancient mariners from Tyre .... Phoenicians (founded Carthage)

Civilization of Crete .... Minoan

Greek war in Asia Minor, c. 1260 B.C. .... Trojan War

Ancient stone building Indians of Central America, c. 1000 B.C.

.... Olmecs

Games started in Greece, 776 B.C. .... Olympics

Legal law giver to Athens, 621 B.C. .... Draco

Settlers of central Italy, 550 B.C. .... Etruscans

Counting table built b Chinese, 550 B.C. .... Abacus

Religion founded by Lao Tzu, 520 B.C. .... Taoism

Sparta and Athens war starting 431 B.C. .... Peloponnesian War

King of Macedonia, 336 B.C. .... Alexander the Great

Alexander's father .... Phillip of Macedonia

Riddle Alexander solved .... Gordian Knot

Site of great library, c. 290 B.C. .... Alexandria

Rome-Carthage wars starting 264 B.C. .... Punic Wars

Greek center of the world .... Oracle at Delphi

Ancient Egyptian "City of the Sun" .... Heliopolis

Carthaginian who invaded Italy, 218 B.C. .... Hannibal

Hannibal's father .... Hamilcar

Egyptians who ruled from 323 to 30 B.C. .... The Ptolemies

Ancient Egyptian book, found in tombs .... Book of the Dead

500 years of Egyptian rulers, 26th to 21st century B.C. ..... Old Kingdom

Ancient Egyptian capitals .... Memphis, Thebes

Ancient Egyptian obelisk .... Cleopatra's Needle

Ikhnaton's wife .... Nefertiti

Egyptian insect talisman .... Scarab (beetle)

Central Asia caravan route, c. 110 B.C. .... Silk Road

Empire of Darius and Xerxes .... Persian Empire

Persian throne .... Peacock throne

Ancient capital of Laconia .... Sparta

Ancient people of Tigris-Euphrates region .... Sumerian

Hittite or Sumerian wedge-shaped form of writing .... Cuneiform

Ancient land "between two rivers" .... Mesopotamia

Ancient Japanese warrior .... Samurai (those who serve)

Man-made relic .... Artifact

Artifact that was key to decipherment of Egyptian heiroglyphs

.... Rosetta Stone

Original location of Elgin Marbles .... Parthenon

Modern location of Ur and Palmyra .... Syria

4 The Animal Kingdom

Classifications of Animals: Example

Kingdom	Animal
Phylum	Cordate
Class	Mammal
Order	Primate
Family	Hominoidea
Genus	Homo Sapiens
Species	Human Being

Animal Facts:

World's tallest animal	Giraffe
World's second-tallest animal	Elephant
World's fastest animal	Cheetah
World's second-fastest animal	Pronghorn antelope
World's fastest two-footed animal	Ostrich
Longest living animal	Giant tortoise
Longest living mammal	Man
Second longest living mammal	Elephant
Largest living animal	Blue whale
Toothless whale with two blowholes	Baleen
Whale with long flippers	Humpback
Whale with unicorn-like projection	Narwhal
Orc or orca	Killer whale
Deepest-diving whale	Sperm whale
Lowest animal in food chain	Plankton
"Sea cow"	Manatee
Manatee relative	Dugon
Sea lion, seal, and walrus family	Pinniped
Largest pinniped	Elephant seal
Male and female pinniped which have tusks	Walrus
"Mud puppy" and "hellbender"	Salamanders
Largest amphibian	Japanese salamander
Number of hearts in an octopus	Three
Freshwater crustacean	Crayfish (crawdad)
Oyster, clam, and mussel species	Bivalves
Freshwater pearl source	Mussels
"Bluepoint" bivalve	Oyster
"Cherrystone" bivalve	Clam
Stone and snow sea creatures	Crabs
Animal with largest eye	Giant squid
Sea hedgehog	Sea urchin
Crab with one big claw	Fiddler crab

Crab that uses a discarded shell	Hermit crab
Crab and scorpion family	Arthropod
Cone gastropod	Snail
Best-swimming bear	Polar bear
Largest bears	Polar and Kodiak bears
South America's only bear	Speckled bear
Animals of Australia	Marsupials
Eucalyptus-eating marsupial	Koala (not a bear)
North America's only marsupial	Opossum (possum)
Baby kangaroo	Joey
The kangaroo's smaller relative	Wallaby
Marsupial with the strongest jaws	Tasmanian Devil
"Hairy nosed" marsupial	Wombat
Symbol of the World Wildlife Fund	(Giant) Panda
North American panda relative	Racoon
South American racoon relative	Coati
Source of mohair	Goat
Camelopard a.k.a.	Giraffe
Giraffe's South American relative	Okapi
Himalayan ox	Yak
Wooly ox of northern Canada and Greenland	Musk-ox
Long-horned European member of goat family	Ibex
Burchell's animal	Zebra
Thompson's animal	Gazelle
South African gazelle	Springbok
World's largest antelope	Eland
Gnu	Wildebeest
"Ship of the desert"	Camel
One-humped camel	Dromedary
Two-humped camel	Bactrian
Smallest member of camel family	Vicuna (South America)
South American's largest member of camel family	Llama
Llama relative raised for wool	Alpaca
Narrow-snouted crocodile of Asia	Gavial
World's largest snake	Python
Western Hemisphere's largest snake	Anaconda
Adder and rattlesnake family	Vipers
Egyptian cobra	Asp
World's longest poisonous snake (Southeast Asia)	King cobra
Cobra killer	Mongoose
Turtle shell	Carapace
World's largest lizard	Komodo dragon
Western hemisphere's largest lizard	Iguana
Small lizard with suction cup feet	Gecko
Lizard of Galapagos Islands	Marine iguana
Venomous lizard of US southwest	Gila monster

4 | *The Animal Kingdom*

Great apes	Gorillas, chimpanzees, orangutans
Two types of gorilla	Mountain and lowland
Dominant male gorilla	Silverback
Great ape of Borneo and Sumatra	Orangutan
Pan family great ape	Chimpanzee
Chimpanzee's close relative	Bonobo
Monkey of Madagascar	Lemur
Tailless macaques of Gibralter	Barbary apes
Monkey with red nose and blue cheeks	Mandril
Asian monkey used in research	Rhesus monkey
Monkey that can be heard for several miles	Howler monkey
Long-armed monkey with prehensile tail	Spider monkey
Long-armed ape of southeast Asia	Gibbon
Small new-world monkey	Marmoset
Smallest monkey	Pygmy marmoset
Slow, hanging tree-dweller of South America	Sloth
South American long-snouted mammal	Tapir
South American fur-bearing rodent	Chinchilla
The hippopotamus' smaller relative	Pygmy hippopotamus
Only venomous mammal	Duckbilled platypus
Only egg-laying mammals	Duckbilled platypus and spiny anteater (echidna)
Flying mammal	Bat
Blood-sucking bat	Vampire bat
Navigational method of bats	Echo location
African cat-like mammal	Civet
"Golden" African predator	Golden Jackal
Spotted "laughing" carnivore	Hyena
World's largest rodent	Capybara
North America's largest rodent	Beaver
"Golden" chubby-cheeked rodent	Golden hamster
Arboreal rodent	Squirrel
Rodent from Mongolia	Gerbil
Suicidal rodent from Antarctica	Lemming
Ermine, ferret, and badger family	Weasel
Largest member of deer family	Moose
Only deer family member where both sexes have horns	Caribou
Graceful antelope	Gazelle
Prairie wolf	Coyote
Cow-like	Bovine
Goat-like	Hircine
Bear-like	Ursine
Fox-like	Vulpine
Wolf-like	Lupine
Sheep-like	Ovine
Pig-like	Porcine

Group of rabbits .... Warren
Group of moose .... Lodge
Caudal vertebrae in animals .... Tail

Birds:

The study of birds .... Ornithology
Largest bird, with largest eggs (flightless) .... Ostrich
Large, flightless South American bird .... Rhea
Large, flightless Australian bird .... Emu
Fastest bird .... Peregrine falcon*
Name for New Zealand flightless bird and native fruit .... Kiwi
Adelie, emperor, and king bird .... Penguins
Snow, Canadian, and blue breeds .... Geese
North Atlantic "sea-parrot" .... Puffin
Brown and white "Fishhawk" bird .... Osprey
Nocturnal singing bird .... Nightingale
Only North American bird that hibernates .... Whippoorwill
North America's most common dove .... Mourning dove
"Gooney bird," unlucky to sailors .... Albatross
Trumpeter, mute, coscoroba and whistling .... Swans
Sandhill and whooping birds .... Cranes
Tallest bird of North America .... Whooping crane
Redwing and grackle birds .... Blackbirds
Golden and bald type of bird .... Eagle
Bird that mimics other birds .... Mocking bird
Ruby-throated bird, only bird that can fly backwards .... Hummingbird
Smallest bird .... Bee hummingbird
South American vulture .... Andean condor
South American bird with largest bill .... Toucan
"Laughing jackass" of Australia .... Kookaburra
Shangri-la bird .... Bird of paradise
Largest member of crow family .... Raven
"Scarlet" parrot .... Macaw
Purple-black Asian bird that mimics humans .... Mynah bird
Yellow songbird .... Gold finch
Downy duck that can dive to 180 feet .... Eider
Black-footed and red-footed sea bird .... Booby
Arizona bird that can run 15 miles per hour .... Roadrunner
Sacred Egyptian bird .... Ibis
Mythical bird that rose from the ashes .... Phoenix
Bird that migrates from arctic to antarctic .... Arctic tern
Most common domesticated bird .... Chicken
Young swan .... Cygnet
Young pigeon .... Squab
*Some sources list the split-tailed swift as the fastest bird

4   *The Animal Kingdom*

Pigeon extinct since 1914 .... Passenger pigeon
Large penguin-like bird, extinct since 1850 .... Great auk
Large, flightless extinct land pigeon .... Dodo
First known feathered bird to become extinct .... Archeopteryx
Flying dinosaur .... Pterodactyl
Legendary bird encountered by Sinbad .... Roc

Cats:

World's largest cat .... Tiger
The Americas' largest cat .... Jaguar
Most popular breed of domesticated cat .... Persian
"Clouded" cat .... Clouded leopard
Pointed-eared cat .... Lynx
Lynx North American relative with short tail .... Bobcat
Tailless cat named for an island .... Manx
Other names for Cougar .... Mountain lion, puma
Ethiopian domestic cat .... Abyssinian
Nearly-hairless cat .... Sphinx cat
Cat with "tiger" coat .... Tabby
Southeast Asian domestic cat .... Siamese
Fever caused by parvo-virus .... Distemper
Swollen lymph nodes .... Cat scratch fever

Dogs:

Tallest dog .... Irish wolfhound
Smallest domestic breed .... Chihuahua
Most common registered breed .... Labrador retriever
Dog of the Netherlands .... Keeshond
Non-barking African dog .... Basenji
Chinese royal dog .... Pekingese
Chinese wrinkled-skin dog .... Shar-pei
"Lion dog" of Chinese nobles .... Shih tzu
Ancient Chinese dog with lion-like mane .... Chow chow
Mediterranean island lap dog .... Maltese
Stag hunting dog .... Deerhound
Loose skinned dog used in finding people .... Blood hound
Tibetan dog .... Lhasa apso
Fluffy white Siberian breed .... Samoyed
Sled dog with blue eyes .... Siberian husky
Japanese guard dog .... Akita
Whippet breed .... Greyhound
Queen Victoria's dog .... Collie
French "butterfly" dog .... Papillon
St. John's dog .... Labrador retriever
Russian wolfhound .... Borzoi

Dog named after eastern U.S. bay .... Chesapeake Bay retriever
South African-bred dog .... Rhodesian ridgeback
South African wild hunting dog .... Cape hunting dog
Large dog from Swiss Alps .... St. Bernard
Australian wild dog .... Dingo
World's premier sheep dog .... Border collie
Silky and Yorkshire breeds .... Terrier
Largest terrier .... Airedale terrier
Irish, Gordon, and English breeds .... Setter
"Toto's" breed (from Wizard of Oz) .... Cairn terrier
Richard Nixon's dog .... Checkers
FDR's dog .... Fala
George Bush's dog .... Millie
German Shepherd with TV show .... Rin Tin Tin
Dog from *Petticoat Junction* who later made movies .... Benji
George Jetson's dog .... Astro
Sgt. Preston's dog .... (Yukon) King
Dog in *Call of the Wild* .... Buck
RCA trademark dog .... Nipper
Top American dog show .... Westminster Kennel Club
Number of breeds recognized by AKC 156
World's longest dogsled race .... Iditarod

Fish:

The study of fish .... Ichthyology
Sargasso sea fish .... Eel
Blood-sucking eel .... Lamprey
Skipjack fish .... Tuna
Pollock and haddock type .... Cod
"Tiger of the sea" .... Barracuda
Mako, tope and nurse types .... Shark
Largest fish .... Whale shark
Largest predatory fish .... Great white shark
Fish that attaches itself to a shark .... Remora
South American predatory fish .... Piranah
Devil fish .... Manta ray
Recently discovered prehistoric fish .... Coelacanth
Caviar comes from this fish .... Sturgeon
"Freshwater shark" .... Pike
Fish that inflates when threatened .... Puffer fish
Brook and rainbow fish .... Trout
Sepia ink fish .... Cuttlefish
Full name for "Musky" .... Muskellunge
Muskellunge family .... Pike
Thai aquarium fish .... Fighting fish
Species that has ability to change color .... Grouper

4   *The Animal Kingdom*

Largest salmon .... Chinook
Pipe fish relative; male carries young in its pouch .... Sea horse
Fish that spawn on beach under full moon .... Grunion
Most poisonous fish .... Rock fish
Fish in *The Old Man and the Sea* .... Marlin
Fish disease characterized by white spots .... Ich

Horses:

Horse belonging to:
Roy Rogers .... Trigger
Dale Evans .... Buttermilk
The Lone Ranger .... Silver
Tonto .... Scout
Tom Mix .... Tony
Hopalong Cassidy .... Topper
Sergeant Preston .... Rex
Gene Autry .... Champion
The Cisco Kid .... El Diablo
Robert E. Lee .... Traveler
John Tyler .... General
U.S. Grant .... Cincinnati
Duke of Wellington .... Copenhagen
Napoleon .... Marengo
Alexander the Great .... Bucephalus
Don Quixote .... Rosinante
Wild Bill Hickock .... Buckshot
El Cid .... Babieca
Richard III .... White Surry
Caligula .... Incitatus

Other horse facts:
The horse in George Orwell's *Animal Farm* .... Boxer
Son of War Admiral .... Man-O-War
First horse to win $1,000,000 .... Citation
Painted horse .... Pinto
Bedouin horse .... Arabian
Smallest British breed .... Shetland
Horse named after Scottish river .... Clydesdale
Horse bred by the Nez Perce Indians .... Appaloosa
Horse bred in Vienna .... Lippizaner
Original wild horse of U.S. west .... Mustang
Spanish-bred horse used by Conquistadores .... Andelusian
Portuguese bred horse .... Lisitano
Tennessee "stepping" horse .... Tennessee Walker
Oklahoma City horseshow horse .... Morgan horse

Horse racing's triple crown events:

Kentucky Derby (The Run for the Roses)	Churchill Downs; Louisville
Preakness (The Run for the Black-Eyed Susans)	Pimlico, Maryland
Belmont Stakes (The Run for the Carnations)	Belmont Racetrack; Belmont, New York

Triple Crown Winners:

1978	Affirmed
1977	Seattle Slew
1973	Secretariat
1948	Citation
1946	Assault
1943	Count Fleet
1941	Whirlaway
1937	War Admiral
1935	Omaha
1930	Gallant Fox
1919	Sir Barton

Horse Racing's most winning jockey	Laffitt Pincay, Jr.
Horse Racing's second-most winning jockey	Willie Shoemaker
Youngest Triple Crown winning jockey	Steve Cauthen
First woman jockey in Horse Racing Hall of Fame	Judy Krone
He rode Whirlaway and Citation to the Triple Crown	Eddie Arcaro

Insects:

Study of insects	Entomology
Giant green darner	Dragonfly
Queen Alexandra's birdwing	Butterfly
"Regal" migrating insect	Monarch butterfly
Hair insect	Louse
Insect fiber	Silk
Causes African sleeping sickness	Tse-tse fly
Egyptian sacred beetle	Scarab
"Pious" predator insect	Praying mantis
Cellulose-digesting insect	Termite
These were a Biblical "scourge"	Locusts
Cotton bowl-eating insect	Boll weevil
Cause of malaria	Anopheles mosquito
First domesticated insect	Honey bee
South American fungus-growing ant	Leaf-cutter ant
European beetle with powerful pincers	Stag beetle
Mexican jumping bean larva	Moth
Chemical ants use to communicate	Pheromone
Butterfly collector	Lepidopterist
Insects studied by Thomas Hunt Morgan	Fruit flies

5 *Anniversary Gifts*

First .... Paper

Second .... Cotton

Third .... Leather

Fourth .... Linen

Fifth .... Wood

Sixth .... Iron

Seventh .... Copper

Eighth .... Bronze

Ninth .... Pottery

Tenth .... Tin

Eleventh .... Steel

Twelveth .... Silk

Thirteenth .... Lace

Fourteenth .... Ivory

Fifteenth .... Crystal

Twentieth .... China

Twenty-fifth .... Silver

Thirtieth .... Pearls

Thirty-fifth .... Coral

Fortieth .... Rubies

Forty-fifth .... Sapphires

Fiftieth .... Gold

Sixtieth .... Diamonds

Seventy-fifth .... Platinum

Architechture 6

Designer of :

US Capital and Boston State House .... Charles Bulfinch
Vietnam War Memorial .... Maya Lin
West tower of Westminster Abbey .... Christopher Wren
Glass Pyramid at the Louvre .... I. M. Pei
Geodesic dome .... R. Buckminster Fuller
Central Park in New York City .... Charles Law Olmsted
Guggenheim Museum .... Frank Lloyd Wright
Layout for Washington, D.C. .... Pierre L'Enfant
White House .... James Hoban
Barcelona Chair .... Mies Van Der Rohe
Tulip Chair .... Eero Saarinen
St. Paul's Cathedral, 1669 .... Christopher Wren
Bauhaus building (Germany) .... Walter Gropius
Taj Mahal .... Shah Jihan
World Trade Center arch .... Minoru Yamasaki
TWA terminal at JFK airpost .... Eero Saarinen
Woolworth Building in New York City .... Gilbert Cass
Presidential palace in Brasilia .... Oscar Neimeyer
Imperial Hotel in Japan .... Frank Lloyd Wright
He influenced Frank Lloyd Wright .... Louis Henry Sullivan
New Reich Chancellery .... Albert Speer
Gateway Arch in St. Louis .... Eero Saarinen
"Less is more" style .... Mies Van Der Rohe
High pitched roof that bears his name .... François Mansard

Other facts:

Types of columns .... Ionic, Doric, Corinthian
"Flying" support .... Buttress
Covered, arched walkway at a monastery .... Cloister
Covered walk supported by columns .... Portico
Central stone of an arch .... Keystone
Horizontal beam supported at only one end .... Cantilever
Hagia Sofia architecture style .... Byzantine
Architectural style of Notre Dame Cathedral .... Gothic
Gothic exterior beastly figures .... Gargoyles
Mid-ninethteenth century English style .... Victorian
Architectural style popular between 1875-1914 .... Art Nouveau
Architectural style popular in the 1920's and 30's .... Art Deco (Chrysler Building)
Swiss architect who designed houses on stilts .... La Corbousier
Riverboat, bridge and Mississippi River jetty designer .. James Eads

7 *Art And Artists*

Art Terms:

Ancient Greek art using decorative tiles.................... Mosaic
Decorative style of 12th to 16th century .... Baroque
18th century style of light colors and irregular curves
.... Rococo (Watteau)
Sensational style of the 1830's .... Romanticism
French style of the late 19th century .... Impressionism (Van Gogh, Monet)
Style popular at the turn of the 20th century .... Post-impressionism (Cezanne)
Emotional style of the early 20th century .... Expressionism (Munch)
"Wild" style of the 20th century .... Fauvism (Matisse)
Style popular in Zurich during early 20th century ..... Dadaism (Duchamp, Arp)
Modern artistic style using metals, 1920's and '30's . Art deco (Empire State Building)
Geometric style .... Cubism (Picasso, Braque)
Non-representational 20th century abstract style .... Abstract art (Mondrian)
Dreamlike effect style .... Surrealism (Dali, Magritte)
Artistic style using splashing and pouring of paint ... Abstract expressionism
                                                                                  (Pollock, de Kooning)
Style of 1950s and 60s using celebrity images .... Pop art (Warhol, Liechtenstein)
Abstract art of optical illusion .... Op art
Dry painting.. Sand painting
Wet plaster painting .... Fresco
Body art... Tattoo
Bone or ivory carvings .... Scrimshaw
Paint with egg yolk binder .... Tempera
Quick-drying paints developed in 1960's .... Acrylics

Artists and their Art:

Bartholdi, Frederic (French) .... *Statue of Liberty*
Borglum, Gutzon (American).................................... *The carvings at Mt. Rushmore*
Botticelli, Sandro (Italian) .... *The Birth of Venus*
Brancusi, Constantin (Romanian) .... *Bird in Space*
Braque, Georges (French) .... *Violin and Pitcher*
Cassatt, Mary (American impressionist) .... *The Conversation*
Cellini, Benvenuto (Italian) .... *Perseus With the Head of Medusa*
Cezanne, Paul.. *Still Life With Basket of Apples*
Constable, John (English) .... *Brighton Beach*
Dali, Salvador (Spanish surrealist) .... *The Persistence of Memory*
David, Jacques-Louis (French).................................. *The Death of Marat*
.... *The Death of Socrates*
Degas, Edgar (French) .... *Statue of a Real Girl*
.... *Rehearsal at the Ballet*

Delecroix, Eugéne (French) .... *Liberty Leading the People*
Donatello (Italian) .... *David* (in bronze)
Duchamp, Marcel (French, chess player) .... *Nude Descending a Staircase*
El Greco (Spanish) .... *View of Toledo*
French, Daniel Chester (American) .... *The Minuteman*
.... *Lincoln* (seated at the Lincoln Memorial)
Gainsborough, Thomas (English) .... *The Blue Boy*
Gauguin, Paul (French, lived in Tahiti) .... *Tahitian Women*
Goya, Francisco (deaf Spaniard) .... *The Bulls of Bordeaux*
.... *The Invasion of Spain*
.... *The 2nd of May*
.... *Nude Maja*
.... *Clothed Maja*
Hogarth, William (American) .... *The Rake's Progress* series
Holbein, Hans, the Younger (English) .... *Henry VIII*
Homer, Winslow (American seascape painter) .... *The Gulf Stream*
.... *Breezing Up*
Hopper, Edward (American) .... *Nighthawks*
Leonardo da Vinci (Italian, left-handed painter, buried in France)
.... *Mona Lisa* (*La Jaconde*)
.... *The Last Supper*
.... *Adoration of the Magi*
Manet, Édouard (French) .... *A Bar at the Folies-Bergéres*
.... *Olympia*
Matisse, Henri (French) .... *The Dance*
Michelangelo (Italian) .... *David* (sculpture in marble)
.... *The ceiling of the Sistine Chapel*
.... *The Last Supper*
.... *The Rebellious Slave*
.... *Pieta* (sculpture)
Millet, Jean-Francois (French) .... *The Gleaners*
Monet, Claude (from Giverny, France) .... *Le Havre Harbor*
.... *The Water Lilies*
.... *Luncheon on the Grass*
.... *The Rouen Cathedral*
.... *Regatta*
Munch, Edvard (Norwegian) .... *The Scream*
Picasso, Pablo (Spanish) .... *Gertrude Stein*
.... *Les Noces de Pierrette*
.... *Guernica*
Raphael (Italian) .... *School of Athens*
Rembrandt (van Rijn, Dutch) .... *The Night Watch*
.... *Aristotle Contemplating the Bust of Homer*
.... *Jacob Wrestling with an Angel*
Remington, Frederick (American sculptor) .... *The Cheyenne*
.... *The Scout*

7   *Art and Artists*

Renoir, Pierre-Auguste (French) .... *Les Parapluies*
Rivera, Diego (Mexican Muralist) .... *The Agrarian Leader Zapata*
.... *Man at the Crossroads* (mural)
Rodin, August (French sculptor) .... *The Thinker (Le Penseur)*
.... *The Burghers of Calais*
.... *Age of Bronze*
.... *Man With a Broken Nose*
.... *The Kiss*
Rousseau, Henri (French) .... *Sleeping Gypsy*
Rubens, Peter Paul (Dutch) .... *Venus and Adonis*
.... *Adoration of the Maji*
.... *Descent from the Cross*
Segal, George (American sculptor) .... *The Diner*
Seurat, Georges (French pointillist) .... *La Grande Jatte*
Toulouse-Lautrec, Henri de (French) .... *At the Moulin Rouge*
Turner, William (English) .... *The Shipwreck*
Velázquez, Diego (Spanish) .... *Phillip IV of Spain*
Van Dyck, Anthony (Flemish) .... *Charles I of England*
Van Gogh, Vincent (Dutch, lived in France)
.... *The Potato Eaters*
.... *Portrait of Dr. Gachet* (sold for $75 million at Christie's in N.Y. 1990)
.... *Sunflowers* (sold for $36.2 million at Sotheby's in New York, 1987)
.... *Starry Night* (subject of Don Maclean song)
.... *Cornfield and Cypress Trees*
.... *Irises* (sold for $49 million at Sotheby's in New York, 1987)
.... *Red Vineyard* (the only painting he sold)
Verrocchio, Andrea del (Italian) .... *Madonna and Child*
.... *Bronze Boy with Dolphin*
Whistler, James (American)
.... *The Artist's Mother: Arrangement in Gray and Black (Whistler's Mother)*
Wood, Grant (American) .... *American Gothic*
Wyeth, Andrew (American) .... *Christina's World*
.... *Helga* series

Other Facts:

Venetian 16th century Renaissance painter .... Titian

Venetian 16th mannerist fresco painter .... Tintoretto

Mirror writing artist .... Leonardo da Vinci

Russian-born painter of Biblical works .... Marc Chagall

Portrait painter of George Washington .... Gilbert Stewart

Action or drip painter .... Jackson Pollock

Impressionist painter of dancers in motion .... Edgar Degas

Elderly painter of rural scenes .... Grandma Moses

Artist who cut off his ear .... Vincent Van Gogh

Painted men in bowler hats .... René Magritte

Flemish painter of fleshy nudes .... Peter Paul Rubens

Dutch domestic scenes painter .... Jan Vermeer

American painter western skies and flowers .... Georgia O'Keeffe

American painter of babies and mothers .... Mary Cassatt

British sculptor of reclining figures .... Henry Moore

John Constable's rival .... William Turner

August Rodin's student and lover .... Camille Claudell

Mobile maker .... Alexander Calder

Dora Mar posed for him .... Pablo Picasso

Marylin Monroe pop artist .... Andy Warhol

Diego Rivera's wife .... Frida Kahlo

Painter of sporting events in bright colors .... Leroy Nieman

"Painter of Lights" .... Thomas Kincade

"Kinetic art" .... Mobiles

Romanian bridge wrapper .... Cristo

Painter of flags .... Jasper Johns

19th century French landscape painter's school ...... Barbizon School

Landscape painters of the Catskill Mountains ...... Hudson River School

French site of ancient cave paintings .... Lascaux

Spanish site of ancient cave paintings .... Alta Mira

Court Painter for:

Henry VIII .... Hans Holbein the Younger

Charles I .... Anthony Van Dyck

Philip IV of Spain .... Diego Velázquez

Napoleon .... Jacques Louis David

Francis I of France .... Leonardo da Vinci

Astronomy and Space

Planets And Their Moons:

Mercury: The second-smallest planet
- Closest to the sun; no moons
- Orbital period: 88 days

Venus: The "greenhouse effect" planet
- No moons
- Probes: Venera (Russian)
- Orbital period: 225 days

Earth: The only planet not named after a mythological figure
- One moon, walked on by twelve astronauts from the Apollo program
- Lunar probe: Surveyor

Mars: The red planet
- Moons: Phobos (largest) and Demos
- Probes: Ranger and Pathfinder
- Volcano: Olympus Mons (largest known volcano in the solar system)
- Orbital period: 1.9 years

Jupiter: The largest planet; larger than all others put together
- Distinguishing feature: a great red spot (a huge storm bigger than Earth)
- Galilean moons: Io, Europa, Castillo, and Ganymede (largest moon in the solar system)
- Jupiter has at least eleven other smaller moons
- Probes: Voyager I & II, Galileo
- Orbital period: 12 years

Saturn: The ringed planet
- Moons: Titan (moon with mysterious atmosphere) and at least 20 others.
- Probes: Voyager I & II, Cassini (launched in 1997)
- Orbital period: 29 years

Uranus:
- Moons: Titania, Oberon, Umbriel, Ariel, Miranda, and ten others (Thirteen of Uranus' fifteen moons are named after Shakespearian characters).
- Probe: Voyager II
- Discoverer: William Herschel, 1781
- Orbital period: 84 years

Neptune: The blue planet
- Moons: Triton, Nereid and others.
- Distinguishing feature: the great blue spot
- Probe: Voyager II

- Discoverer: Johann Galle, 1856
- Orbital period: 165 years

Pluto: The smallest planet
  (there is debate about whether Pluto is an actual planet)
  - Moon: Charon
  - Discoverer: Clyde Taumbaugh (on calculations from Percival Lowell,
    the "PL" in Pluto)
  - Orbital period: 248 years

Other facts:

American astronomer	Edwin Hubble
American female astronomer	Maria Mitchell
Danish astronomer	Tycho Brahe
English astronomer royal	Sir Edmund Halley
English astronomer family	Herschel
French astronomer family	Cassini
German astronomer	Johannes Kepler
Greek astronomer (2nd century)	Ptolemy
Italian astronomer	Galileo (Galilei)
Polish astronomer	Copernicus
U.S. space station	Skylab
Russian space station	Mir ("peace" in Russian)
First man in space	Yuri Gagarin
First woman in space	Valentina Tereshkova
First space walk	Alexei Leonov
First American in space (suborbital)	Alan Shepard
Second American in space (suborbital)	Gus Grissom
Third American in space (three orbits)	John Glenn
First American woman in space	Sally Ride
First American to walk in space	Edward White
First American woman to walk in space	Kathryn Sullivan
American who has longest duration in space	Shannon Lucid
First man to walk on the moon	Neil Armstrong
Second man to walk on the moon	Buzz Aldrin
Apollo 13 commander	James Lovell
Oldest U.S. astronaut, launched in 1998	John Glenn (77 yrs. old)
Man who played golf on the moon	Alan Shepard
First space shuttle crew	Young and Crippen
Frist female space shuttle commander	Eileen Collins
First satellite, 1957	Sputnik
First U.S. satellite	Explorer I
First weather satellite	Tiros
First communications satellite	Echo I
First telecommunications satellite	Telstar

8　*Astronomy and Space*

The sun's halo .... Corona
The sun's "breeze" .... Solar wind
Solar magnetic storms with 11-year cycles .... Sun spots
The Earth's magnetic belt .... Van Allen Belt
Belt between Mars and Jupiter. .... Asteroid belt (possibly a destroyed planet)
Largest known asteroid .... Ceres
Closest major galaxy .... Andromeda (can be seen by naked eye)
Milky Way's satellite galaxies .... Large and Small Magellanic Cloud
Galactic cloud of dust and gas .... Nebula
Nebula named for sea creature .... Crab nebula
"Equine" nebula .... Horse head nebula
"Dog Star", brightest star in the sky .... Sirius
North star or pole star .... Polaris
Closest star .... Proxima Centauri* (4.1 light years)
Stars known as "seven sisters" .... Pleiades
Theory of the expanding universe .... Big Bang theory
Moon probe .... Surveyor
Mars probes .... Mariner and Pathfinder
Pathfinder mobile rover .... Sojourner
Jupiter probe .... Galileo
Saturn probe .... Cassini
"Grand tour of planets" probes .... Voyager I & II
First man-made object to leave the solar system .... Pioneer 10
One-person U.S. space program .... Mercury
Two-person U.S. space program .... Gemini
Three-person U.S. space program .... Apollo
Apollo 11 landing module .... Eagle
Reusable U.S. space vehicle .... Space Shuttle
Space shuttle names .... Enterprise (atmospheric tests
　　　　　only), Columbia, Challenger, Atlantis, Discovery, Endeavor
1983 book chronicling the U.S. space program .... *The Right Stuff*
Comet that returns every 76 years .... Halley's Comet
Comet that struck Jupiter in 1994 .... Shoemaker-Levy 9
Comet visible for several months in 1996 .... Hale-Bopp
Highly touted comet that fizzled in 1973 .... Comet Kahoutek

* There seems to be confusion among major publications about the closest star to our solar system. Some publications list Proxima Centauri as the closest star, while others state that the five star system Alpha Centauri is the closest star. The reason for this confusion is Proxima Centauri is the closest of the five individual stars in the multiple Alpha Centauri system.

Awards 9

The Four Top Entertainment Awards:

Film	Oscar
Television	Emmy
Theater	Tony
Music	Grammy

The only people to win all four awards	Rita Moreno, Barbra Streisand
Tony Award's full name	Antoinette Perry Award
National Hockey League championship	Stanley Cup
International soccer championship	World Cup
Super Bowl trophy	Lombardi Trophy
Given to the best college football player	Heisman Trophy
Yachting's top award	America's Cup
Given to baseball's best pitcher	Cy Young Award
Outstanding amateur athletic award	Sullivan Award
ESPN's annual awards	ESPY's
World team golf award	Ryder Cup
World team tennis award	Davis Cup
Highest award given by US government	Congressional Medal of Honor
Highest civilian award given by US government	(Presidential) Medal of Freedom
Great Britain's highest military award	Victoria Cross
Off-Broadway theater award	Obie
Given for the best television commercial	Clio
Mystery writer's award	Edgar (named after Poe)
London's Tony award	Olivier (named for Lawrence Olivier)
U.S. poetry award presented by Yale University	Bollinger Prize
Award for broadcasting	Peabody Award
Science fiction literature award	Hugo Award
Outstanding cartoonist award	Reuben Award
National Geographic Society award	Hubbard Award
Given for best children's illustration	Caldecott Medal
Outstanding teacher award	Golden Apple
Planned Parenthood Federation award	Maggie (named for Margaret Sanger)
MacArthur Foundation award	Genius Grant
Mason's award	Order of the Eastern Star
Fashion design award	Perry Ellis Award
Award from the Columbia School of Journalism	Pulitzer Prize
Prizes awarded annually in Stockholm, Sweden	Nobel Prizes*
Two original Nobel Prizes	Chemistry and Physics
Other Nobel Prizes	Peace, Literature, Economics, Physiology/Medicine

* Only the Nobel Peace Prize is awarded in Oslo, Norway

10 *The Bible*

The Old Testament:

Biblical unit of weight	Shekel
Biblical unit of length	Cubit
First book of Bible named after a tribe	Leviticus
Book that tells of the destruction of Jerusalem	Lamentations
First five books of Bible	Pentateuch (Torah)
Last book of Old Testament	Malachi
Books named after women	Esther, Ruth
Book of wisdom, written by David	Psalms
Book written by Solomon	Proverbs
First book, alphabetically	Amos
Book with shortest name	Job
Animals that spoke	The serpent of Eden, Balaam's ass
Adam and Eve's sons	Cain, Abel, Seth
Oldest man in Bible	Methuselah (969 years)
Hunter in Genesis	Nimrod
Cities destroyed by fire and brimstone	Sodom and Gomorrah
His wife was turned into a pillar of salt	Lot
Tower in Genesis	Tower of Babel
Noah's sons	Shem, Ham, Japheth
Mountain where ark came to rest	Ararat
Birds Noah sent out from the ark	Dove, raven
Father of Israel or The Father of Many Nations	Abraham
Abraham's wife	Sarah
Abraham's oldest son, father of all Muslims	Ishmael
Abraham's son, father of Jacob	Isaac
Abraham's nephew	Lot
Isaac's wife	Rebeccah
Isaac's twin sons	Jacob and Esau
He wrestled with an angel	Jacob
Jacob's wives	Rachel and Leah
Rachel's sons	David and Benjamin
Zipporah's husband	Moses
Father of Zipporah, priest of the Midianites	Jethro
Brother of Moses	Aaron
Sister of Moses	Miriam
Number of years the Israelite were in Egypt	Four Hundred
Mountian where Moses received Ten Commandments	Mount Sinai
Chest containing the Ten Commandments	Ark of the Covenant
Food supplied to the Israelites	Manna and quail
Moses sent this spy into Canaan	Caleb

Leader of Israelites after Moses .... Joshua
Land "flowing with milk and honey" .... Canaan
Walled city conquered by Joshua .... Jericho
He defeated the Midianites with 300 men .... Gideon
Haman's wife .... Esther
Ruth's mother-in-law .... Naomi
Ruth husband .... Boaz
Righteous man from Uz .... Job
Prophet taken to heaven on a chariot of fire .... Elijah
Prophet from Nineveh, swallowed by "great fish" .... Jonah
Prophet who advised Saul .... Samuel
Prophetess who helped the Israelites in Canaan .... Deborah
Dogs ate her flesh .... Jezebel
Jezebel's husband .... Ahab
Man taken to the Valley of the Bones .... Ezekial
First king of Israel .... Saul
Saul's son .... Jonathan
King after Saul .... David
David's father .... Jesse
David slew this Philistine giant .... Goliath
David's great grandmother .... Ruth
David's love .... Bathsheba
Bathsheba's husband, sent off to war by David .... Uriah the Hittite
David's sons .... Absalom, Solomon
David played this instrument .... Lyre (harp)
King of Babylon who destroyed Jerusalem .... Nebuchadnezzar
He interpreted Nebuchadnezzar's dream .... Daniel
They were thrown into the fiery furnace .... Shadrach, Meshach, Abednego
Biblical horn .... Shofar

The New Testament:

The four Gospels .... Matthew, Mark, Luke, John
Shortest Gospel .... Mark
Book that tells story of Jesus' birth .... Matthew
First book after Gospels .... Acts (of the Apostles)
Last book .... Revelation
Author of Revelations .... John
Author of Acts .... Luke (the physician)
The one who preceeded Jesus .... John the Baptist
Mother of John the Baptist .... Elizabeth
Father of John the Baptist .... Zechariah
She called for the head of John the Baptist .... Salomé
Where John the Baptist baptised Jesus .... Jordan River
Jewish king who ordered the death of male babies .... Herod (the Great)
Birthplace of Jesus .... Bethlehem
Wise men who came to Bethlehem .... Magi (not used in Bible)

10 *The Bible*

Names of the three wise men .... Caspar, Balthazar, Melchior
Gifts the wise men brought to Jesus .... Gold, Frankincense, Myrrh
Home city of Jesus .... Nazareth
Language of Jesus .... Aramaic
Mother of Jesus .... Mary
Mother of Mary .... Anne
Mary's husband .... Joseph
Angel who appeared before Mary .... Gabriel
City where Jesus performed first miracle .... Cana (turned water into wine)
Jesus' sermon, found in books of Matthew and Luke .... Sermon on the Mount
Eight blessings found in the Sermon on the Mount .... Beatitudes
The first apostle .... Andrew
Apostle brothers who were fishermen .... Peter and Andrew
Apostle brothers, "the sons of thunder" .... John and James
Apostle Jesus called "The Rock" .... Peter
Apostle who betrayed Jesus .... Judas Iscariot
Means of Judas' death .... Hung himself
Tax collector Apostle .... Matthew
Apostle who doubted Jesus' resurrection .... Thomas
Apostle who denied Jesus three times .... Peter
Apostle who replaced Judas .... Matthias
Man who was stoned to death, first Christian martyr .... Stephen
Man Jesus raised from the dead .... Lazarus ("God has helped")
Place where Jesus was arrested .... Garden of Gethsemene
Where Garden of Gethsemene is located .... Mount of Olives
Crime Jesus was charged with .... Blasphemy
Man who defended Jesus .... Nicodemus
Judean Procurator; he "washed his hands" of Jesus' death
.... Pontius Pilate
High priests that sent Jesus to Pilate .... Annas and Caiphas
Criminal released instead of Jesus .... Barabbas
Hill where Jesus was crucified .... Calvary
Man who provided a tomb for Jesus .... Joseph of Arimathea
She witnessed Jesus' resurrection .... Mary Magdalene
Number of days between Jesus' resurrection and transfiguration
.... Forty
The two who appeared at Jesus' transfiguration .... Moses and Elisha
Formerly Saul, who wrote much of New Testament .... Paul
Paul's occupation .... Tentmaker
Island where Paul was ship wrecked .... Malta
Companion and messinger of Paul .... Timothy
The last battle in the book of Revelation .... Armageddon
The four horsemen of the apocalypse .... War, Famine, Pestilence, Death
Shortest verse in the Bible .... Jesus wept (John 11:35)
Biblical scrolls found in 1947 .... Dead Sea Scrolls
Location of Dead Sea Scrolls .... Qumran

Black History 11

First Black:

U.S. Poet Laureate	Maya Angelou
To win Pulitzer Prize for Poetry	Gwendolyn Brooks
To win Pulitzer Prize for Literature	Alice Walker
Awarded Nobel Prize for Literature	Toni Morrison
Awarded Nobel Peace Prize	Ralph Bunche
Singer at the Metropolitan Opera	Marian Anderson
Miss America	Vanessa Williams
Grammy winner	Harry Belafonte
Female Grammy winner	Ella Fitzgerald
Academy Award winner	Hattie McDaniel
U.S. Ambassador to United Nations	Andrew Young
Supreme Court Justice	Thurgood Marshall
Attorney General	Jocelyn Elders
Chairman of Joint Chiefs of Staff	Colin Powell
Congresswoman	Shirley Chisholm
Woman in the Senate	Carol Mosley-Braun
To reach the North Pole	Matthew Henson
In space	Leon Bluford, Jr.
Female in space	Mae Jemeson
Starring role on television	Diahann Carroll (for *Julia*)
Coach in any professional sport	Bill Russell
Major League baseball coach	Frank Robinson
All-American athlete	Paul Robeson
Heavyweight boxing champion	Jack Johnson
Masters golf champion	Tiger Woods
To win at Wimbledon	Althea Gibson
Major League Baseball player (19th century)	Moses Fleetwood Walker
Major League Baseball player (20th century)	Jackie Robinson
American League baseball player (20th century)	Larry Doby
In the NBA	Nate "Sweetwater" Clifton
To hold a patent (corn harvester)	Henry Blair
Mayor of Cleveland	Carl Stokes
Mayor of Chicago	Harold Washington
Mayor of New York City	David Dinkins
Mayor of Los Angeles	Tom Bradley
Mayor of Detroit (five times)	Coleman Young
Female mayor of Washington, D.C.	Sharon Pratt Kelly
Mayor of Atlanta	Maynard Jackson
To enroll at the University of Mississippi	James Meredith
Flying squadron	Tuskegee Airmen (WWII)

11   *Black History*

Other facts:

Man killed at Boston Massacre	Crispus Attucks
Female preacher, abolitionist and activist	Sojourner Truth
Orator and former slave	Frederick Douglass
Preacher who led 1831 insurrection against slavery	Nat Turner
Underground railroad "conductor"	Harriet Tubman
Male tennis champion	Arthur Ashe
The "Ambassador of love"	Pearl Bailey
Playwright born in Harlem, 1924	James Baldwin
"One O'clock Jump" band leader	Count Basie
President of Southern Christian Leadership Conference after Martin Luther King	Ralph Abernathy
Founder of *Ebony* and *Jet* magazines	John Johnson
Former Urban League head and Clinton advisor	Vernon Jordan
19th century educator; founder of Tuskegee Inst.	Booker T. Washington
Peanut cultivator	George Washington Carver
Aid in developing blood banks	Charles Drew
The voice of Darth Vader	James Earl Jones
Rat Pack member	Sammy Davis, Jr.
Chairwoman of the Congressional Black Caucus	Maxine Waters
Texas congresswoman, 1972-78	Barbara Jordan
Female figure skater	Debi Thomas
Miss America, 1991	Debbye Turner
Rainbow Coalition leader	Jesse Jackson
O.J. Simpson's defense lawyer	Johnny Cochran
Prosecutor in O.J. Simpson trial	Christopher Darden
CNN Washington anchor	Bernard Shaw
Founder of The American Dance Theater	Alvin Ailey
Soprano at Metropolitan Opera, 1976-85	Leontyne Price
NAACP founder, 1909	W.E.B. DuBois
NAACP representative murdered in Mississippi, 1965	Medgar Evers
Medal awarded by NAACP	Spingarn Medal
Fund founded at Tuskegee Institute, 1944	United Negro College Fund
Nationalist leader assassinated in 1965	Malcolm X
Nation of Islam leader	Louis Farrakhan
Huey Newton and Bobby Seal's party, founded 1966	Black Panthers
Black Panther leader and newspaper editor	Eldridge Cleaver
He coined the term "black power"	Adam Clayton Powell
City of the 1955 bus boycott	Montgomery
Woman who initiated the Montgomery bus boycott	Rosa Parks
George W. Bush's National Security Advisor	Condoleezza Rice
City high school integratd, 1956	Little Rock
University integrated in 1962	University of Alabama

Business and Industry 12

Headquarters of:

Monsanto	St. Louis, MO
Proctor & Gamble	Cincinnati, OH
Heinz	Pittsburgh, PA
Boeing	Seattle, WA
Saturn auto plant	Springhill, TN
Tyson Foods	Springdale, AK
Nike	Beaverton, OR
Anheuser-Busch	St. Louis, MO
Coca-Cola	Atlanta, GA
Nieman-Marcus	Dallas, TX
Goodyear	Akron, OH
Rubbermaid	Worster, OH
Federal Express	Memphis, TN
Eastman Kodak	Rochester, NY
Land-O-Lakes	Minneapolis, MN
General Electric	Schenectady, NY
Jack Daniels	Lynchburg. TN
Tandy	Fort Worth, TX
USX	Pittsburgh, PA
Pillsbury	Minneapolis, MN
Quaker Oats	Cedar Rapids, IA
Kellogg	Battle Creek, MI
Berlitz	Providence, RI
Ben and Jerry's Ice Cream	Waterbury, CT

Other facts:

St. Petersburg, Russia jewelry firm	Fabergé
Delaware chemical company	DuPont
Capital Cities network	ABC
Parent company of CBS	Westinghouse
Parent company of NBC	General Electric
Pancake brand started in 1893	Aunt Jemima
Standard Oil of New Jersey	Exxon
Auto maker who declared bankruptcy in 1940	Preston Tucker
"Flying Colors" airline that went bankrupt in 1981	Braniff
Dutch airline; the world's oldest	KLM
Brazil's airline	Varig
Israel's airline	El Al
Russian airline	Aeroflot
Scandinavian airline	SAS

12   *Business and Industry*

Germany's airline	Lufthansa
Belgian airline	Sabena
Hong Kong's airline	Cathay Pacific
Switzerland's airlines	Crossair, Swissair
Australia's airline	Qantas
Spain's airline	Iberia
Top U.S. shipping company	Federal Express
Top U.S. rental car company	Enterprise
Top U.S. prescription medicine outlet	Walgreen's
Top-selling U..S. motor oil company	Pennzoil
Largest U.S. tire and rubber company	Goodyear
Largest U.S. chemical company	DuPont
Second largest U.S. chemical company	Dow
Largest U.S. cirarette maker	Phillip Morris
Ray Ban sunglasses maker	Bausch and Lomb
Pony Express owners	Wells Fargo
Billboard ad company and newspaper chain owner	Gannett
Company that uses the Red Cross symbol	Johnson & Johnson
Bennett Cerf's publishing company	Random House
Maine company with outdoor gear catalogues	L.L. Bean
San Francisco high tech catalogue company	Sharper Image
U.S. largest mail order company	Montgomery Ward
U.S. largest exporter	Boing
Maker of Cheerios	General Mills
Vermont ice cream maker	Ben And Jerry's
"All Natural" ice cream maker	Breyers
German aspirin company	Bayer
Owner of *Jeopardy!* and Columbia-Tri Star	Sony
Arkansas frozen foods company	Tyson
Lean Cuisine maker	Stouffer's
Top soy sause maker	Kikoman
Little Rock yogurt chain	TCBY
They had the first roasted coffee in cans, 1878	Chase and Sandbourne
Coffee brand named after a Memphis hotel	Maxwell House
Spam maker	Hormel
World's largest spice company	McCormack and Co.
Largest electric razor company	Norelco
Maker of the C90 super computer	Cray Research
Dallas semiconductor company	Texas Instruments
Scotch Tape-brand maker	3M
Company that built the Queen Elizabeth	Cunard
North Dakota computer merchant	Gateway
French maker of disposable lighters and razors	Bic
Largest U.S. maker of pasteurized orange juice	Tropicana
Largest U.S. maker of fruit juices	Ocean Spray

Etch-a-Sketch maker .... Ohio Art
Barbie maker .... Mattel
GI Joe maker .... Hasbro
First yoyo maker .... Duncan
Hula Hoop maker .... Wham-O
Leading maker of processed turkey products .... Louis Rich
Company whose symbol is a monocled peanut .... Planters
Maker of Zima.. Coors
Maker of Viagra .... Pfizer
Only major motorcycle maker in U.S. .... Harley-Davidson
Credit reporting firm and rocket engine builder .... TRW
"Kleenex" maker .... Kimberly-Clark
First company to mass-market baby foods .... Gerber
World's largest food company .... Nestle
Banana Republic and Old Navy owner .... The Gap
Former name of Chiquita brands... United Fruit Company
Former chairman of Occidental Petroleum .... Armand Hammer
Walt Disney CEO .... Michael Eisner
Apple CEO .... Steve Jobs
Steve Jobs' original partner .... Steve Wozniak
Former Microsoft CEO .... Bill Gates
Bill Gates' original partner .... Paul Allen
Current Microsoft CEO .... Steve Ballmer
Dell Computer CEO .... Michael Dell
Amazon CEO .... Jeff Bezos
AMR CEO .... Robert Crandall
QVC CEO .... Barry Diller
Ford CEO .... Jacques Nasser
Berkshire Hathaway CEO .... Warren Buffett
Chrysler chairman, 1979-92 .... Lee Iacocca
Founder of Wendy's Restaurants .... Dave Thomas
Founder of McDonalds' Restaurants... Ray Kroc
Founder of TWA .... Howard Hughes
Founder of CBS .... William Paley
Founder of Kodak... George Eastman
Founder of FOX entertainment .... Rupert Murdoch
Founder of Paramont Pictures .... Adolph Zukor
Founded Hawaiian Pineapple Company in 1901 .... James Dole
Founded American Fur Company in 1808 .... John Jacob Astor
Founded Chicago's largest department store, 1881 .... Marshall Field
Aaron Ward's middle name.. Montgomery
WWI flier and Eastern Airlines chairman .... Eddie Rickenbacker
Astronaut and Eastern Airlines chairman .... Frank Borman
State that incorporates half of the Fortune 500 companies .... Deleware

13 *Celebrity Relatives*

Alfred Stieglitz' wife	Georgia O'Keeffe
Andrea Mitchell's husband	Alan Greenspan
Andrew Shue's sister	Elizabeth Shue
Anjelica Huston's grandfather	Walter Huston
Barbara Bach's husband	Ringo Starr
Beau and Jeff Bridges' father	Lloyd Bridges
Blake Edward's wife	Julie Andrews
Bruce Boxleitner's wife	Melissa Gilbert
Carolyn Bessette's husband	John F. Kennedy, Jr.
Cecil B. DeMille's niece	Agnes DeMille
Charlie Sheen's older brother	Emilio Estevez
Christopher Plummer's daughter	Amanda Plummer
Clint Black's wife	Lisa Hartman
Daniel Day Lewis' father-in-law	Arthur Miller
Danny DeVito's wife	Rhea Perlman
David Cassidy's stepmother	Shirley Jones
Dyan Cannon and Cary Grant's daughter	Jennifer Grant
Eddie Fisher and Debbie Reynolds' daughter	Carrie Fisher
Emilio Estevez's father	Martin Sheen
Erskine Caldwell's wife	Margaret Bourke-White
Eugene O'Neill's son-in-law	Charlie Chaplin
F. Scott Fitzgerald's wife	Zelda
Fernando Lamas' son	Lorenzo Lamas
Francis Ford Coppola's nephew	Nicholas Cage
Francis Ford Coppola's sister	Talia Shire
Franz Liszt's son-in-law	Richard Wagner
Helen Hayes' husband	Charles MacArthur
Helen Hayes' son	James MacArthur
Isabella Rossellini's mother	Ingrid Bergman
Jane Pauley's husband	Gary Trudeau
Jessica Tandy's husband	Hume Cronyn
Joan Collins' sister	Jackie Collins
Joan Fontaine's sister	Olivia de Havilland
Joanne Woodward's husband	Paul Newman
Julia Roberts' brother	Eric Roberts
Julie Nixon's husband	David Eisenhower
Kelly Preston's husband	John Travolta
Kiefer Sutherland's father	Donald Sutherland
Kim Basinger's husband	Alec Baldwin
Kyra Sedgewick's husband	Kevin Bacon
Larry Hagman's mother	Mary Martin
Lillian Gish's sister	Dorothy Gish

Liza Minnelli's mother .... Judy Garland
Loretta Lynn's sister .... Crystal Gayle
Loretta Young's brother-in-law .... Ricardo Montalban
Lynda Bird Johnson's husband .... Charles Robb
Maria Shriver's cousin .... Caroline Kennedy
Maria Shriver's husband .... Arnold Schwarzenegger
Mary Livingston's husband .... Jack Benny
Mel Brooks' wife .... Anne Bancroft
Melanie Griffith's mother .... Tippi Hedren
Melanie Griffith's husband .... Antonio Banderas
Mia Farrow's mother .... Maureen O'Sullivan
Michael Douglas' father .... Kirk Douglas
Natasha Richardson's husband .... Liam Neeson
Orson Welles' wife .... Rita Hayworth
Jon Voight's daughter .... Angelina Jolie
Gwneth Paltrow's mother .... Blythe Danner
Phyllis Rashad's sister .... Debbie Allen
Faith Hill's husband .... Tim McGraw
Tim McGraw's father .... Tug McGraw
Whitney Houston's cousin .... Dionne Warwick
Warren Beatty's sister .... Shirley Maclaine
Brad Pitt's wife .... Jennifer Anniston
Will Smith's wife .... Jada Pinkett
Steve Allen's wife .... Jayne Meadows
Steven Speilberg's wife .... Kate Capshaw
Ted Hughes' wife .... Sylvia Plath
Ted Danson's wife .... Mary Steenburgen
Tony Curtis' daughter .... Jamie Lee Curtis
Vanessa Redgrave's daughter .... Natasha Richardson
Vanessa Redgrave's sister .... Lynn Redgrave
Vic Morrow's daughter .... Jennifer Jason Leigh
Will Durant's wife .... Ariel Durant
Ann Baxter's grandfather .... Frank Lloyd Wright
Barbra Streisand's husband .... James Brolin
Patty Duke's son .... Sean Astin
Peter Graves' brother .... James Arness
Renzo Rossellini's brother .... Roberto Rossellini
Rhea Perlman's husband .... Danny DeVito
Sophia Loren's husband .... Carlo Ponti
Jackie Coogan and Harry James were married to her ....
.... Betty Grable
Jason Robards and Humphrey Bogart were married to her
.... Lauren Bacall
Arthur Miller and Joe DiMaggio were married to her ......
.... Marilyn Monroe

14 *Cinema*

Top Grossing Films of All Time*:
1. Titanic
2. Star Wars
3. Star Wars Episode One: The Phantom Menace
4. E.T.- The Extraterrestrial
5. Jurassic Park
6. Forest Gump
7. The Lion King
8. Return of the Jedi
9. Independence Day
10. The Empire Strikes Back

* Based on sales in U.S. theaters

Actors and Their Roles:

"The Little Tramp"	Charlie Chaplin
Silent screen swashbuckler	Douglas Fairbanks, Sr.
Silver screen swashbuckler	Errol Flynn
Silent film star of *Cleopatra* and *A Fool There Was*	Theda Bara ("The Vamp")
Silent film star of *Phantom of the Opera*, "The Man of a Thousand Faces."	Lon Chaney, Sr.
Silent German horror film, 1919	*The Cabinet of Dr. Caligari*
Charlie Chaplin's film set in the Klondike	*The Gold Rush*
He played "The Sheik"	Rudolph Valentino
He played *Don Juan* in 1926	John Barrymore
Fritz Lang's 1926 silent masterpiece	*Metropolis*
Actress with longest film career	Lillian Gish (75 years)
Royal family of American stage	The Barrymores
The original *Odd Couple*	Walter Matthau & Jack Lemmon
Olympic swimmers who played Tarzan	Buster Crabbe & Johnny Weissmuller
Original *Great Gatsby* star	Alan Ladd
The first talkie	*The Jazz Singer*
The Jazz Singer star	Al Jolson
First color movie, 1935	*Becky Sharp*
First wide screen movie, 1953	*The Robe*
Original *Lawrence of Arabia*	Peter O'Toole
King's Row and *Bedtime for Bonzo* actor	Ronald Reagan
Night of the Iguana and *Where Eagles Dare* actor	Richard Burton
The Miracle Worker and *The Graduate* actress	Ann Bancroft
Rebel Without a Cause and *Giant* actor	James Dean

Fort Apache and *The Grapes of Wrath* actor .... Henry Fonda
On the Waterfront and *Mutiny on the Bounty* actor .... Marlon Brando
An American in Paris and *Singin' in the Rain* actor .... Gene Kelly
Gigi and *An American In Paris* actress .... Leslie Caron
Mary Poppins and *Victor/Victoria* actress .... Julie Andrews
The World of Susie Wong and *Stalag 17* actor .... William Holden
The Misfits and *Some Like it Hot* actress............................ Marilyn Monroe
Stagecoach and *The Quiet Man* actor .... John Wayne
Natural Born Killers and *White Men Can't Jump* actor
.... Woody Harrelson
A Star is Born and *Meet Me in St. Louis* actress .... Judy Garland
True Lies and *Halloween* series actress .... Jamie Lee Curtis
Conan the Barbarian and *The Terminator* actor .... Arnold Schwarzenegger
The Client and *Thelma and Louise* actress .... Susan Sarandon
Cyrano de Bergerac and *Green Card* actor .... Gerard Depardieu
The Net and *Speed* actress .... Sandra Bullock
City Slickers and *Forget Paris* actor .... Billy Crystal
The Color of Money and *Top Gun* actor .... Tom Cruise
Addams Family and *Back to the Future* actor .... Christopher Lloyd
Aliens and *Gorillas in the Mist* actress .... Sigourney Weaver
Prizzi's Honor and *The Addams Family* actress .... Angelica Huston
The Goodbye Girl portrayer .... Marsha Mason
Easy Rider and *Ulee's Gold* actor .... Peter Fonda
Terms of Endearment and *Steel Magnolias* actress .... Shirley MacLaine
Parenthood and *Father of the Bride* actor .... Steve Martin
Rocky and *The Clash of the Titans* actor .... Burgess Meredith
Dirty Dancing and *Ghost* actor .... Patrick Swayze
Raging Bull and *Casino* actor .... Robert De Niro
Jurassic Park and *Independence Day* actor .... Jeff Goldblum
Apollo 13 and *A Few Good Men* actor .... Kevin Bacon
Primary Colors and *Dolores Claiborne* actress .... Kathy Bates
The Fugitive and *Men In Black* actor .... Tommy Lee Jones
My Cousin Vinny and *Goodfellas* actor .... Joe Pesci
Reds and *Dick Tracy* actor .... Warren Beatty
Back to the Future and *Doc Hollywood* actor .... Michael J. Fox
Deep Impact and *The Shawshank Redemption* actor .... Morgan Freeman
Pretty Woman and *An American Gigolo* actor .... Richard Gere
The Natural and *The Sting* actor .... Robert Redford
Zorro and *The Wild, Wild West* actress.............................. Catherine Zeta-Jones
Sleepless in Seattle and *When Harry Met Sally* actress .... Meg Ryan
Lethal Weapon and *Predator II* actor................................. Danny Glover
Mask and *The Witches of Eastwick* actress .... Cher
Same Time Next Year and *Catch 22* actor .... Alan Alda
Bugsy and *Bonnie and Clyde* actor .... Warren Beatty
Legends of the Fall and *Seven Years in Tibet* actor .... Brad Pitt
Edward Scissorhands and *Sleepy Hollow* actor .... Johnny Depp

14 *Cinema*

Body Heat and *Kiss of the Spider Woman* actor .... William Hurt
Four Weddings and a Funeral and *Green Card* actress .... Andie MacDowell
Splash and *Roxanne* actress .... Daryl Hannah
Scent of a Woman and *The Godfather* actor .... Al Pacino
Batman and *The Doors* actor .... Val Kilmer
Manhattan and *Annie Hall* actress .... Diane Keaton
Ferris Bueller's Day Off and *Godzilla* actor .... Matthew Broderick
The Mask and *The Grinch* actor .... Jim Carrey
Die Hard and *The Sixth Sense* actor .... Bruce Willis
Glengarry Glen Ross and *Grumpy Old Men* actor ..... Jack Lemmon
Prince of Tides and *Yeltl* astress .... Barbra Streisand
Alice Doesn't Live Here Anymore star .... Ellen Burstyn
Othello and *What's Love Got to do With It* actor .... Laurence Fishburne
Men in Black and *Independence Day* actor .... Will Smith
Tootsie and *Little Big Man* actor .... Dustin Hoffman
Prizzi's Honor and *Peggy Sue Got Married* actress ... Kathleen Turner
Jaws and *Close Encounters of the Third Kind* actor .... Richard Dreyfuss
Private Benjamin and *Death Becomes Her* actress .... Goldie Hawn
Apocalypse Now and *The Great Santini* actor .... Robert Duvall
Dirty Harry and *The Outlaw Josey Wales* actor .... Clint Eastwood
Jaws and *All That Jazz* actor .... Roy Scheider
Fatal Attraction and *Hamlet* actress .... Glenn Close
Hunt for Red October and *Diamonds are Forever* actor .... Sean Connery
Sister Act and *The Color Purple* actress .... Whoopi Goldberg
Doctor Zhivago and *Star Wars* actor .... Alec Guinness
Forget Paris and *Terms of Endearment* actress .... Debra Winger
Pulp Fiction and *Broken Arrow* actor .... John Travolta
Jewel of the Nile and *Twins* actor .... Danny DeVito
Fried Green Tomatoes and *Cocoon* actress .... Jessica Tandy
Wall Street and *War of the Roses* actor .... Michael Douglas
Accidental Tourist and *Thelma and Louise* actress .... Geena Davis
Big and *A League of Their Own* actor .... Tom Hanks
Apollo 13 and *Glengarry Glen Ross* actor .... Ed Harris
Howard's End and *Legends of the Fall* actor .... Anthony Hopkins
Amadeus and *Animal House* actor .... Tom Hulce
Basic Instinct and *Total Recall* actress .... Sharon Stone
A Few Good Men and *The Witches of Eastwick* actor .... Jack Nicholson
Lorenzo's Oil and *48 Hours* actor .... Nick Nolte
Lilies of the Field and *The Blackboard Jungle* actor .... Sidney Portier
Howard's End and *Henry V* actress .... Emma Thompson
Malcolm X and *Glory* actor .... Denzel Washington
The Player and *The Shawshank Redemption* actor .... Tim Robbins
Pretty Woman and *The Pelican Brief* actress .... Julia Roberts
Edward Scissorhands and *Little Women* actress .... Winona Ryder
Coal Miner's Daughter and *Crimes of the Heart* actress ...... Sissy Spacek
Caddyshack and *Fletch* actor .... Chevy Chase

Groundhog Day and *Ghostbusters* actor .... Bill Murray
The Blues Brothers and *Ghostbusters* actor .... Dan Aykroyd
The Blues Brothers and *Animal House* actor .... John Belushi
Star Wars and *Shampoo* actress .... Carrie Fisher
Good Will Hunting and *Dead Poets Society* actor ...... Robin Williams
The Great Gatsby and *Hannah and Her Sisters* actress .... Mia Farrow
Barbarella and *The Electric Horseman* actress .... Jane Fonda
Air Force One and *The Fugitive* actor .... Harrison Ford
Wall Street and *Hot Shots, Part Deux* actor .... Charlie Sheen
Snake Eyes and *Forrest Gump* actor .... Gary Sinise
Cliffhanger and *Judge Dredd* actor .... Sylvester Stallone
Striptease and *Ghost* actress .... Demi Moore
Beverly Hills Cop and *48 Hours* actor .... Eddie Murphy
Places in the Heart and *Norma Rae* actress .... Sally Field
The Naked Gun and *Airplane* actor .... Leslie Nielsen
Water World and *The Bodyguard* actor .... Kevin Costner
The Bridges of Madison County and *Silkwood* actress .... Meryl Streep
Nell and *Contact* actress .... Jodie Foster
Rob Roy and *Star Wars: The Phantom Menace* actor .... Liam Neeson
Henry V and *Hamlet* actor (modern) .... Kenneth Branagh
Braveheart and *The Road Warrior* actor .... Mel Gibson
A Fish Called Wanda and *Ice Storm* actor .... Kevin Kline
Twister and *As Good as it Gets* actress .... Helen Hunt
Mambo Kings and *Evita* actor .... Antonio Banderas
Two *Sabrina* actresses .... Audrey Hepburn &
                                                                                      Julia Ormond
Three *Batman* actors .... Michael Keaton, Val Kilmer,
                                                                                      George Clooney
Six James Bond actors..........................Peter Sellers, George Lazenby, Sean Connery,
                                                      Roger Moore, Pierce Brosnan, Timothy Dalton
He portrayed "Q" in 17 James Bond Films .... Desmond Llewellyn

Directors:
Woody Allen .... *Annie Hall* (Oscar)
.... *Manhattan*
.... *Sleeper*
.... *Play It Again, Sam*
.... *The Purple Rose of Cairo*
.... *Bullets Over Broadway*
.... *Crimes and Misdeamours*
.... *Hannah and Her Sisters*
Robert Altman .... *M*A*S*H*
.... *Short Cuts*
.... *The Player*
Richard Attenborough .... *Gandhi* (Oscar)
.... *A Chorus Line*

14 Cinema

John Avildsen .... *Rocky* (Oscar)
Lionel Barrymore .... *Madame X*
Warren Beatty .... *Reds*
Roberto Benigni .... *Life is Beautiful* (Oscar)
Robert Benton .... *Kramer vs. Kramer* (Oscar)
Ingmar Bergman .... *Persona*
.... *The Seventh Seal*
Bernardo Bertolucci .... *The Last Emperor* (Oscar)
.... *Last Tango in Paris*
James L. Brooks .... *Terms of Endearment* (Oscar)
Tim Burton .... *Nightmare Before Christmas*
.... *Edward Scissorhands*
.... *Mars Attacks*
.... *Sleepy Hollow*
James Cameron .... *The Terminator*
.... *Terminator II: Judgement Day*
.... *Aliens*
.... *Titanic* (Oscar)
Michael Camino .... *The Deer Hunter* (Oscar)
Frank Capra .... *It's a Wonderful Life*
.... *You Can't Take it With You* (Oscar)
.... *It Happened One Night* (Oscar)
.... *Mr. Deeds Goes To Town* (Oscar)
John Carpenter .... *Halloween I, II, III, ...*
.... *Scream I, II*
Charlie Chaplin .... *The Gold Rush*
.... *City Lights*
.... *Limelight*
.... *The Great Dictator*
Francis Ford Coppola .... *The Godfather I ,II & III* (Oscar, II)
.... *Apocalypse Now*
.... *Peggy Sue Got Married*
.... *Bram Stoker's Dracula*
Kevin Costner .... *Dances With Wolves* (Oscar)
Wes Craven .... *Nightmare on Elm Street I, II, III ...*
Michael Crichton .... *West World*
George Cukor .... *My Fair Lady* (Oscar)
.... *Gaslight*
Michael Curtez .... *Casablanca* (Oscar)
Cecil B. DeMille .... *Sunset Boulevard*
.... *Cleopatra*
.... *The Ten Commandments*
.... *The Greatest Show on Earth*
Jonathan Demme .... *The Silence of the Lambs* (Oscar)
.... *Scarface*
.... *The Untouchables*

Brian De Palma	*Mission Impossible*
	The Untouchables
Clint Eastwood	*Unforgiven* (Oscar)
	The Bridges of Madison County
Federico Fellini	*La Dolce Vita*
Robert Flaherty	*Nanook of the North*
Victor Fleming	*Gone With the Wind* (Oscar)
	The Wizard of Oz
John Ford	*The Grapes of Wrath* (Oscar)
	How Green Was My Valley (Oscar)
	The Informer (Oscar)
	The Quiet Man (Oscar)
	Fort Apache
	Stagecoach
Milos Forman	*One Flew Over the Cuckoo's Nest* (Oscar)
	Amadeus (Oscar)
Bob Fosse	*All That Jazz*
	Cabaret (Oscar)
William Friedkin	*The French Connection* (Oscar)
Mel Gibson	*Braveheart* (Oscar)
Jean-Luc Godard	*Breathless*
D. W. Griffith	*Birth of a Nation*
George Roy Hill	*The Sting* (Oscar)
	Butch Cassidy and the Sundance Kid
	Slaughterhouse Five
Alfred Hitchcock	*Rebecca*
	Rear Window
	Psycho
	Frenzy
	Strangers on a Train
	North By Northwest
	Vertigo
	Notorious
Ron Howard	*Cocoon*
	Apollo 13
John Huston	*Treasure of the Sierra Madre* (Oscar)
	Prizzi's Honor
	The Faltese Falson
	The African Queen
Norman Jewison	*In the Heat of the Night*
	Moonstruck
Lawrence Kasdan	*The Big Chill*
	Body Heat
Elia Kazan	*On the Waterfront* (Oscar)
	Gentlemen's Agreement (Oscar)
	A Streetcar Named Desire

14 *Cinema*

Stanley Kubrick	*2001: A Space Odyssey*
	Dr. Strangelove
	Spartacus
	Clockwork Orange
	The Shining
	Full Metal Jacket
	Eyes Wide Shut
Akira Kurosawa	*The Seven Samurai*
	Roshomon
	Ran
Fritz Lange	*M*
David Lean	*The Bridge on the River Kwai* (Oscar)
	Dr. Zhivago
	A Passage to India
	Lawrence of Arabia (Oscar)
Barry Levinson	*Rain Man* (Oscar)
	The Natural
	Good Morning, Vietnam
George Lucas	*Star Wars*
	American Graffiti
	Star Wars: The Phantom Menace
Joseph L. Mankiewicz	*Letter to Three Wives* (Oscar)
	All About Eve (Oscar)
	Guys and Dolls
Penny Marshall	*Awakenings*
	Big
	A League of Their Own
Anthony Mingella	*English Patient* (Oscar)
Vincent Minnelli	*Gigi* (Oscar)
	An American in Paris
Mike Nichols	*Who's Afraid of Virginia Woolf*
	The Graduate (Oscar)
	Silkwood
	Working Girl
	Postcards from the Edge
Alan Parker	*Midnight Express*
	Mississippi Burning
Wolfgang Peterson	*In the Line of Fire*
	Air Force One
Sam Peckinpah	*The Wild Bunch*
Roman Polanski	*Chinatown*
	Rosemary's Baby
Sidney Pollack	*Out of Africa* (Oscar)
	The Electric Horseman
	Tootsie

Robert Redford .... *Ordinary People* (Oscar)
.... *A River Runs Through It*
.... *Quiz Show*
Rob Reiner .... *When Harry Met Sally....*
.... *Misery*
.... *A Few Good Men*
Jerome Robbins..................... *West Side Story* (Oscar)
Sir Carol Reed .... *Oliver* (Oscar)
Tom Richardson .... *Tom Jones* (Oscar)
Franklin Schaffner............... *Patton* (Oscar)
Martin Scorsese .... *Raging Bull*
.... *The Last Temptation of Christ*
.... *Cape Fear*
.... *Goodfellas*
.... *Taxi Driver*
Ridley Scott .... *Alien*
.... *Thelma and Louise*
.... *G. I. Jane*
.... *Blade Runner*
Mack Sennett........................ *Keystone Kops* series
John Schlesinger .... *Midnight Cowboy* (Oscar)
Steven Spielberg .... *Duel* (TV movie)
.... *Close Encounters of the Third Kind*
.... *E.T.-The Extra-Terrestrial*
.... *The Color Purple*
.... *Jaws*
.... *Poltergeist*
.... *Raiders of the Lost Ark*
.... *Indiana Jones and the Temple of Doom*
.... *Indiana Jones and the Last Crusade*
.... *Empire of the Sun*
.... *Jurassic Park*
.... *Jurassic Park: The Lost World*
.... *Schindler's List* (Oscar)
.... *Saving Private Ryan* (Oscar)
George Stevens .... *A Place in the Sun* (Oscar)
.... *Giant* (Oscar)
Oliver Stone .... *Platoon* (Oscar)
.... *Born on the 4th of July* (Oscar)
.... *The Doors*
.... *JFK*
.... *Natural Born Killers*
.... *Wall Street*
Barbra Streisand .... *Prince of Tides*
.... *The Mirror Has Two Faces*
.... *Yentl*

14 *Cinema*

Quentin Tarantino .... *Pulp Fiction*
.... *Reservoir Dogs*
.... *Jackie Brown*
François Truffaut .... *Small Change*
Orson Welles........................... *Citizen Kane*
.... *Macbeth* (1948)
.... *The Magnificent Ambersons*
Lina Wertmuller .... *Seven Beauties*
Billy Wilder .... *The Lost Weekend* (Oscar)
.... *The Apartment* (Oscar)
.... *Sunset Boulevard*
Robert Wise............................ *The Sound of Music* (Oscar)
Ed Wood .... *Plan 9 From Outer Space*
William Wyler .... *Mrs. Miniver* (Oscar)
.... *The Best Years of Our Lives* (Oscar)
.... *Ben Hur* (Oscar)
.... *Wuthering Heights*
.... *Funny Girl*
Franco Zeffirelli .... *Taming of the Shrew*
Robert Zemeckis.................... *Forrest Gump* (Oscar)
.... *Cast Away*
Fred Zinnemann .... *From Here to Eternity* (Oscar)
.... *A Man for All Seasons* (Oscar)
.... *The Day of the Jackal*
.... *High Noon*
David Zucker .... *Airplane!*
.... *Ghost*

The Oscars:

Films to win most Oscars (11) .... *Ben Hur*
.... *Titanic*
Films nominated for most Oscars (14) .... *All About Eve*
.... *Titanic*
Most nominated films to receive no Oscars (11) .... *The Turning Point*
.... *The Color Purple*
Three films to win top five Oscars .... *It Happened One Night*
.... *One Flew Over the Cuckoo's Nest*
.... *Silence of the Lambs*
Four time winner of Best Actress Oscar .... Katharine Hepburn
Four time winner of Best Director Oscar .... John Ford
Three time winner of Best Supporting Actor Oscar .... Walter Brennen
Two time winners of Best Actor Oscar .... Spencer Tracy (back to back)
.... Frederic March
.... Garry Cooper
.... Marlin Brando
.... Dustin Hoffman

.... Jack Nicholson
.... Tom Hanks (back to back)
Two time winners of Best Actress Oscar .... Bette Davis
.... Louise Rainer (back to back)
.... Vivian Leigh
.... Ingrid Bergman
.... Glenda Jackson
.... Jane Fonda
.... Sally Field
.... Jodie Foster
Youngest Best Supporting Actress winner .... Tatum O'Neal (10 yrs.)
Youngest Best Actress winner .... Marlee Matlin (20 yrs.)
Oldest Best Actress winner .... Jessica Tandy (80 yrs.)
Oldest Best Actor winner .... Henry Fonda (76 yrs.)
Oldest Best Supporting Actor winner .... George Burns (80 yrs.)
Individual with most non-acting Oscars .... Walt Disney (27 plus 6 special)
Fashion designer with most Oscars .... Edith Head (8)
Only film and its sequel to win Best Picture Oscar .... *The Godfather I & II*
First film and only silent film to win Best Picture, 1927 ... *Wings*
Frederic March Best Actor film, 1931-32 .... *Dr. Jekyll and Mr. Hyde*
Charles Laughton Best Actor film, 1932-33 .... *Private Life of Henry VIII*
Clark Gable Best Actor film, 1934 .... *It Happened One Night*
Claudette Colbert Best Actress film, 1934 .... *It Happened One Night*
Bette Davis Best Actress film, 1935 .... *Dangerous*
Louise Ranier Best Actress film, 1936 .... *The Great Ziegfield*
Spencer Tracy Best Actor film, 1937 .... *Captains Courageous*
Louise Ranier Best Actress film, 1937 .... *The Good Earth*
Spencer Tracy Best Actor film, 1938 .... *Boys Town*
Bette Davis Best Actress film, 1938 .... *Jezebel*
Robert Donat Best Actor film, 1939 .... *Goodbye Mr. Chips*
Vivian Leigh Best Actress film, 1939 .... *Gone With the Wind*
Hattie McDaniel Best Supporting Actress film, 1939 .... *Gone With the Wind*
Jimmy Stewart Best Actor film, 1940 .... *The Philadelphia Story*
Ginger Rogers Best Actress film, 1940 .... *Kitty Foyle*
Gary Cooper Best Actor film, 1941 .... *Sergeant York*
Joan Fontaine Best Actress film, 1941 .... *Suspicion*
James Cagney Best Actor film, 1942 .... *Yankee Doodle Dandy*
Greer Garson Best Actress film, 1942 .... *Mrs. Miniver*
Paul Lukas Best Actor film, 1943 .... *Watch on the Rhine*
Jennifer Jones Best Actress film, 1943 .... *Song of Bernadette*
Bing Crosby Best Actor film, 1944 .... *Going My Way*
Ingrid Bergman Best Actress film, 1944 .... *Gaslight*
Ray Milland Best Actor film, 1945 .... *The Lost Weekend*
Joan Crawford Best Actress film, 1945 .... *Mildred Pierce*
Fredric March Best Actor film, 1946 .... *The Best Years of Our Lives*
Ronald Colman Best Actor film, 1947 .... *A Double Life*

14 *Cinema*

Loretta Young Best Actress film, 1947 .... *The Farmer's Daughter*
Laurence Olivier Best Actor film, 1948 .... *Hamlet*
Walter Huston Best Supporting Actor film, 1948 .... *Treasure of the Sierra Madre*
Broderick Crawford Best Actor film, 1949 .... *All the King's Men*
Jose Ferrer Best Actor film, 1950 .... *Cyrano de Bergerac*
Humphrey Bogart Best Actor film, 1951 .... *The African Queen*
Vivien Leigh Best Actress film, 1951 .... *A Streetcar Named Desire*
Gary Cooper Best Actor film, 1952 .... *High Noon*
Shirley Booth Best Actress film, 1952 .... *Come Back Little Sheba*
William Holden Best Actor film, 1953 .... *Stalag 17*
Audrey Hepburn Best Actress film, 1953 .... *Roman Holiday*
Marlon Brando Best Actor film, 1954 .... *On the Waterfront*
Grace Kelly Best Actress film, 1954 .... *Country Girl*
Ernest Borgnine Best Actor, 1955 .... *Marty*
Anna Magnani Best Actress film, *1955*............................ *The Rose Tatoo*
Yul Brynner Best Actor film, 1956 .... *The King and I*
Ingrid Bergman Best Actress film, 1956 .... *Anastasia*
Alec Guiness Best Actor film, 1957 .... *The Bridge on the River Kwai*
Joanne Woodward Best Actress film, 1957 .... *The Three Faces of Eve*
David Niven Best Actor film, 1958 .... *Separate Tables*
Susan Hayward Best Actress film, 1958............................. *I Want to Live*
Charlton Heston Best Actor film, 1959............................. *Ben Hur*
Simone Signoret Best Actress film, 1959 .... *Room at the Top*
Bert Lancaster Best Actor film, 1960 .... *Elmer Gantry*
Elizabeth Taylor Best Actress film, 1960 .... *Butterfield 8*
Maximilian Schell Best Actor film, 1961 .... *Judgement at Nuremberg*
Sophia Loren Best Actress film, 1961 .... *Two Women*
Gregory Peck Best Actor film, 1962 .... *To Kill a Mockingbird*
Ann Bancroft Best Actress film, 1962 .... *The Miracle Worker*
Sidney Poitier Best Actor film, 1963 .... *Lilies of the Field*
Patricia Neal Best Actress film, 1963 .... *Hud*
Rex Harrison Best Actor film ,1964 .... *My Fair Lady*
Julie Andrews Best Actress film, 1964 .... *Mary Poppins*
Lee Marvin Best Actor film, 1965 .... *Cat Ballou*
Julie Christie Best Actress film, 1965 .... *Darling*
Paul Scofield Best Actor film, 1966 .... *A Man for All Seasons*
Elizabeth Taylor Best Actress film, 1966 .... *Who's Afraid of Virginia Woolf?*
Rod Steiger Best Actor Film, 1967 .... *In the Heat of the Night*
Katharine Hepburn Best Actress film, 1967 .... *Guess Who's Coming to Dinner?*
Cliff Robertson Best Actor film, 1968 .... *Charley*
Katharine Hepburn Best Actress film, 1968 (tie) .... *The Lion in Winter*
Barbra Streisand Best Actress film, 1968 (tie) .... *Funny Girl*
John Wayne Best Actor film, 1969 .... *True Grit*
Maggie Smith Best Actress film, 1969 .... *The Prime of Miss Jean Brodie*
George C. Scott Best Actor film, 1970 .... *Patton*
Glenda Jackson Best Actress film, 1970 .... *Women in Love*

Gene Hackman Best Actor film, 1971 .... *The French Connection*
Jane Fonda Best Actress film, 1971 .... *Klute*
Marlon Brando Best Actor film, 1972 .... *The Godfather*
Liza Minnelli Best Actress film, 1972 .... *Cabaret*
Jack Lemmon Best Actor film, 1973 .... *Save the Tiger*
Glenda Jackson Best Actress film, 1973 .... *A Touch of Class*
Art Carney Best Actor film, 1974 .... *Harry and Tonto*
Ellen Burstyn Best Actress film, 1974 .... *Alice Doesn't Live Here Anymore*
Jack Nicholson Best Actor film, 1975 .... *One Flew Over the Cuckoo's Nest*
Louise Fletcher Best Actress film, 1975 .... *One Flew Over the Cuckoo's Nest*
Peter Finch Best Actor film, 1976 .... *Network* (posthumous award)
Faye Dunaway Best Actress film, 1976 .... *Network*
Richard Dreyfuss Best Actor film, 1977 .... *The Goodbye Girl*
Diane Keaton Best Actress film, 1977 .... *Annie Hall*
Jon Voight Best Actor film, 1978 .... *Coming Home*
Jane Fonda Best Actress film, 1978 .... *Coming Home*
Dustin Hoffman Best Actor film, 1979 .... *Kramer vs. Kramer*
Sally Field Best Actress film, 1979 .... *Norma Rae*
Robert De Niro Best Actor film, 1980 .... *Raging Bull*
Sissy Spacek Best Actress film, 1980 .... *Coal Miner's Daughter*
Henry Fonda Best Actor film, 1981 .... *On Golden Pond*
Katharine Hepburn Best Actress film, 1981 .... *On Golden Pond*
Meryl Streep Best Actress film, 1982 .... *Sophie's Choice*
Ben Kingsley Best Actor film, 1982 .... *Gandhi*
Lou Gossett, Jr. Best Supporting Actor film, 1982 .... *An Officer and a Gentleman*
Robert Duvall Best Actor film, 1983 .... *Tender Mercies*
Shirley MacLaine Best Actress film, 1983 .... *Terms of Endearment*
F. Murray Abraham Best Actor film, 1984 .... *Amadeus*
Sally Field Best Actress film, 1984 .... *Places in the Heart*
William Hurt Best Actor film, 1985 .... *Kiss of the Spider Woman*
Geraldine Page Best Actress film, 1985 .... *Trip to Bountiful*
Paul Newman Best Actor film, 1986 .... *The Color of Money*
Marlee Matlin Best Actress film, 1986 .... *Children of a Lesser God*
Michael Douglas Best Actor film, 1987 .... *Wall Street*
Cher Best Actress film, 1987 .... *Moonstruck*
Dustin Hoffman Best Actor film, 1988 .... *Rain Man*
Jodie Foster Best Actress film, 1988 .... *The Accused*
Daniel Day-Lewis Best Actor film, 1989 .... *My Left Foot*
Jessica Tandy Best Actress film, 1989 .... *Driving Miss Daisy*
Jeremy Irons Best Actor film, 1990 .... *Reversal of Fortune*
Kathy Bates Best Actress film, 1990 .... *Misery*
Anthony Hopkins Best Actor film, 1991 .... *Silence of the Lambs*
Jodie Foster Best Actress film, 1991 .... *Silence of the Lambs*
Jack Palance Best Supporting Actor film, 1991 .... *City Slickers*
Al Pacino Best Actor film, 1992 .... *Scent of a Woman*
Jessica Lange Best Actress film, 1992 .... *Blue Sky*

Marisa Tomei Best Supporting Actress film, 1992 .... *My Cousin Vinny*
Holly Hunter Best Actress film, 1993 .... *The Piano*
Tom Hanks Best Actor film, 1993 .... *Philadelphia*
Martin Landau Best Supporting Actor film, 1994 .... *Ed Wood*
Tom Hanks Best Actor film, 1994 .... *Forrest Gump*
Nicolas Cage Best Actor film, 1995 .... *Leaving Las Vegas*
Susan Sarandon Best Actress film, 1995 .... *Dead Man Walking*
Geoffrey Rush Best Actor film, 1996 .... *Shine*
Frances McDormand Best Actress film, 1996 .... *Fargo*
Juliette Binoche Best Supporting Actress film, 1996 .... *The English Patient*
Jack Nicholson Best Actor film, 1997 .... *As Good as it Gets*
Helen Hunt Best Actress film, 1997 .... *As Good as it Gets*
Roberto Benigni Best Actor film, 1998 .... *Life is Beautiful*
Gwyneth Paltrow Best Actress film, 1998 .... *Shakespeare in Love*
Kevin Spacey Best Actor film, 1999 .... *American Beauty*
Hilary Swank Best Actress film, 1999 .... *Boys Don't Cry*

Best Pictures:

1927-28 .... *Wings*

1928-29 .... *Broadway Melody*

1929-30 .... *All Quiet on the Western Front*

1930-31 .... *Cimarron*

1931-32 .... *Grand Hotel*

1932-33 .... *Cavalcade*

1934 .... *It Happened One Night*

1935 .... *Mutiny on the Bounty*

1936 .... *The Great Ziegfield*

1937 .... *The Life of Emile Zola*

1938 .... *You Can't Take it With You*

1939 .... *Gone With the Wind*

1940 .... *Rebecca*

1941 .... *How Green Was My Valley*

1942 .... *Mrs. Miniver*

1943 .... *Casablanca*

1944 .... *Going My Way*

1945 .... *The Lost Weekend*

1946 .... *The Best Years of Our Lives*

1947 .... *Gentlemen's Agreement*

1948 .... *Hamlet*

1949 .... *All the King's Men*

1950 .... *All About Eve*

1951 .... *An American in Paris*

1952 .... *The Greatest Show on Earth*

1953 .... *From Here to Eternity*

1954 .... *On the Waterfront*

1955 .... *Marty*

1956 .... *Around the World in 80 Days*

1957 .... *The Bridge on the River Kwai*

1958 .... *Gigi*

1959 .... *Ben Hur*

1960 .... *The Apartment*

1961 .... *West Side Story*

1962 .... *Lawrence of Arabia*

1963 .... *Tom Jones*

1964 .... *My Fair Lady*

1965 .... *The Sound of Music*

1966 .... *A Man for All Seasons*

1967 .... *In the Heat of the Night*

1968 .... *Oliver*

1969 .... *Midnight Cowboy*

1970 .... *Patton*

1971 .... *The French Connection*

1972 .... *The Godfather*

1973 .... *The Sting*

1974 .... *The Godfather II*

1975 .... *One Flew Over the Cuckoo's Nest*

1976 .... *Rocky*

1977 .... *Annie Hall*

1978 .... *The Deer Hunter*

1979 .... *Kramer vs. Kramer*

1980 .... *Ordinary People*

14 *Cinema*

1981	*Chariots of Fire*
1982	*Gandhi*
1983	*Terms of Endearment*
1984	*Amadeus*
1985	*Out of Africa*
1986	*Platoon*
1987	*The Last Emperor*
1988	*Rain Man*
1989	*Driving Mrs. Daisy*
1990	*Dances With Wolves*
1991	*Silence of the Lambs*
1992	*Unforgiven*
1993	*Schindler's List*
1994	*Forrest Gump*
1995	*Braveheart*
1996	*The English Patient*
1997	*Titanic*
1998	*Shakespeare in Love*
1999	*American Beauty*

Cities 15

Largest Cities in:

THE UNITED STATES
1. New York
2. Los Angeles
3. Chicago
4. Houston
5. Philadelphia
6. San Diego
7. Detroit
8. Dallas
9. Phoenix
10. San Antonio

THE WORLD
1. Mexico City
2. Tokyo
3. Sao Paulo
4. Shanghai
5. Buenos Aires
6. Beijing
7. Paris
8. Seoul
9. Cairo
10. Moscow

World's Largest Metropolitan Areas*
1. Tokyo/Yokohama
2. New York City
3. Sao Paulo
4. Mexico City
5. Shanghai
6. Bombay
7. Los Angeles
8. Beijing
9. Calcutta
10. Seoul

* Author's Note: The world's largest cities are very difficult to gauge. If Yokohama is included as part of Tokyo, then Tokyo becomes the world's largest city. New York within its city limits does not make the top ten list, but when the entire metro area is considered, then it becomes the world's second largest city. It is this way with all the cities on the list. If the greater metropolitan area is included or left out, then the list changes. That is why there are two separate lists.

US Cities:

Northernmost state capital	Juneau, AK
Southernmost state capital	Honolulu, HI
Easternmost state capital	Augusta, ME
Westernmost state capital	Honolulu, HI
Northernmost state capital of the 48 states	Olympia, WA
Southernmost state capital of the 48 states	Austin, TX
Westernmost state capital of the 48 states	Salem, OR

15 Cities

Oldest state capital	Santa Fe, NM
State capital with the largest population	Phoenix, AZ
State capital with the smallest population	Montpelier, VT
State capital covering the largest area	Juneau, AK
Oldest U.S. city	St. Augustine, FL
The City of Brotherly Love	Philadelphia, PA
The "Biggest Little City in the World"	Reno, NV
City of Lakes	Minneapolis, MN
Alamo city	San Antonio, TX
The Big Peach	Atlanta, GA
Chocolate capital of the world	Hershey, PA
The Hub of the Universe	Boston, MA
Motor City	Detroit, MI
Pittsburgh of the South	Birmingham, AL
Rubber capital of the world	Akron, OH
Windy City	Chicago, IL
Wright brothers' hometown	Dayton, OH
Omaha's twin city	Council Bluffs, IA
Michigan city named for an Indian chief	Pontiac
Washington city named for an Indian chief	Seattle
The Queen City	Cincinnati, OH
Beacon Street city	Boston, MA
Beale Street city	Memphis, TN
Athens of the South	Nashville, TN
Crescent city	New Orleans, LA
Windsor, Ontario's sister city	Detroit, MI
Bagdad by the Bay	San Francisco, CA
Sunshine city	St. Petersburg, FL
First capital of California	San Jose
Tennessee "Manhattan Project" city	Oak Ridge
Tennessee World's Fair city	Knoxville (named for John Knox)
End of the Oregon Trail	Astoria, OR (named for John J. Astor)
City of Roses	Portland, OR
The Witch City	Salem, MA
The Crossroads of the West	Salt Lake City, UT
The Disney City	Orlando, FL
Mt. Washington overlooks this city	Pittsburgh, PA
Stone Mountain overlooks this city	Atlanta, GA
New Mexico ski resort	Taos
Alabama port	Mobile
Georgia port	Savannah
New Hampshire port	Portsmouth
Maine port	Portland
Mississippi port	Biloxi

South Carolina port	Charleston
Pennsylvania Great Lakes port	Erie
Minnesota Great Lakes port	Duluth
Indiana Great Lakes port	Gary
Johns Hopkins University city	Baltimore, MD
Mayo Brothers Clinic city	Rochester, MN
Lincoln Park Zoo city	Chicago, IL
Insurance capital of the world	Hartford, CN
NASA city in Alabama	Huntsville
The streets in *Monopoly* are found here	Atlantic City, NJ
Rhode Island jazz festival city	Newport
Cradle of Jazz	New Orleans, LA
Gateway to the West	St. Louis, MO
Highest incorporated city in the U.S.	Leadville, CO
Comstock Lode city	Virginia City, NV
U.S. city with the most fountains	Kansas City, MO
Kansas City, MO sister city	Kansas City, KS
Kansas penitentiary city	Leavenworth
South Dakota frontier city	Deadwood
Pabst Mansion city	Milwaukee, WI
Wisconsin city meaning "clear water"	Au Clair
OK Corral city	Tombstone, AZ
Gardner Museum city	Boston, MA
Field Museum city	Chicago, IL
Will Rogers Museum city	Claremore, OK
J. Paul Getty Museum city	Malibu, CA
Eisenhower Museum city	Abilene, KS
6th Floor Museum city	Dallas, TX
Lake Superior Museum of Transport city	Duluth, MN
City served by Logan Airport	Boston, MA
City served by Skye Harbor Airport	Phoenix, AZ
City served by Ronald Reagan Airport	Washington, D.C.
City served by John Wayne Airport	Long Beach (Orange County)
City served by Love Field	Dallas, TX
City served by Midway Airport	Chicago, IL
City served by Will Rogers & Wiley Post Airports	Tulsa, OK
Home of the Peale Museum	Philadelphia, PA
Home of the Field Museum	Chicago, IL
Home of the Heard Museum	Phoenix, AZ
Home of the Frick Museum	Pittsburgh, PA
Home of the Ringling Brothers Museum	Sarasota, FL
Home of the Norman Rockwell Museum	Stockbridge. MA
Home of the Colorado Ski Museum	Vail
Home of The Smithsonian	Washington, D.C.

15 *Cities*

World Cities:

World's oldest walled city .... Jericho
World's oldest continuously inhabited city .... Damascus
World capital highest in elevation .... La Paz
Northernmost world capital .... Reykjavik
Southernmost world capital .... Wellington
City with the most fountains .... Rome
The Waltz City .... Vienna
The Jewel of the Adriatic .... Venice
The City of Lights .... Paris
The Pearl of the Orient .... Manila
The City of Bridges .... Stockholm
City formerly known as Christiania .... Oslo
City formerly known as Tenochtitlan .... Mexico City
City formerly known as Philadelphia .... Amman, Jordan
City formerly known as Edo .... Tokyo
City formerly known as New Amsterdam .... New York City
City formerly know as Fort York.................................. Toronto
City formerly known as Batavia .... Jakarta
City formerly known as Leningrad .... St. Petersberg
City formerly known as Lutentia .... Paris
City formerly known as Danzig .... Gdansk
City formerly known as Constantinople .... Istanbul
City formerly known as Angora .... Ankora
City formerly known as Saigon .... Ho Chi Minh City
City formerly known as Rangoon .... Yangon
City formerly known as Salsbury .... Harare
Home of the world's tallest building .... Kuala Lumpur, Malaysia
Home of the Hagia Sophia .... Istanbul
Home of the Taj Mahal .... Agra, India
Home of the Hermitage.. St. Petersburg, Russia
Home of the Rijksmuseum .... Amsterdam
Home of the Benaki Museum .... Athens
Home of the Effizi Museum and the Bargello .... Florence
Home of the Victoria and Albert Museum .... London
Home of the Prado .... Madrid
Home of the Tretykov Museum .... Moscow
Home of the Guggenheim Museum .... New York
Home to the Kon Tiki Museum .... Oslo
Interpol headquarters... Paris
NATO headquarters .... Brussels
WHO headquarters .... Geneva
Where Nobel Prizes (except Peace) are awarded .... Stockholm
Where Nobel Peace Prize is awarded .... Oslo

Civil War 16

First capital of the Confederacy	Montgomery, AL (Cradle of the Confederacy)
Capital after Montgomery	Richmond, VA
President of Confederate States of America (C.S.A.)	Jefferson Davis
Vice president of C.S.A.	Alexander Stephens
Number of states in the Confederacy	Eleven
Number of states in the Union	Twenty-three
Lincoln's first choice to head Union Army	Robert E. Lee
C.S.A. general; "Old Jube"	Jubilee Anderson Early
C.S.A. general who captured Fort Sumter	P. G. T. Beauregard
C.S.A. general; victor at Shenandoah Valley	Stonewall Jackson
Union general; "Fighting Joe"	Joseph Hooker (term "hooker" came from his female camp followers)
Union general; "Uncle Billy"	William Tecumseh Sherman
Union general; "Little Phil"	Phillip Sheridan
Union general with "mutton chop" sideburns	Ambrose Burnside (Rhode Island governor)
Union general who resigned ashead of the Union Army, 1861	Winfield Scott
Union army chief relieved in 1862	George McClellan ("Little Mac")
Union general who was Buchanan's V.P.	John C. Breckinridge
Union admiral who captured Mobile Bay, 1864	David Farragut
Union general who captured Atlanta	William T. Sherman
Superintendent of Union Army nurses	Dorothea Dix
Female surgeon who received Congressional Medal of Honor	Mary Walker
"Angel of the battlefield"	Clara Barton
Female "Spy of the Cumberland"	Pauline Cushman
Confederate female spy	Belle Boyd
Underground railroad conductor; "Moses" of her people	Harriet Tubman
Man who led raid on Harper's Ferry, 1859	John Brown
Slave involved in a Supreme Court decision	Dred Scott
Civil War detective agency	Pinkerton's ("We never sleep")
Line dividing slave and free states	Mason-Dixon line
States along the Mason-Dixon line	Border States
First state to secede from the Union	South Carolina
Last state to secede from the Union	Virginia
First state to rejoin the Union	Tennessee
Last state to rejoin the Union	Georgia
Union ironclad	Monitor

16 | *Civil War*

Confederate ironclad	Merrimack
Merrimack's other name	Virginia
Ill-fated C.S.A. submarine	Hunley
"The Breadbasket of the Confederacy"	Shenandoah Valley
Infamous Confederate POW camp	Andersonville (in GA)
Confederate train hijacked by the North	The General
Site of first Civil War battle in April, 1861	Fort Sumter
First major battle of the war, July, 1861	First Manassas (Bull Run), Virginia
Tennessee battle site, April, 1862	Shiloh (won by U.S. Grant's army)
"Road to Richmond" battle, Feb.-June, 1862	Shenandoah Valley Campaign
Virginia battle site, Aug., 1862	Second Manassas (Bull Run, won by Jackson's army)
Bloodiest battle in American history, Sept. 1862	Antietam, MD
Lawrence, KS raiders from Missouri, 1863	Quantrill's Raiders (including Jesse James)
Battle where Stonewall Jackson lost an arm	Fredericksberg
Battle where Stonewall Jackson was killed, May 1863	Chancellorsville, TN
Mississippi River battle site, March-July 1863	Vicksburg, MS
Pennsylvania battle site, July 1863	Gettysburg
Union commander at Gettysburg	George Meade
Confederate commander at Gettysburg	Robert E. Lee
Gettysburg ridge defended by Union Armies	Seminary Ridge
Gettysburg "charge"	Pickett's Charge
Gettysburg ridge Pickett charged up	Cemetery Ridge
Place where Lee surrendered, April 1865	Appomattox (Court House)
Farm where Lee met Grant to sign the surrender	Wilmer McLean's
Rebuilding the South after the war	Reconstruction
Confederate inaugural song	*Dixie*
Theater where Lincoln was shot	Ford's Theater
Lincoln was shot while watching this play	*Our American Cousin*
Man who shot Lincoln	John Wilkes Booth
Doctor who set Booth's broken leg	Samuel Mudd
Woman hung for Lincoln's death	Mary Surratt
Only person executed for war crimes	Henry Wirz, Andersonville P.O.W. commandant
Term for southern sympathizers in the north	Copperhead
Northern opportunists in the South after the war	Carpetbaggers
Civil War photographer	Matthew Brady
20th century Civil War historian	Bruce Catton
Group of Civil War veterans	Grand Army of the Republic

Colleges and Universities 17

University Locations:

American University	Washington, DC
Arizona State University	Tempe, AZ
Ball State	Muncie, IN
Baylor	Waco, TX
Bradley	Peoria, IL
Brandeis	Waltham, MA
Brigham Young	Provo, UT
Bowdoin	Brunswick, ME
Cal Tech	Pasadena, CA
Carnegie Mellon	Pittsburgh, PA
The Citadel	Charleston, SC
Columbia	New York City, NY
Creighton	Omaha, NB
DePaul	Chicago, IL
Drake	Des Moines, IA
Duke	Durham, NC
Emory	Atlanta, GA
Florida State University	Tallahassee, FL
Fordham	New York City, NY
Gallaudet	Washington, D.C.
Georgetown	Washington, D.C.
George Washington	Washington, D.C.
Georgia State University	Atlanta, GA
Gonzaga	Spokane, WA
Holy Cross	Worcester, MA
Howard	Washington, D.C.
Illinois State University	Normal, IL
Johns Hopkins University	Baltimore, MD
Julliard School	New York City, NY
Kansas State University	Manhattan, KS
Lehigh	Bethlehem, PA
Liberty	Lynchburg, VA
Louisiana State University	Baton Rouge, LA
Marquette	Milwaukee, WI
Massachusetts Institute of Technology (MIT)	Cambridge, MA
McGill	Montreal, Quebec, Canada
Miami of Ohio	Oxford, Ohio
North Carolina State	Raleigh, NC
Northwestern	Evanston, IL
Notre Dame	South Bend, IN
Michigan State University	East Lansing, MI

17 *Colleges and Universities*

Mississippi (Ole Miss) .... Oxford, MS
Ohio State University .... Columbus, OH
Oklahoma State University .... Stillwater, OK
Old Dominion .... Norfolk, VA
Oral Roberts .... Tulsa, OK
Penn State .... State College, PA
Purdue .... West Lafayette, IN
Rice .... Houston, TX
Rutgers .... New Brunswick, NJ
St. Johns .... Jamaica, NY
Seton Hall .... South Orange, NJ
Scripp's Institute of Oceanography .... San Diego, CA
Southern Methodist University (SMU) .... Dallas, TX
Spelman .... Atlanta, GA
Temple .... Philadelphia, PA
Texas A&M .... College Station, TX
Texas Christian University (TCU) .... Fort Worth, TX
Tufts .... Medford, MA
Tulane .... New Orleans, LA
University of Alabama .... Tuscaloosa, AL
University of Arkansas .... Fayetteville, AR
University of Arizona .... Tempe, AZ
University of Florida .... Gainesville, FL
University of Georgia .... Athens, GA
University of Illinois .... Urbana, IL
University of Iowa .... Iowa City, IA
University of Maryland .... College Park, MD
University of Kansas .... Lawrence, KS
University of Kentucky .... Lexington, KY
University of Michigan .... Ann Arbor, MI
University of Montana .... Missoula, MT
University of New Mexico .... Albuquerque, NM
University of North Carolina .... Chapel Hill, NC
University of Oklahoma .... Norman, OK
University of Oregon .... Eugene, OR
University of Rhode Island .... Kingston, RI
University of Texas .... Austin, TX
University of Utah .... Salt Lake City, UT
University of Vermont .... Burlington, VT
University of Virginia .... Charlottesville, VA
University of Washington .... Seattle, WA
University of Wyoming .... Laramie, WY
Vanderbilt .... Nashville, TN
Vassar (member of the "Seven Sisters") .... Poughkeepsie, NY
Villanova .... Villanova, PA
Wake Forest .... Winston-Salem, NC

Colleges and Universities **17**

Washington University .... St. Louis, MO
Willamette .... Salem, OR
Xavier .... Cincinnati, OH

The Ivy League:

Brown University .... Providence, RI
Columbia University (formerly Kings College) .... New York, NY
Cornell University .... Ithaca, NY
Dartmouth University .... Hanover, NH
Harvard University .... Cambridge, MA
Penn .... Philadelphia, PA
Princeton University .... Princeton, NJ
Yale .... New Haven, CT

Other Facts:

Oldest U.S. university.. Harvard
Second oldest U.S. university .... William & Mary
First U.S. business school .... Wharton
University that awards the Pulitzer Prize .... Columbia University
CUNY .... City Univ. of New York
Home to Hoover Tower and the Golden Spike .... Stanford
The first coed college in the U.S. .... Oberlin College
Presidential college of New Hampshire......................... Franklin Pierce College
Ronald Reagan's Illinois college .... Eureka
Mass. college named after Supreme Court justice .... Brandeis
U.S. largest school for the deaf .... Gallaudet
JFK's university.. Harvard
Harvard absorbed this college in 1999 .... Radcliff
Richard Nixon's Law School .... Duke
Bill Clinton's Law School .... Yale
"New England brain trust" .... MIT
George Bush's university .... Yale
Hillary Clinton attended this college .... Wellesley
University founded by Thomas Jefferson .... University of Virginia
College founded by Marshall Field .... University of Chicago
San Francisco Bay University .... Berkeley
University with bonfire accident, 1999 .... Texas A&M
Name for conference of seven colleges .... Seven Sisters
University attended by Rhodes Scholars .... Oxford
James VI's university .... University of Edinburgh
World's oldest university .... Heidelberg, Germany
Paris university.. Sorbonne
Fidel Castro studied law here .... University of Havana

18 *Composers*

Bach, Johann Sebastian (German baroque composer)
.... *Brandenburg Concertos 1-6*
.... *The Well Tempered Clavier*
.... *Toccata and Fugue*
.... *Goldberg Variations*
Barber, Samuel (American)
.... *School for Scandal*
.... *Adagio for Strings*
Beethoven, Ludwig von (German)
.... *Eroica Symphony #3*
.... *Pastoral Symphony #6*
.... *Choral Symphony #9 (Ode to Joy)*
.... *Egmont Overture*
.... *Fidelio (his only opera)*
.... *Moonlight Sonata*
.... *"Emperor" Piano Concerto #5*
.... *Für Elise*
Berlioz, Hector (French)
.... *Symphonie Fantastique*
.... *Damnation of Faust*
.... *Les Troyens* (opera)
Bizet, Georges (French)
.... *Carmen* (opera, set in Seville)
.... *L'Arlésienne*
Borodin, Alexandr (Russian)
.... *Prince Igor* (opera)
Brahms, Johannes (German)
.... *Hungarian Dances*
.... *Lullaby*
Britten, Benjamin (British)
.... *Billy Budd* (opera)
Chabrier, Alexis (French)
.... *España*
Chopin, Frederic (Polish)
.... Numerous scherzos, etudes and mazurkas
Copeland, Aaron (American)
.... *Appalachian Spring*
.... *Fanfare for the Common Man*
.... *Billy the Kid* (opera)
.... *Music for a Great City*

Debussy, Claude (French)
.... *Clair de Lune*
.... *La Mer*
.... *Prelude, Afternoon of a Faun*
Donizetti, Gaetano (Italian)
.... *Lucia di Lammermoor* (opera)
Dvorak, Antonin (Czech, Bohemian)
.... *The New World Symphony*
.... *Humoresque*
Elgar, Edward (English)
.... *Pomp and Circumstance*
.... *Enigma Variations*
Gershwin, George (American)
.... *Rhapsody in Blue*
.... *Porgy and Bess* (opera)
.... *An American in Paris*
Grieg, Edvard (Norwegian)
.... *Peer Gynt*
.... *Piano Concerto in A Minor*
Grofe, Ferd (American)
.... *The Grand Canyon Suite*
Gounod, Charles (French)
.... *Faust* (opera)
Handel, George Friedrich (German oratorio composer, lived at times in England)
.... *Messiah*
.... *Water Music*
.... *Music for Royal Fireworks*
Haydn, Franz Joseph (Austrian, nickname "Papa")
.... *The Creation*
.... *"Surprise" Symphony #94*
.... *"Military" Symphony #100*
.... *"The Clock" Symphony #101*
Herbert, Victor (Irish-American)
.... *Babes in Toyland* (opera)
Holst, Gustav (English)
.... *The Planets*
Humperdink, Ingelbert (German)
.... *Hansel and Gretel*
Khachaturian, Aram (Soviet-American)
.... *Sabre Dance*
Ruggiero Leoncavallo (Italian)
.... *I Pagliacci* (opera)
Liszt, Franz (Hungarian)
.... *Hungarian Rhapsody*
Massenet, Jules (French)
.... *Thaïs*

18 *Composers*

Mendelssohn, Felix (German, lived for a time in Scotland)
.... *A Midsummer Night's Dream Overture*
.... *Violin Concerto in E Minor*
.... *Hebrides Overture*

Menotti, Carlo (20ᵗʰ century Italian)
.... *Amahl and the Night Visitors* (opera)

Mozart, Wolfgang Amadeus (Austrian, wife Maria Anna)
.... *The Magic Flute*
.... *Symphony #40 in G Minor*
.... *Jupiter Symphony #41*
.... *Elvira Madigan*
.... *The Marriage of Figaro (opera)*
.... *Cosi Fan Tutte (opera)*
.... *Don Giovanni (opera)*
.... *Eine Kleine Nachtmusik (A Little Night Music)*

Mussorgsky, Modest (Russian)
.... *Night on Bare (Bald) Mountain*
.... *Pictures at an Exhibition*
.... *Boris Godunov (opera)*

Orff, Carl (German)
.... *Carmina Burana*

Offenbach, Jacques (German)
.... *Tales of Hoffman*
.... *Orpheus in the Underworld*

Pachelbel, Johann (German)
.... *Canon*

Prokofiev, Sergei (Russian)
.... *Peter and the Wolf*
.... *Romeo and Juliet* (opera)

Puccini, Giacomo (Italian)
.... *Madam Butterfly* (opera)
.... *Tosca* (opera)
.... *La Boheme* (opera)
.... *Turandot* (unfinished opera)

Rachmaninov, Sergei (Russian)
.... *Rhapsody on a Theme of Paganini*
.... *Piano Concerto #2*
.... *Piano Concerto #3* (used in movie *Shine*)

Ravel, Maurice (French)
.... *Bolero*
.... *Mother Goose Suite*

Respighi, Ottorino (Italian)
.... *The Pines of Rome*
.... *Ancient Airs and Dances*

Rimsky-Korsakov, Nikolai (Russian)
.... *Flight of the Bumble Bee*
.... *Scheherazade*
Rossini, Gioacchino (Italian)
.... *William Tell Overture*
.... *The Barber of Seville*
St. Saens, Camille (French)
.... *Dance Macabre*
.... *The Carnival of the Animals*
.... *Symphony #3, The Organ*
Satie, Erik (French)
.... *Gymnopedie*
Schubert, Franz (Austrian lieder composer)
.... *Ave Maria*
.... *"The Trout"* for string quintet
.... *The Great Symphony*
.... *The Unfinished Symphony*
Sibelius, Jean (Finnish)
.... *Finlandia*
Smetana, Bedrich (Czechoslovakian)
.... *The Bartered Bride* (opera)
.... *Ma Vlast* (My Country)
Sousa, John Philip (American)
.... *Stars and Stripes Forever*
Strauss, Johann II ("The Waltz King", Austrian)
.... *Die Fledermaus* ("The Bat")
.... *The Blue Danube Waltz*
.... *Tales From the Vienna Woods*
Strauss, Richard (Austrian)
.... *Don Juan* (opera)
.... *Thus Spake Zarathustra* (opera,
                                                            (theme to *2001: A Space Odyssey*)
.... *Don Quixote* (opera)
.... *Der Rosenkavalier* (opera)
.... *Salomé* (opera)
Stravinsky, Igor (Russian)
.... *Firebird*
.... *Rite of Spring*
.... *Petrushka* (puppet ballet)
Suppé, Franz von (Austrian)
.... *Poet and Peasant Overture*
Tchaikovsky, Peter (Russian)
.... *The Nutcracker* (ballet)
.... *Swan Lake* (ballet)
.... *1812 Overture*

18 *Composers*

.... *Romeo and Juliet*
.... *Symphony #6 (Pathetique)*
.... *Eugene Onegin* (opera)
Verdi, Giuseppe (Italian)
.... *Aida* (opera)
.... *La Traviata* (opera)
.... *Rigoletto* (opera)
.... *Il Trovatore* (opera)
.... *The Anvil Chorus*
Vivaldi, Antonio (Italian)
.... *The Four Seasons*
Wagner, Richard (German operatic composer)
.... *Tannhauser* (opera)
.... *Parsifal* (opera)
.... *Tristan and Isolde* (opera)
.... *Lohengrin* (opera)
.... *The Ring of Nibelungen* (*The Ring Cycle,* opera)
.... *The Flying Dutchman*
.... *Ride of the Valkyries*
Weill, Kurt (German)
.... *The Threepenny Opera*

Other Facts:

Franz Lizst's son-in-law .... Richard Wagner
Composer and antagonist to Mozart .... Antonio Salieiri
He loved author George Sand .... Frederic Chopin
12 tone music inovator .... Arnold Schoenberg
Composer buried at Westminster Abby ... George Friedrich Handel
Beethoven's only opera .... *Fidelio*
Dvorak symphony that got its name because it premiered in New York
.... *The New World Symphony*
Stravinsky symphony that caused a riot at its premier
.... *Rite of Spring*

Author's note: For anyone unfamiliar with classical music and wanting to start a music collection, the selections in this section contain some of the most beautiful classical pieces ever written. Happy listening!

Countries 19

Countries by area and population:

Largest in area
1. Russia
2. Canada
3. China
4. United States
5. Brazil
6. Australia
7. India
8. Argentina
9. Kazakstan
10. Sudan

Largest in population
1. China
2. India
3. United States
4. Indonesia
5. Brazil
6. Russia
7. Japan
8. Pakistan
9. Bangladesh
10. Nigeria`

Countries of the world:

Afghanistan
    Capital .... Kabul
    Freedom fighters... Mudjaheddin
    Ruling party .... Taliban
    Mountain pass .... Khyber Pass

Albania
    Capital .... Tirana
    Royalty .... King Zog
    Nobel Peace Prize winner .... Mother Teresa

Algeria (former French colony)
    Capital .... Algiers
    16th century fortress .... Casbah

Andorra
    Capital .... Andorra la Vella
    Mountains .... Pyrenees
    Principal language .... Catalan

Angola (former Portuguese colony)
    Capital .... Luanda
    Indigenous people .... Bantu
    Language .... Portuguese

Antigua & Barbuda (largest of Caribbean Leeward Islands)
    Capital .... St. John's

19   *Countries*

Argentina

Capital	Buenos Aries
Currency	Peso
Religion	Roman Catholic
Language	Spanish
Desert	Atacama (world's driest place)
Mountain	Aconcagua (shared with Chile)
River	Rio de la Plata ("river of silver")
Strait	Strait of Magellan
Southern plateau	Patagonia
Plains	The Pampas
Southern island shared with Chile	Tierra del Fuego ("land of fire")
Site of 1982 war	Falkland Islands
Falkland Islands Argentine name	Malvinas
Cowboys	Gauchos
Gaucho weapon	Bola
President 1946-55, 1973-74	Juan Peron
Juan Peron's second wife, died 1972	Evita (Eva) Peron
Juan Peron's third wife and president 1974-76	Isabelle Peron
Tennis star	Gabriela Sabatini

Armenia

Capital	Yereyan
Mountains	Caucasus

Australia (only nation to encompass an entire continent, world's sixth largest country)

Nickname	"The Land Down Under"
Capital	Canberra
Prime Minister, 1991-96	Bob Hanke
Prime minister, 1996-	John Howard
States:	New South Wales
	Victoria
	Queensland
	South Australia
	Western Australia
	Tasmania
Currency	Dollar
Largest city	Sydney
Second largest	Melbourne
Western Australia city	Perth
North coast city	Darwin
Harbor Bridge location	Sydney
Sydney airport	Kingsford Smith Airport
Sydney Harbor landmark	The Opera House
Largest island	Tasmania
Longest river	Darling River*
Lake	Lake Eyre

* Some sources list the Murry River as Australia's longest river

Bay .... Botany Bay
Eastern sea .... Tasman Sea
Color changing landmark .... Ayres Rock (Ulura)
Wild dog .... Dingo
Native people .... Aborigines
Aboriginal rite .... Walkabout
Aborigine weapon .... Boomerang
Stagnant water .... Billabong
Actor .... Paul Hogan
Singer .... Olivia Newton John
Opera singer .... Nellie Melba
Female author .... Colleen McCullough
Super model .... Elle McPherson
Tennis grand slam winner .... Margaret Court
Media Magnate .... Rupert Murdoch
Olympic sites: Summer 1956 .... Melbourne
                 Summer 2000 .... Sydney
Gum tree .... Eucalyptus
Eucalyptus eater .... Koala Bear
Duckbilled mammal .... Platypus
Reef .... Great Barrier Reef

Austria
Capital and largest city .... Vienna (The Waltz City)
Dynasty, 1247-1918 .... Hapsburg (or Habsburg)
Currency .... Shilling
Winter Olympics site, 1964 and 1976 .... Innsbruck
Newspaper .... *Wiener Zuting*
U.N. Secretary-General .... Kurt Waldheim
Composer .... Wolfgang Amadeus Mozart
Mozart's birthplace .... Salzburg
Actor .... Arnold Schwarzenegger
Holy Roman Empress .... Maria Theresa
Vienna psychoanalysis pioneer .... Sigmund Freud

Azerbaijan
Capital .... Baku
Mountains .... Caucasus
Lake .... Caspian Sea
World chess champion, 1985-2000 .... Garry Kasparov

Bahamas
Capital and largest city .... Nassau
Second largest city .... Freeport
Nassau island .... New Providence
Largest island .... Andros
Columbus' original landing point .... San Salvador

Bangladesh (formerly East Pakistan)
Capital .... Dhaka

19 *Countries*

Bay	Bay of Bengal
Language	Bengali

Belarus (former SSR)

Capital	Minsk
Religion	Eastern Orthodox
Currency	Ruble

Belgium (won its independence from the Netherlands)

Capital and largest city	Brussels (NATO headquarters)
Largest port	Antwerp (major diamond processing center)
City of treaty that ended War of 1812	Ghent
Currency	Franc
Religion	Roman Catholic
WW I cemetery	Flanders Field
Language	Flemish
Ethnic groups	Flemings, Walloons
Flemish cartographer	Mercator
Flemish painter	Sir Anthony Van Dyck (beard named after him)
Surrealist	Rene Magritte
Artist who taught van Dyke	Peter Paul Rubens
Fictional detective	Hercules Poirot
Cheese	Limburger
Current king	Alfred II
Other royalty	Leopold I & II, Baudouin
Colony	The Belgian Congo

Belize (formerly British Honduras)

Capital	Balmopan

Bermuda

Capital	Hamilton

Bolivia (Formerly Upper Peru, named after Simon Bolivar)

Legal capital	Sucre
Administrative capital	La Paz ("The Peace", highest world capital in elevation)
Religion	Roman Catholic
Language	Spanish
Lake	Titicaca
Mineral held in large deposits	Tin

Bosnia-Herzegovina

Capital	Sarajevo
Author of teen diary	Zlata (Frankovich)

Botswana (formerly Bechuanaland)

Capital	Gaborone
Desert	Kalahari
Swamp	Okavango

Brazil (largest country in South America)
>   Capital .... Brasilia
>   Former capital .... Rio de Janeiro
>   Rio beaches .... Copacabana and Ipanima
>   Religous statue overlooking Rio .... Christ the Redeemer
>   Largest city .... Sao Paulo
>   Language .... Portugese
>   Religion .... Roman Catholic
>   Currency .... Cruzeiro
>   Dance .... Tango
>   River.. Amazon
>   Stadium (world's largest) .... Maracana Stadium
>   Royalty .... Pedro I & II
>   Actress who wore fruit on her head .... Carmen Miranda

Brunei
>   Island .... Borneo
>   Ruler (by decree) .... The Sultan of Brunei

Bulgaria
>   Capital .... Sofia
>   Royalty .... King Boris III

Burkina Faso (formerly Upper Volta)
>   Capital .... Ouagadougou

Cambodia (former Kampuchea)
>   Capital .... Phnom Penh
>   Religion .... Buddhism
>   Ancient empire.................................... Khmer Empire
>   Communist organization .... Khmer Rouge
>   Khmer Rouge leader, died in 1998 .... Pol Pot
>   Ancient Buddhist temple.............................. Angkor Wat
>   Royalty .... King Norodom Sihanouk

Canada (world's second largest country)
>   *Provinces:* .... *Capitals:*
>   Alberta.. Edmonton
>   British Columbia................................. Victoria (The Garden City)
>   Manitoba (the Prairie Province) .... Winnipeg
>   New Brunswick (borders Maine) .... Fredericton
>   Newfoundland (Canada's newest province) .... St. Johns
>   Nova Scotia (New Scotland) .... Halifax
>   Ontario .... Toronto
>   Prince Edward Island (the Cradle of the Waves) .. Charlottetown
>   Quebec (the Maple Syrup Province)................. Quebec
>   Saskatchewan .... Regina
>
>   *Territories:*
>   Northwest Territory........................... Yellowknife
>   Yukon Territory (borders Alaska) .... Whitehorse

19 *Countries*

Other facts:

Capital	Ottawa
Largest city	Toronto
Second largest city	Montreal
Largest province	Quebec
National anthem	*O, Canada*
Largest Island	Baffin Island
Northern most island	Ellesmere Island
British Columbian island	Vancouver Island
Longest river	Mackenzie
Currency	Dollar
Toronto tower	CN (Canadian National) Tower
French-Canadian prime minister, 1968-79, 1980-84	Pierre Trudeau
Conservative prime minister, 1984-93	Brian Mulroney
Female prime minister, 1993	Kim Campbell
Liberal prime minister, 1993-	Jean Chretien
NW Territory lake	Great Slave Lake
Nova Scotia island	Cape Breton
Nova Scotia french area	Acadia
Nova Scotia ship builder	Cunard (founded 1787)
Newfoundland air traffic control center	Gander
Montreal University	Magill
Comedian and actor	Jim Carrey
Snowbird singer	Anne Murray
Game show host	Alex Trebek
Number of provinces	Ten
Alberta national park	Banff
Alberta rodeo	Calgary Stampede
Banff lake	Lake Louise
Yukon gold rush area	Klondike
Capitals named for Queen Victoria	Victoria and Regina

Chad

Capital	N'djamena
Desert	Sahara

Chile (southernmost South American country)

Capital	Santiago
Revolutionary leader, 1817-23	Bernardo O'Higgins
Marxist president, 1970-73	Salvador Allende
Salvador Allende's wife and author	Isabelle Allende
Man who overthrew Allende	Augusto Pinochet
Currency	Peso
Mountain	Aconcagua (with Argentina)
Desert	Atacama (world's driest place)
Southern island	Tierra del Fuego (with Argentina)
Pacific island	Easter Island (Papa Nui)

Poet .... Pablo Neruda
Mineral held in large deposits .... Copper

China (world's third largest country)
Capital .... Beijing (formerly Peking)
Largest city .... Shanghai
Currency .... Yuan
Major language dialects .... Cantonese and Mandarin
Ancient Northern China .... Cathay
Ancient philosopher .... Confucius
Last emperor .... Pu-Yi
Dynasty 1368-1644 .... Ming Dynasty
Communist revolutionary leader .... Mao Tse-tung
Premier under Mao Tse-tung .... Chou Enlai
Head of government, 1976-92 .... Deng Xiaoping
Current premier .... Jiang Zamin
Youth military .... Red Guard
Chinese-American architect .... I. M. Pei
Chinese-American sleuth .... Charlie Chan
Chinese self defense .... Kung-fu
Desert .... Gobi
Longest river .... Yangtze
Second longest river .... Yellow
Counting table .... Abacus
Chinese root .... Ginseng
Site of world's largest McDonalds' restaurant .... Beijing
Beijing square .... Tiananmen Square
Beijing temple .... Temple of Heaven
Beijing central area .... Forbidden City
Violent uprising, 1900 .... Boxer Rebellion
Industrial objective, 1956 .... Great leap forward
Egalitarian movement, 1966 .... Cultural revolution
Art of furniture arranging .... Feng Shui

Columbia (only South American country with Caribbean and Pacific coasts)
Capital .... Bogota
Currency .... Peso
Religion .... Roman Catholic
Author .... Gabriel Marquez
Drug cartels .... Cali, Medellin

Congo, Republic of
Capital .... Brazzaville

Congo, Democratic Republic of (formerly Zaire)
Capital .... Kinshasa
River .... Congo

Costa Rica
Capital and largest city .... San Jose
President, 1986- .... Oscar Arias Sanchez (Nobel Peace Prize, 1987)

19 *Countries*

Croatia

Capital	Zagreb (last in alphabetical order)

Cuba (largest island in Caribbean)

Capital	Havana
Head of government, 1959-	Fidel Castro
Former dictator, overthrown by Castro	Fulgencio Batista
Castro's revolutionary aide	Che Guevera
Castro's brother	Raul
U.S. Naval base	Guantanamo Bay (Gitmo)
Site of failed invasion, 1961	Bay of Pigs
Brothers pitching major league baseball	Livan and Orlando Hernandez
World high jump record holder	Javier Sodomayer

Cyprus

Capital	Nicosia
First president	Archbishop Makarios
Mythical king	Pygmalion

Czech Republic (formerly part of Czechoslovakia)

Capital	Prague (City of 1000 Spires)
Prague cathedral	St. Vitus
President, 1992-93, 1993-	Vaclav Havel
Leader during Prague Spring, 1968	Alexander Dubcek
Region	Bohemia
New World Symphony or Bohemian composer	Antonin Dvorak
The Bartered Bride composer	Bedrich Smetana
Female tennis star	Martina Navratilova
Male tennis star	Ivan Lendl

Denmark

Capital and largest city	Copenhagen
Peninsula	Jutland
Royalty	Queen Margarethe II
Ruling house	Orange
Currency	Kröne
Overseas regions	Greenland and Faroe Islands
Flag	Dannenbrög (world's oldest flag)
Astronomer	Tycho Brahe
Philosopher	Søren Kierkegaard
Explorer	Vitus Bering (Bering Sea and Strait)
Physicist	Niels Bohr
Author	Isak Dinesen (Karen Blixen)
Short story writer	Hans Christian Anderson
Piano comic	Victor Borge
National drink	Acabee
Copenhagen Harbor figure	The Little Mermaid
Copenhagen amusement park	Tivoli Gardens

Dominican Republic (where Columbus is buried)
        Capital .... Santo Domingo
        Island .... Hispaniola (second largest island
                                                                                        in Caribbean)

East Germany (now part of Germany)
        Capital .... East Berlin
        Dividing wall .... Berlin Wall
        Berlin Wall crossing point .... Brandenburg Gate
        Figure skater .... Katarina Witt

Ecuador (yes, the equator runs through it)
        Capital .... Quito
        Currency .... Sucre
        Language .... Spanish
        Second most widely spoken language .... Quechuan
        Islands .... Galapagos Islands

Egypt
        Capital and largest city .... Cairo (largest city in Africa)
        Second-largest city .... Alexandria (founded by
                                                                                        Alexander the Great)
        Ancient capitals .... Memphis, Thebes
        Dam .... Aswan High Dam
        Aswan Dam lake .... Lake Nasser
        River .... Nile
        Canal .... Suez
        Currency .... Pound
        Largest pyramid .... Khufu (a.k.a. Cheops)
        King, 1932-52 .... King Farouk
        Man who overthrew King Farouk, 1952 .... Abdul Nasser
        President, 1970-81 .... Anwar Sadat (won Nobel Peace
                                                                                        Prize, 1979)
        President, 1981- .... Hosni Mubarak
        Amenhotep III's son, 17th century BC .... Akhenton
        Akhenton's wife .... Nefertiti
        King who died at age 18, c. 1350 BC................ Tutankhamen (King Tut)
        Book found in ancient tombs .... Book of the Dead
        3rd to 6th B.C.dynasties .... Old Kingdom
        18th to 30th B.C.dynasties .... New Kingdom
        19th dynasty rulers .... Ramses II, Seti I
        15th to 18th B.C. century dynasty....................... Mamluk
        King who fathered 160 children .... Ramses II
        Christian sect .... Coptic Church

El Salvador (only Central American country without a Caribbean coastline)
        Capital .... San Salvador
        President 1980-82, 1984-89 .... Jose Napoleon Duarte

Estonia
        Capital .... Tallinn

19 *Countries*

Ethiopia

Capital	Addis Ababa
Emperor 1930-74	Haile Selassie (a.k.a. Ras Tafari)
Country newly independent from Ethiopia	Eritrea

Fiji (Pacific island group)

Capital	Suva
Largest island	Viti Levu

Finland

Capital	Helsinki (site of Accord on Human Rights)
Gulf	Gulf of Bothnia
Currency	Markka
Northern herdsmen	Lapps
Composer	Jean Sebelius
Finnish-American architect	Eero Saarinen
Runner known as the "Flying Finn"	Paavo Nurmi

France

Capital and largest city	Paris
Southern port	Marseille
Film festival city	Cannes
Brigitte Bardot's tourist city	St. Tropez
Spa city and World War II capital	Vichy
Former seat of the Papacy	Avignon
Stained glass cathedral city	Chartres
Porcelain city	Limoges
National anthem	Les Marseilles
Current government	The Fifth Republic

Fifth Republic leaders:

President, 1958-69	Charles de Gaulle
President, 1969-74	Georges Pompidou
President, 1974-81	Valery Giscard d'Estaing
Socialist president 1981-95	Francois Mitterrand
President 1995-	Jacques Chirac (former Paris mayor)
Premier, 1906-09, 1917-20	Georges Clemenceau
Floral symbol	Fleur-de-Lis
Paris site of the Tomb of the Unknown Soldier	Arc de Triomphe
Paris gardens	Tulleries
Paris river	Seine
Paris' oldest bridge	Pont Neuf
Tourist coast	Cote d'Azur
Mustard region	Dijon
Hot summer month	Thermidor
Empire including France, 900 A.D.	Carolingian
12th century minstrels	Troubadours

Ruling house of France, 987-1328 .... Capetians
Middle age middle class .... Bourgeoisie
Ruling family, 13th to 19th century .... Bourbons
Philosopher and Armine Bejart's lover .... Molière
French Protestants .... Huguenots
Cardinal who opposed the Huguenots, 1629 .... Cardinal Richelieu
Day the Huguenots were massacred .... St. Bartholomew's Day
Philosophical document of the revolution, 1789
.... Declaration of the Rights of Man
Prison stormed by French peasants .... Bastille
Date of the storming of the Bastille .... July 14, 1789
French leader subject of a David painting .... Jean Marat
She killed Marat .... Charlotte Corday
Leader deposed on 9 Thermidor, 1774 .... Maximilian Robespierre
Robespierre's supporters .... Jacobins
The Sun King (Le Roi Solier) .... Louis XIV
Louis XIV's imprisoned brother .... The man in the iron mask
Louis XV's lover .... Madame Pompadour
Louis XVI's Queen .... Marie Antoinette
Marie Antoinette's mother .... Maria Teresa (of the Habsburgs)
Palace built by Louis XIV .... Versailles
Versailles' hall .... Hall of Mirrors
Napoleon's second wife .... Josephine
Napoleon's third wife .... Eugenie
He defeated Napoleon at Waterloo .... Duke of Wellington
Napoleon's brother, king of Rome .... Napoleon II
Napoleon's brother, king of Spain .... Joseph Bonaparte
Napoleon's nephew, emperor of France, 1852-70
.... Napoleon III (Louis Napoleon)
Army captain stripped of honor, 1895 .... Major Dreyfus
He defended Major Dreyfus with *J'Accuse* .... Émile Zola
Island where Major Dreyfus was exiled .... Devil's Island
Trendsetter and actress, 1890's .... Sarah Bernhardt
Philosopher who developed analytical geometry
.... René Descartes
Founder of modern chemistry .... Antionne Lavosier
Grand dictionary lexicographer .... Pierre Larouse
Photography pioneer, 19th century .... Louis Deguarre
Ballooning brothers, 1793 .... Mongolfier brothers
Probably pioneer .... Blaise Pascal
Baby doctor .... Ferdinand Lamaze
Largest auto company .... Renault

Gambia (Africa's smallest mainland country)
Capital .... Banjul
Gabon
Capital .... Libreville

19   *Countries*

Georgia

Capital	Tbilisi
President 1995-	Edvard Shevardnadze
Mountains	Caucasus
Religion	Eastern Orthodox
Sea	Black Sea

Germany

Capital	Berlin
West German capital	Bonn
Port and second largest city	Hamburg
Twin tower cathedral city	Cologne
Oldest European university city	Heidelberg
City destroyed in Allied firestorm	Dresden
Home of Wagner music festival	Bayreuth
Capital of Bavaria	Munich
City known for its baths	Baden Baden
German chancellor, 1871-90	Otto von Bismarck (The Iron Chancellor)
Emperor, 1890-1918	Kaiser Wilhelm (William) II
President of German Republic, 1925-34	Paul von Hindenburg
West German chancellor, 1949-63	Konrad Adenauer (Der Alte)
West German chancellor, 1969-74	Willy Brandt (won Nobel Peace Prize, 1971)
West German chancellor, 1974-82	Helmut Schmidt
West German and German chancellor, 1982-98	Helmut Kohl
German chancellor 1998-	Gerhard Schröeder
Industrial region	Ruhr
Currency	Mark
Hamburg river	Elbe
17th century transcendental philosopher	Immanuel Kant
20th century philosopher	Gestalt
1930's actress	Marlene Dietrich
Physicist	Max Plank
German-American physicist	Albert Einstein
Chemist	Robert Bunsen
Astronomer	Johannes Kepler
Playwright	Bertolt Brecht
Weimar school of arts and crafts	Bauhaus
Bauhaus architect	Walter Gropius
Steel making family	Krupp
Baroque composer	Johann Sebastian (J. S.) Bach
J. S. Bach's composer son	C. P. E. Bach (he had several composer sons, this is most famous)
Noble family	Hohenzollern
Annual Bavarian party	Oktoberfest

16th century Reformation leader .... Martin Luther
19th century publisher .... Baedeker
Airship .... Zeppelin
Airship that set Atlantic crossing record, 1929 .. Graf Zeppelin
Airship that blew up at Lakehurst, NJ, 1937 ..... Hindenburg
Aspirin manufacturer .... Bayer
German terms:
Snout .... Snorkel
Ghostly double .... Doppleganger
Child prodigy .... Wunderkind
Pipe .... Meerschaum
Count .... Graf
Substitute .... Ersatz
Dumplings .... Spaetzle
*More information about Germany is under the category World War II

Ghana (former Gold Coast)
Capital .... Accra
US ambassador .... Shirley Temple Black
UN Secretary-General .... Kofi Annon

Great Britain
Capital and largest city .... London
Second largest city .... Birmingham
Major river .... Thames
National anthem .... *God Save the King (Queen)*
Port where the Beatles originated .... Liverpool
Hot springs city .... Bath
Prime minister, 1997- .... Tony Blair
Tony Blair's Party .... Labour
Prime minister, 1990-97 .... John Major
Prime minister, 1979-90 .... Margaret Thatcher
Major and Thatcher's party .... Conservative
Prime minister, 1955-57 .... Earl Anthony Eden
Prime minister, 1945-51 .... Clement Attlee
Prime minister, 1940-45, 1951-55 .... Sir Winston Churchill
Prime minister, 1937-40 .... Neville Chamberlain
Prime minister, 1916-22 .... David Lloyd-George
Late 19th prime minister four times .... William Gladstone
Prime minister, 1874-80 .... Benjamin Disraeli
Lord protector, 1653-58 .... Oliver Cromwell
Lord chancellor, 1618-26 and philosopher .... Francis Bacon
Rhodes scholars attend this university .... Oxford
Oxford's rival .... Cambridge
Boys prep school, founded 1440 .... Eton
Private residence of British monarchs .... Balmoral Castle
Home of British monarchs .... Buckingham Palace
Palace that burned, 1997 .... Windsor Castle

19 *Countries*

Prince and Princess of Wales home	Kensington Palace
Royal seaside resort	Brighton
Foreign ambassador's residence	St. James Court
London church where monarchs are crowned	Westminster Abby
Westminster Abby cemetery	Poet's Corner
London baroque cathedral (burned 1666)	St. Paul Cathedral
London square with Lord Nelson's statue	Trafalgar Square
London area with statue of Eros	Piccadilly Circus
London wax museum	Madame Tussaud's
London museum with the Rosetta Stone	British Museum
London park known for its orators	Hyde Park
London insane asylum	Bedlam
Conquest of 1066	Norman Conquest
Battle ending the Norman Conquest	Battle of Hastings
Wall hanging depicting Norman Conquest	Bayeux Tapestry
King who signed the Magna Carta, 1215	King John
Place where Magna Carta was signed	Runnymede
Ancient astronomical stone relic	Stonehenge
Stonehenge plain	Salisbury
Man murdered in Canterbury Cathedral	Sir Thomas Beckett
13th century scholar and alchemist	Roger Bacon
1381 John Bull and Watt Tyler tax revolt	Peasant's revolt
1455-85 war	War of the Roses
Opponents in the War of the Roses	Red vs White (York vs Lancaster)
Battle ending War of the Roses	Battle of Bosworth Field
Pact ending War of the Roses	Peace of Westphalia
Place where British fleet defeated Napoleon	Trafalgar
Admiral at Trafalgar	Lord Horatio Nelson
Lord Nelson's lover	Emma Hamilton
British ambassador to Turkey, 1799-1803	Lord Thomas Elgin (Elgin Marbles)
Commander defeated at Khartoum, 1884	Charles (Chinese) Gordon
Explorer who spoke 29 languages and translated *Arabian Nights*	Sir Richard Burton
African explorer who discovered Lake Victoria	John Speke
Man who found David Livingstone	Henry Morton Stanley
Conqueror of India, 1755-56	Robert Clive (of Plassey)
Surveyor General of India, 1830-41	Sir George Everest
Female in Parliament, 1919-45	Lady Nancy Astor
Last Governor General of India, 1947	Lord Mountbatten
Capital of British India	Calcutta
British calvary troops of India	Bengal Lancers
British dungeon in India	Black hole of Calcutta
Mau Mau rebellion country	Kenya
Declaration calling for a Jewish homeland, 1917	Balfour Declaration

17th century diarist .... Samuel Pepys
17th century poet and dramatist .... John Dryden
17th century philosopher .... John Locke
18th century pottery maker .... Josiah Wedgewood
18th century furniture maker .... Thomas Chippendale
19th century anatomist .... Henry Grey
Engraver .... William Hogarth
Romance novelist .... Barbara Cartland
Jockey and mystery writer .... Dick Francis
Landscape painter .... John Constable
Constable's rival .... William Turner
Historian .... Kenneth Clark
Playwright .... Harold Pinter
News service .... Reuters
Insurance Agency .... Lloyd's of London
Encyclopedia, debuting in 1768 .... Encyclopedia Britannica
Barrister .... Lawyer
Nanny's formal name .... Governess
Travel agency founder, 1828 .... Thomas Cook
British West Point .... Sandhurst
British envoy held hostage in Lebanon .... Terry Waite
British ballerina .... Dame Margot Fonteyn
Colonies .... Belize (British Honduras), Kenya,
Nigeria, South Africa, Guyana, India, Hong Kong, Singapore, Canada, Australia,
New Zealand, Fiji, Bahamas, British West Indies (Turks & Caicos), Falkland
Islands

Greece

Capital and largest city .... Athens
Second largest city .... Thessalonika
Largest port .... Piraeus
Prime Minister 1975-89 .... Georgios Papandreou
Last king .... Constantine II
Currency .... Drachma
Religion .... Eastern (Greek) Orthodox
Peninsula .... Peloponnesus
Oracle site .... Delphi
Athens' fortified hilltop .... Acropolis
Acropolis' landmark .... Parthenon
Largest island .... Crete
Ancient Crete capital .... Knossos
Ancient king of Crete .... Minos
Second largest island .... Euboea
Sappho's island .... Lesbos
Tallest mountain .... Olympus
Plain .... Marathon
Mountain pass .... Thermopylae

19 *Countries*

Shipping magnate .... Aristotle Onassis
Greek-American tennis player .... Pete Sampras
Greek-American opera singer .... Maria Callas
Liquor .... Uzzo
Drink .... Mastika
Royalty .... George, Alexander
Greek words:
Treasure .... Thesaurus
Ten words .... Decalogue
Rainbow .... Iris
Single letter .... Monogram
Werewolf .... Lycanthrope
Rug .... Flokati
Love of man .... Philanthropy
Love of trees .... Philodendron
To sell alone .... Monopoly
The masses .... Hoi polloi
People rule .... Democracy
Without pain .... Analgesic
Prefixes:
Geo .... Earth
Mono .... One
Omni .... All
Quasi .... In some sense or degree
Para .... Approximately
Phila .... Love of
Proto .... First
Pseudo .... False
Grenada
Capital .... St. George's
Guatemala
Capital .... Guatemala City
Currency .... Quetzal
Religion .... Roman Catholic
Guinea-Bissau
Capital .... Bissau
Guyana
Capital .... Georgetown
Haiti
Capital .... Port-au-Prince
Island .... Hispaniola
President, 1806-20 .... Henri Christophe
President, 1957-71 .... Francois Duvalier ("Papa Doc")
President, 1971-86 .... Jean Claude Duvalier ("Baby Doc")
President, 1991- .... Jean Bertram Aristide (exiled for
a time in the US)

Honduras (The Banana Republic)
Capital .... Tegucigalpa
Religion .... Roman Catholic
Language .... Spanish
Norther Indians and pyramid builders .... Mayans
Coastal Indians .... Mesquita

Hungary
Capital .... Budapest
Language .... Magyar
Patron saint .... St. Stephen
Year of revolt against Communist government .. 1956
Leader of 1956 revolt .... Imre Nagy
19th century composer and piano virtuoso .... Franz Liszt
20th century composer .... Bela Bartok
Tennis player .... Ilia Nastase
Hungarian-American actress-sisters .... Magda, Zsa Zsa and Eva Gabor

Iceland (originally part of Denmark, over 100 active volcanos)
Capital .... Reykjavik
Currency .... Krona
Major source of energy .... Geothermal
Major religion .... Lutheranism
12th to 13th century literature .... Edda

India (Independent from Britain since 1947)
Capital .... New Delhi
Largest city .... Bombay* (Mumbai)
Currency .... Rupee
Divisional system of society .... Caste system
Agra Shrine .... Taj Mahal
Taj Mahal builder .... Shah Jihan
Prophet of nonviolence, assassinated in 1948 .... Mahatma Gandhi
Gandhi's successor .... Jawaharlal Nehru
Female prime minister, 1980-84 .... Indira Gandhi (Nehru's daughter)
Prime minister, 1984-88 .... Rajiv Gandhi (Indira's son)
Wheel of Law .... Dharma Chakra
Guitar .... Sitar
Sitar player .... Ravi Shankar
Indian-American conductor .... Zubin Mehta
Clarified butter .... Ghee
Spice .... Curry
Site of 1984 Union Carbide disaster .... Bophal
Gandhi's "Children of God" .... The Untouchables
Vivian Leigh's birthplace and tea center .... Darjeeling
Former Portuguese colony .... Goa
*Some publications list Calcutta as India's largest city

19 *Countries*

Indonesia

Capital and largest city	Jakarta
Jakarta's Island	Java
Other main islands	Sumatra, Borneo, New Guinea
Island in *South Pacific* and resort	Bali
Island fighting for independence	East Timor
Volcanic island, erupted in 1883	Krakatoa
President 1999-	Abdurrahman Wahid
Leader forced to resign, 1998	Suharto
Suharto's predecessor	Sukarno

Iran (formerly Persia)

Capital	Teheran
Shah of Iran, 1941-79	Mohammed Reza Pahlavi
Revolutionary government head, 1979-89	Ayatollah Khomeini
President, 1989-	Rafsanjani
Currency	Rial
Police	Savak
Persian prophet, 6th century BC	Zoroaster
Persian poet	Omar Khayyam
Persian empire founder, 548 BC	Cyrus the Great
Persian defeated at Marathon, 490 BC	Darius I
Darius' son, defeated by Athens, 480 BC	Xerxes

Iraq

Capital	Baghdad
President, 1979-	Saddam Hussein
Currency	Dinar
Northern minority group	Kurds

Ireland (The Emerald Isle)

Capital and largest city	Dublin
Second largest city	Cork
Third largest city	Limerick
Glass works city	Waterford
Language	Gaelic
Accent	Brogue
Patron saint	St. Patrick
Dublin college	Trinity
Kissing stone	Blarney Stone
Lakes	Lakes of Killarney
Province with cycle of stories	Ulster
"Little Clover"	Shamrock (what St. Patrick used to describe the Trinity)
Dublin theater and company	Abbey Theater
Moaning spirit	Banshee
Convent	Sisters of Mercy
Physicist and chemist	Robert Boyle (Boyle's law)
8th century book of gospels	Book of Kells

1848-49 disaster .... Potato famine
Rebellion against British rule, 1916 .... Easter Uprising
Olympic swimmer .... Michele Smith
Hunger striker .... Bobby Sands
Writer and poet .... James Joyce
Female writer .... Maeve Binchy
Dramatist and director of Abbey Theater, 1904
.... John Millington Synge
Playwright .... Sean O'Casey
Poet who won Nobel Prize for Literature .... William Butler Yeats
Olympic swimmer .... Janet Evans
Irish-American miners .... "Molly Maguires"

Israel

Capital .... Jerusalem
Former capital and largest city .... Tel Aviv
First prime minister .... David Ben-Gurion
Prime minister, 1999- .... Ehud Barak
Prime minister, 1996-1999 .... Benjamin Netanyahu
Prime minister, 1974-77, 1992-95 .... Yitzhak Rabin (Nobel Peace Prize, 1994)
Prime minister, 1977-83 .... Menachem Begin (Nobel Peace Prize, 1987)
Prime minister, 1984-86, 1995-96 .... Shimon Peres
Foreign minister who wore an eye patch .... Moshe Dayan
Currency .... Shekel
Parliament .... Knesset
Intelligence agency .... Massad
Desert .... Negev
World's saltiest lake .... Dead Sea
River .... Jordan
Collective farm .... Kibbutz
Group that created Israel .... Zionists

Italy

Capital and largest city .... Rome (Roma)
Second largest, capital of Lombardy .... Milan (Milano)
Capital of Piedmont region .... Turin (Turino)
The Jewel of the Adriatic .... Venice (Venezia)
Capital of Tuscany region .... Florence (Firenze)
Northeast Adriatic port .... Trieste
Galileo's birthplace .... Pisa
Columbus' birthplace .... Genoa
Violin manufacturing center .... Cremona
Religion .... Roman Catholic
Currency .... Lire
Longest river .... Poe
Caesar's river .... Rubicon

19 *Countries*

Largest lake .... Lake Garda
Naples island .... Capri
Capri cave .... Blue Grotto
Largest island... Sicily
Sicily capital .... Palermo
Sicily volcano .... Etna
Second largest island .... Sardinia
Mainland volcano.. Vesuvius
Cities Vesuvius buried .... Pompeii and Herculaneum
Central mountains forming the spine of Italy ... Apennines
North central mountains .... Domolites
Countries within its borders .... Vatican City and San Marino
Infamous patron of the arts .... Lucretia Borgia
Revolutionary Red Shirt leader .... Guiseppe Garibaldi
Physicist .... Enrico Fermi
Educator.. Maria Montessori
Tenor from Modena .... Luciano Pavarotti
Electro statics and animal physiology pioneer ... Luigi Galvani
Opera conductor .... Arturo Toscanini
Violin virtuoso .... Niccolo Paganini
Rome river.. Tiber
Rome underground cemeteries .... Catacombs
Rome ancient arena .... Colosseum
Rome steps leading to Villa Burghese .... Spanish Steps
Rome fountain .... Trevi Fountain
Milan ruling family .... Sforza
Milan opera house... La Scala
Florence ruling family .... Medici
Florence river .... Arno
Florence fountain .... Fountain of Neptune
Florence art gallery .... Uffizi Gallery
Florence palace used as an art gallery................. Pitti Palace
Venetian artist .... Titian
Venetian composer .... Antonio Vivaldi
Venetian leader .... Doge
Venetian traveler.. Marco Polo
Venetian landmark bridge .... The Rialto
Venetian bridge on the way to the gallows......... The Bridge of Sighs
Venetian canal .... Grand Canal
Turin auto maker.. Fiat
Turin veil of controversy................................... Shroud of Turin
Comedy of Masks.. Commedia del' Arte
Bell tower .... Campanile

Jamaica (Third largest Caribbean island)

Capital .... Kingston
Resort city .... Montego Bay

City of "eight rivers" .... Ocho Rios
Mountains .... Blue Mountains
Reggae artist .... Bob Marley
Liquor .... Tia Maria
Famous Olympians .... Jamaican Bobsled Team

Japan

Capital .... Tokyo
Ancient Capital .... Kyoto
Largest port .... Yokohama
Largest island... Honshu
Northernmost main island .... Hokkaido
Southernmost main island............................... Kyushu
Parliament .... Diet
Currency .... Yen
Emperor .... Akihito (125th Emperior)
Akihito's father .... Hirohito
Primary religion .... Shinto
Temple .... Pagoda
Sacred mountain .... Mt. Fuji (Mt. Fujiyama)
Ancient ceremony .... Tea ceremony
Flower .... Chrysanthemum
Female professional entertainer .... Geisha
Conductor.. Seiji Ozawa
Director.. Akira Kurosawa
Dramas .... Noh dramas
Drama theater .... Kabuki
Kabuki theater of Tokyo .... Ginza
"Precision" watch maker .... Seiko
Film maker .... Fuji
First pocket radio maker .... Sony
Art of paper folding.. Origami
Art of flower arranging .... Ichybonnet
Art of dwarf tree growing .... Bonsai
Massage .... Shiatsu
Self defense... Judo and Jujitsu
Wrestling .... Sumo
Grill.. Hibachi
Green liquor .... Midori
Lute .... Samisen
Floor mat .... Tatami
Gangster .... Yasuka
Ornamental fish .... Koi
Poison fish .... Fugu
Three line poem .... Haiku
Number of syllables in haiku 17
Hokkaido aborigines .... Ainus

19   Countries

High speed train	Bullet train
Powerful businessman	Tycoon
Added to a name for respect	San
Act of ceremonial suicide	Hara-Kiri
9th to 16th century military dictators	Shoguns
Warrior knights	Samurai

Terms:

Divine wind	Kamikaze
Empty hand	Karate
Exalted gate	Mikado
Long life	Bonzai

Jordan

Capital	Amman (former Philadelphia)
Former name	Trans Jordan
King, 1999-	King Abdul Hussein
King, 1953-99	King Hussein I
King Hussein's wife	Queen Noor (American born)

Kazakhstan (world's largest landlocked country)

Capital	Astana
Currency	Ruble
Space port	Balkanor Cosmodrome (leased by Russia)

Kenya

Capital	Nairobi
Independence leader	Jomo Kenyatta
President, 1978-	Daniel arap Moi
Currency	Shilling
Languages	Swahili and English
Native tribe	Masai
Game reserve	Masai Mara
Tallest mountain	Mt. Kenya

Kuwait

Capital	Kuwait City

Laos

Capital	Vientiane
Religion	Buddhism

Latvia

Capital	Riga

Lebanon

Capital	Beirut
Valley	Bekaa Valley
Tree	Cedar (on their flag, used in building Solomon's temple)
Group of militant Shiite Muslims	Hezbollah

Liberia

    Capital .... Monrovia (named after U.S. president James Monroe)

Libya

    Capital .... Tripoli

    Dictator, 1969- .... Muammar Gaddafi

    Gulf .... Gulf of Sidra

Liechtenstein

    Capital .... Vaduz

Lithuania

    Capital .... Vilnius

Luxembourg

    Capital .... Luxembourg

    Grand Duke .... John

    Grand Duchess .... Carlotta

    Major religion .... Catholicism

Macedonia (formerly part of Yugoslavia)

    Capital .... Skopje

Madagascar (former Malagasy Republic)

    Capital .... Antananarivo

    Monkey .... Lemur

Malaysia

    Capital .... Kuala Lumpur

    Island .... Borneo

    Peninsula .... Malay Peninsula

Mali

    Capital .... Bamako

    River .... Niger

    Ancient trading center .... Timbuktu

Malta

    Capital .... Valletta

    Knights .... Knight's of St. John (Hospitalers)

Martinique (owned by France)

    Capital .... Fort de France

    Dormant volcano .... Mt. Pelee

    City destroyed by Pelee, 1902 .... St. Pierre

Mexico

    Capital and largest city .... Mexico City

    Leader during Mexican-American war .... Santa Anna (one legged)

    Austrian archduke, ruled 1864-67 .... Maximilian

    Maximilian's Belgian wife .... Grand Duchess Carlotta

    Man who overthrew Maximilian .... Benito Juarez

    President who overthrew Juarez, 1887 .... Porfirio Diaz

    Leader of Mexican revolution, 1910-14 .... Emilio Zapata

    President 1988-94 .... Carlos Salinas

    President, 1994-2000 .... Ernesto Zedillo

19 *Countries*

President, 2000- .... Jefe Vincente Fox
Pyramid-building Indians of central Mexico ..... Aztecs
Pyramid-building Indians of the Yucatan .... Mayans
Aztec conqueror .... Hernando Cortez (Marquis del
                                                                        Valle de Oaxaca)
Aztec god .... Quetzaquadl
Stone carving Indians .... Olmecs
State after which a breed of dog was named ...... Chihuahua
Southern state with insurgency .... Chiapas
Caribbean peninsula .... Yucatan
Pacific peninsula .... Baja California
Atlantic gulf .... Gulf of Mexico
Pacific gulf .... Gulf of California (Sea of Cortez)
Yucatan resort .... Cancun
Island off of Yucatan .... Cozumel
Christmas procession .... Peseta
Candy filled toy .... Piñata
Artist-Muralist .... Diego Rivera
Mexican-American male golfer .... Lee Trevino
Mexican-American female golfer .... Nancy Lopez
Late Mexican-American singer .... Selena (Perez)

Monaco
Capital .... Monaco-Ville
Principal income .... Gambling
Gambling city .... Monte Carlo
Current royalty .... Prince Rainier
Renier's children .... Princesses Caroline and
                                                                        Stephanie, Prince Albert
Prince Rainier's spouse .... Princess Grace (Kelly)
Royal house .... Grimaldi
Currency .... Monegasque Franc
Man who broke the bank at Monte Carlo .... Charles Wells

Mongolia
Capital .... Ulan Bator
Desert .... Gobi
Rodent .... Gerbil

Morocco
Capital .... Rabat
Port and largest city .... Casablanca
Well known cities .... Fez, Marrakesh
King who died in 1999 .... King Hassan II
King Hassan II's successor .... King Sedi Mohammed
Rice dish .... Couscous

Mozambique
Capital .... Maputo

Myanmar (former Burma)

Capital .... Yangon (former Rangoon)
United Nations secretary general .... U Thant
Nobel Peace Prize winner, 1996 .... Daw Aung San Suu Kyi
Religion .... Buddhism
River .... Irrawaddy
Bay .... Bay of Bengal

Namibia

Capital .... Windhoek
Desert .... Namib

Nepal

Capital .... Kathmandu
Wild ox .... Yak
"Lost man" of Himalayas .... Yeti (Abominable Snowman)

Netherlands, The

Capital .... The Hague
Largest city .... Amsterdam
Port .... Rotterdam
Pottery making city .... Delft
Currency .... Guilder
Royal house .... Orange
Current Queen .... Beatrix
Beatrix' mother .... Juliana
Juliana's mother .... Wilhelmina
Priest and humanist, 1466-1536 .... Erasmus
Artists .... Piet Mondrian and Rembrandt
Architect .... Mies Van der Rohe
Explorer .... Abel Tasman
Area drained for farmland .... Zuider Zee
Colonies .... Ceylon, Cape Colony, Indonesia,
　　　　　　　　　New York (New Amsterdam),St. Maarten, Surinam, Aruba

New Zealand

Capital .... Wellington
Former capital .... Christchurch
Currency .... Dollar
Mountains .... Southern Alps
Islands .... North Island, South Island
Minor island .... Chatham Island
Strait .... Cook Strait
Explorer .... Sir Edmond Hillary
Bird .... Kiwi
Extinct bird .... Moa
Indigenous people .... Maori
Operatic soprano .... Kiri te Kanawa

19 *Countries*

Nicaragua

Capital	Managua
Lakes	Lake Nicaragua, Lake Managua
Dictator ousted in 1979	Anastasio Somoza
Communist rebels	Sandinistas
Rebel leader and president	Daniel Ortega
Rebels against Sandinista government	Contras
Female president, 1990-97	Violeta Chamorro

Nigeria

Capital	Abuja
Former capital and largest city	Lagos
Breakaway republic	Biafra

North Korea

Capital	Pyongyang
Head of government, 1948-94	Kim Il-Sung
Head of government, 1994-	Kim Jong Il
U.S. ship captured in 1968	Pueblo

Northern Ireland (part of Great Britain)

Capital	Belfast
Northern port	Londonderry
Actor	Liam Neeson

Norway

Capital and largest city	Oslo (former Christiana)
Second largest city	Bergen
Currency	Kröne
Island	Spitsbergen
Betrayer of Norway	Vidkun Quisling
Composer	Edvard Grieg
Playwright	Heinrich Ibsen
Explorer	Roald Amundsen
Artist	Edvard Munch ("Screaming Artist")
Actress	Liv Ullman
Olympic figure skater	Sonja Henie
Ethnologist	Thor Heyerdahl
Royal names	Haakon, Harold

Pakistan

Capital	Islamabad
Former Capital, largest city and port	Karachi
Currency	Rupee
President, 1977-88	Ul-Haq Zia
Prime minister, 1988-90, 1993-96	Benazir Bhutto
Northern disputed territory	Kashmir

Panama (originally part of Columbia)

Capital	Panama City
Currency	Balboa
General and strongman (now in a U.S. prison)	Manuel Noriega

Papua New Guinea
    Capital .... Port Moresby
Paraguay (landlocked in South America)
    Capital .... Asuncion
Peru (South America's western most country)
    Capital .... Lima
    President, 1992- .... Alberto Fujimori
    Indians .... Incas
    Incan dialect .... Ketchua
    Incan city in Andes... Macchu Picchu
Philippines, The
    Capital and largest city .... Manila
    Former capital .... Quezon City
    Currency .... Peso
    Largest island.. Luzon
    Luzon peninsula (WWII battle site) .... Bataan
    Manila Bay island .... Corregidor
    Largest religious group .... Roman Catholic (only Christian
                                       majority Asian country)
    Second largest religious group .... Islam
    Territorial governor, 1901 .... William Howard Taft
    Deposed president .... Ferdinand Marcos
    Marcos' wife, known for thousands of shoes ..... Imelda
    Exiled and assassinated activist .... Benigno (Ninoy) Aquino
    Female President, 1986-92 ....Corazon Aquino
                                       (Benigno's wife)
    President, 1992-98 .... Fidel Ramos
    President, 1998- .... Joseph Estrada
    Former U.S. airbase .... Clark
    Former U.S. navy base .... Subic Bay
    Volcano .... Mt. Pinitubo
Poland
    Capital and largest city .... Warsaw
    Former capital .... Krakow (home of John Paul II)
    Port .... Gdansk (a.k.a. Danzig)
    Currency .... Zloty
    River.. Vistula
    Gdansk shipyard.. Lenin shipyard
    Union .... Solidarity
    Union leader and president, 1990-95 .... Lech Walesa (won Nobel Peace
                                       Prize)
    Composer and pianist .... Frédéric Chopin
    Astronomer .... Nicolaus Copernicus
    Pianist and Prime Minister, 1919 .... Ignace Paderewski
    Dance .... Polonaise

19 *Countries*

Portugal

Capital	Lisbon
Currency	Escudo
River	Tagus
Atlantic island group	Azores
Dictator, 1933-68	António Salazar
Instructor to future explorers	Prince Henry the Navigator
Royal names	Alfonso, Pedro
Wine	Port
Wine valley	Douro
Colonies	Angola, Goa, Macau (returned to China in 1998), Indonesia, Formosa (Taiwan), Brazil, Cape Verde, Mozambique,Uruguay

Romania *(former Moldavia)*

Capital	Bucharest
Mountains	Transylvanian Alps (Carpathians)
Sculptor	Constantin Brancusi
Nomadic people	Gypsies
Mad king	Ludwig II
Royalty	Carol I, Carol II
Dictator deposed in 1989	Nikolae Ceausescu
Gymnast	Nadia Comaneci
Gymnastics coach	Bela Karolyi

Russia *(Europe's most populous and largest country)*

Capital and largest city	Moscow
Largest port	St. Petersburg (former Leningrad)
Currency	Ruble
Flag colors	Red, white and blue
Longest river	Volga (longest in Europe)
St. Petersburg river	Neva
Siberian lake	Lake Baikal (world's deepest lake)
Former newspaper	*Pravda* (truth)
News agency	Tass
Breakaway republic	Chechnya
World's longest railroad	Trans Siberian Railroad
Trans Siberian Railroad terminals	Moscow to Vladivostok
Father of Soviet H bomb	Andrei Sakharov
Poet	Aleksandr Pushkin
Dramatist	Nikolai Gogol
Exiled author	Aleksandr Solzhenitsyn
Mad monk	Grigori Rasputin
Lenin's majority	Bolshevik
Labor camp	Gulag
Jeweled egg maker	Fabergé
Triangular guitar	Balalaika
Confederation	Commonwealth of Independent States

Royal family .... Romanov
"Terrible" tsar, 1547-64 .... Ivan the Terrible
"Great" tsar, 1682-1725 .... Peter the Great
"Great" tsarina, 1762-96, built the Hermitage .. Catherine the Great
Last Romanov tsar, 1894-1918 .... Nicholas II
Interim prime minister, ousted in 1917 .... Alexander Kerensky
Soviet dictator, 1918-24 .... Vladimir Lenin
Soviet dictator, 1929-53 .... Josef Stalin
Soviet premier, 1953-64 .... Nikita Khruschev
Soviet premier, 1964-82 .... Leonid Brezhnev
Soviet premier, 1982-84 .... Yuri Andropov
Soviet premier, 1984-85 .... Constantine Chernyenko
Soviet premier, 1985-91 .... Mikhail Gorbachev (won Nobel
                                                                     Peace Prize, 1990)
Russian president, 1991-1999 .... Boris Yeltsin
Russian president, 1999- .... Vladimir Putin
Nobel Peace Prize winner, 1975 .... Andrei Sakharov

Rwanda
Capital .... Kigali
Majority tribe .... Hutu
Minority tribe .... Tutsi

San Marino (The Serene Republic, found entirely within the borders of Italy)
Saudi Arabia (largest country in middle east, world's largest oil producer)
Capital .... Riyadh
Islamic holy cities .... Mecca, Medina
Currency .... Riyal
Saudi Arabia founder and king, 1925-53 .... Ibn Saud
King, 1982- .... King Fahd
King, 1975-82 .... King Khalid
King, 1964-75 .... King Faisal
Peninsula .... Arabian Peninsula (world's
                                                                     largest peninsula)

Scotland (part of Great Britain)
Capital .... Edinburgh
Largest city .... Glasgow
Ancient name .... Caledonia
City and breed of cattle .... Aberdeen
River .... Tay
Islands .... Inner and Outer Hebrides,
                                                                     Orkney Islands
Highest mountain .... Ben Nevis
Hills .... Lammermoors
"Brave hearted" leader .... William Wallace
Jacobites supported him .... Bonnie Prince Charlie
Royal house .... Stuart
Robert I royal house .... Bruce

19 *Countries*

Scottish "Robin Hood" .... Rob Roy
Inventors .... James Watt and Alexander
                                                                 Graham Bell
Philosopher and historian .... David Hume
Tea Magnate .... Sir Thomas Lipton
Steel magnate and philanthropist .... Andrew Carnegie
Poet and songwriter .... Robert Burns (Caledonia's poet)
Robert Burns' love .... Mary Campbell
Naturalist .... John Muir
Missionary in Africa and explorer .... David Livingstone
Samuel Johnson's mentor .... James Boswell
Cabinet maker .... Duncan Fife
Protestant leader .... John Knox
Author who died in Samoa .... Robert Louis Stevenson
Botanist .... David Douglas (Douglas fir)
Pole tossing game .... Caber tossing
Dance .... Highland fling

Senegal
Capital .... Dakar

Sierra Leone (translated-mountain lion)
Capital .... Freetown

Singapore (smallest country in Asia, originally part of Malaysia)
Capital .... Singapore
Currency .... Dollar
Famous hotel .... Raffles (where the Singapore
                                                                 Sling was invented)

Slovakia (formerly part of Czechoslovakia)
Capital .... Bratislava

Somalia (located on the "horn of Africa")
Capital .... Mogadishu

South Africa
Capitals:
  Executive .... Pretoria
  Legislative .... Cape Town
  Judicial .... Bloemfontein
Indian Ocean port .... Durban
National park .... Kruger National Park
River .... Orange
Southern cape .... Cape of Good Hope
Provinces .... Natal, Orange Free State,
                                                                 Transvaal, Cape Province
Currency .... Rand
Gold coin .... Krugerrand
Former segregation policy .... Apartheid
Farmer .... Boer
19th century Boer leader .... Paul Kruger

Playwright .... Athol Fugard
Actress and dancer .... Juliet Prowse
Martyred leader .... Steven Biko
Nonviolence advocate and Nobel Peace Prize winner, 1984
.... Desmond Tutu
President, 1984-89 .... Pieter Botha
Prime minister, 1989-93 and Nobel Peace Prize winner, 1993
.... F. W. DeKlerk
Prime minister, 1993- and Nobel Peace Prize Winner, 1993
.... Nelson Mandela
Mandela's former wife .... Winnie Mandela
Cape Colony prime minister, 1898 .... Cecil Rhodes
Heart transplant doctor .... Dr. Christiaan Barnard
Female author .... Nadine Gordimer
Female barefoot runner .... Zola Budd

South Korea
Capital .... Seoul
Currency .... Won
President, 1993- .... Kim Dae Jung (Noble Peace Prize)
President, 1948-60 .... Syngman Rhee
President assassinated in 1979 .... Park Chung-Hee
Dividing parallel to the north .... 38th parallel
Major city in the southeast .... Pusan
Allied invasion site .... Inchon
Korean War armistice site, 1953 .... Panmunjom
Symbol on flag .... Yin and Yang
Female golfer .... Se Ri Pak

Spain
Capital .... Madrid
Mediterranean port, capital of Catalonia .... Barcelona
Southern port .... Cadiz
Currency .... Peseta
Mediterranean islands .... Balearic Islands (Ibiza, Majorca)
Peninsula .... Iberia
French border mountains .... Pyrenees
Central mountains .... Sierra Nevada
Tourist coast .... Costa del Sol
13th to 15th century tribunal .... Inquisition
Grand Inquisitor .... Torquemada
Conqueror of Moorish Valencia in 1091 .... El Cid
Windmill region .... La Mancha
Indigenous people of Northern Spain .... Basque
Dialect of northern Spain .... Catalan
Islamic sect .... Moors
Last Moorish kingdom .... Granada
Granada citadel .... Alhambra

19 *Countries*

King Ferdinand's region of central Spain .... Castile
Queen Isabella's region of northeast Spain .... Aragon
Ferdinand and Isabella's daughter .... Catherine of Aragon
Spanish fleet, 1588 .... Spanish Armada
16ᵗʰ century military adventurers .... Conquistadors
Toledo artist .... El Greco
The Uprising of the 2ⁿᵈ of May painter .... Francisco Goya
Islamic art .... Moorish
Cubist .... Pablo Picasso
Guitarist .... Andres Segovia
Cellist .... Pablo Casals
Fortified wine .... Sherry
National sport .... Bull fighting
General .... Francisco Franco
King .... Juan Carlos
Royalty names .... Alfonso XIII, Phillip II

Sri Lanka (former Ceylon)
Capital .... Columbo
Language .... Singhalese
Minority separatists .... Tamils
Author .... Arthur C. Clarke
Main export .... Tea

Surinam (former Dutch Guyana)
Capital .... Paramaribo
Mountains .... Wilhelmina Mountains
Currency .... Guilder
Well known city .... New Amsterdam

Sudan (largest country in Africa, 10ᵗʰ largest in the world)
Capital .... Khartoum
Rivers .... Nile, White Nile, Blue Nile

Sweden
Capital .... Stockholm
Port and ship building center .... Göteborg
University .... Uppsala
Currency .... Krona
U.N. secretary-general .... Dag Hammarskjöld
1970's singing group .... ABBA
Swedish nightingale .... Jenny Lind
Playwright .... August Strindberg
Prize fighter .... Ingemar Johansson
Botanist .... Carolus Linnaeus (taught at
                                                                           Uppsala)
Assassinated leader .... Olaf Palm
Diplomat who saved 100,000 during holocaust
.... Raoul Wallenberg
Director .... Ingmar Bergman

Actor .... Max Von Sydow
Actress .... Greta Garbo
Buxom actress.. Anita Ekberg
Auto maker .... Volvo
Royal names .... Christina, Oscar, Carl Gustav
Feast .... Smorgasbord
Turnip .... Rutabaga

Switzerland (former Helvetia)
Capital .... Bern
Largest city .... Zurich
Currency .... Franc
Zurich airport .... Lugano
Geographical districts .... Cantons (23 total)
Lakes .... Lake Geneva, Lake Zurich
Rivers ....·Rhine, Rhone
The "Gnomes of Zurich" .... Bankers
Mountain .... Matterhorn
Protestant reformer.. John Calvin
Philosopher .... Jean Jacques Rousseau
Male psychiatrist .... Carl Jung
Female psychiatrist .... Elisabeth Kübler-Ross
Long wooden horn .... Alpinhorn
Tennis player .... Martina Hingis

Syria
Capital .... Damascus
President, 1971-2000 .... Hafez al-Assad
Southern high ground, held by Israel .... Golan Heights

Taiwan (largest country in the world that is not a member of the United Nations)
Capital .... Taipei
Island .... Formosa

Tanzania
Capital. .... Dodoma
Former capital .... Dar es Salaam
Union of these former countries .... Tanganyika and Zanzibar
Language .... Swahili
National Park .... Serengeti National Park
Mountain .... Kilimanjaro

Thailand (former Siam)
Capital .... Bangkok
Northern city .... Chang Mai
Currency .... Baht
Religion .... Buddhism
Royalty .... King Bhumibol
Resort island .... Phuket
Peninsula .... Malay Peninsula

19 *Countries*

Tibet (part of China)

    Capital .... Lhasa

    Spiritual leader .... Dalai Lama (won Nobel Peace Prize)

Trinidad & Tobago

    Capital .... Port-of-Spain

Tunisia (northern most country in Africa)

    Capital .... Tunis

    Ancient city .... Carthage

Turkey

    Capital .... Ankara

    Port and largest city .... Istanbul (formerly Byzantium and Constantinople)

    Currency .... Lira

    Peninsula .... Gallipoli

    River... Meander

    Mountain .... Mt. Ararat

    Lake... Lake Van

    Empires .... Byzantine, Ottoman

    President, 1923-38 .... Kemal Ataturk

    He renamed Byzantium Constantinople, 330 AD

    .... Constantine I

    Byzantine empire ruler, 527-65 .... Justinian I

    "Magnificent" Ottoman ruler, 1520-66 .... Suleyman the Magnificent

    Istanbul inlet .... Golden Horn

    Istanbul Strait... Bosporus

    Istanbul shrine.. Hagai Sophia (Santa Sophia)

    Istanbul Mosque .... The Blue Mosque

Uganda

    Capital .... Kampala

    Israeli raid city .... Entebbe

    Former dictator .... Idi Amin

Ukraine (Europe's second largest country)

    Capital .... Kiev

    Peninsula .... Crimea

    Horse solder .... Cossack

    Sea .... Black Sea

    Plains.. Steppes

    Mountains .... Carpathians

    Nuclear power plant .... Chernobyl (site of accident in 1986)

    Chicken dish .... Chicken Kiev

United Arab Emirates (U.A.E.)

    Capital .... Abu Dhabi

Uruguay

    Capital .... Montevideo

    Currency .... Peso

Uzbekistan
    Capital .... Tashkent
    Sea .... Aral Sea
Vatican, The (world's smallest country)
    Capital .... Vatican City
    Vatican basilica .... St. Peter's Basilica
    Vatican chapel .... Sistine Chapel
Venezuela (named after Venice, Italy)
    Capital .... Caracas (birth place of
                         Simone Bolivar)
    Currency .... Bolivar
    River .... Orinoco
Vietnam
    Capital .... Hanoi
    Southern capital .... Ho Chi Minh City (former
                         Saigon)
    Currency .... Dong
    Rivers .... Mekong, Red River
    Gulf .... Tonkin
    Central port .... Da Nang
    Bay .... Cam Ranh
    Site of French defeat, 1954 .... Dien Bien Phu
    North Vietnam leader, 1945-69 .... Ho Chi Minh
    South Vietnam leader and Nobel Peace Prize winner, 1973
    .... Le Duc Tho

Wales (part of Great Britain)
    Capital .... Cardiff
    Mineral found in large deposits .... Slate
    Poet .... Dylan Thomas
    Actor .... Richard Burton
    Welsh for James .... Iago
    Welsh for William .... Liam
Yugoslavia
    Capital .... Belgrade
    President, 1998-2000 .... Slobodan Milosevic
    Republics .... Serbia, Montenegro
    Breakaway province .... Kosovo
Zaire (see Congo, Democratic Republic of)
Zambia (former Northern Rhodesia)
    Capital '.. Lusaka
Zimbabwe (former Rhodesia, named after Cecil Rhodes)
    Capital .... Harare (former Salisbury)
    Head of government, 1987- .... Robert Mugabe
    Last Rhodesian prime minister .... Ian Smith

20 *Dance*

Dances:

Andelusian (gypsy) dance	Flamenco
Argentine (seductive) dance	Tango
English-Irish dance	Jig
Bohemian dance	Polka
Brazilian dances	Lambada and Samba
Cuban line dance	Conga
Polish national dance	Mazurka
Spanish dance with one hand over head	Bolero
Spanish dance with castanets	Fandango
Italian dance	Tarantella
Tango relative	Mambo
"Vulgar" French dance	Can Can
Court dance of Louis XIV	Minuet
3/4 time Viennese dance	Waltz
1940s-50s jive dance	Jitterbug
Sailor's dance	Hornpipe
Court dance	Pavan

Other Facts:

1911 Igor Stravinsky puppet ballet	*Petrushka*
Other Stravinsky ballets	*Firebird, The Rite of Spring*
Peter Tchaikovsky ballets	*Swan Lake, Sleeping Beauty*
Moscow Square ballet theater	Bolshoi
St. Petersburg ballet theater	Kirov
Joffrey Ballet's current home	Chicago
British ballet theater	Royal Ballet
George Balanchine established this theater	New York City Ballet
Ukranian-born dancer who came to the U.S. in 1916	Vaslav Nijinsky
Theater Baryshnikov directed from 1980-89	American Ballet Theater
Defected from the Kirov Ballet in 1961	Rudolph Nureyev
Defected from the Bolshoi Ballet in 1974	Mikhail Baryshnikov (Misha)

Ballerina who defected from the Kirov Ballet in 1970 .. Natalia Makarova

Impresario who founded Ballet Russe .... Sergei Diaghilev

British ballerina known as Margot Hookham .... Margot Fonteyn

Classic 1948 ballet film .... *The Red Shoes*

West Side Story and *Fiddler on the Roof* choreographer ..

.... Jerome Robbins

Choreographer *of Rodeo* and *Oklahoma!* .... Agnes de Mille

Appalachian Spring choreographer .... Martha Graham

Grand Hotel choreographer .... Tommy Tune

Movie *Hair* choreographer .... Twyla Tharp

Singin' in the Rain dancer and choreographer .... Gene Kelly

Afternoon of a Faun choreographer .... Vaslav Nijinsky

Chicago Ballet founder .... Maria Tallchief

American Dance Theater founder .... Alvin Ailey

Moscow School of Dance founder .... Isadora Duncan (she died
when her scarf got caught in an auto tire)

Native American ballerinas from Oklahoma .... Maria and Marjorie Tallchief

Dying Swan ballerina .... Anna Pavlova

Maria Tallchief's husband .... George Balanchine

Vernon Castle's ballroom dancing partner .... Irene (Foote) Castle

Tap dancer who danced with Shirley Temple .... Bill "Bojangles" Robinson

Black, St. Louis-born dancer who lived in France .... Josephine Baker

Famous fan dancer .... Sally Rand

Famous burlesque stripper .... Gypsy Rose Lee

Top Hat and *The Gay Divorcee* dancer .... Fred Astaire

Fred Astaire's sister .... Adele Astaire

Dance Party host .... Arthur Murray

The Tap Dance Kid star .... Savion Glover

Denishawn Dance School founders .... Ted Shawn and Ruth St. Denis

Radio City Music Hall dancers .... Rockettes

Number of classical ballet positions .... Five

Ballet move bending at the knee .... Plié

Ballet move extending one leg straight back 90 degrees

.... Arabesque

Ballet dance for two .... Pas de deux

21 *Explorers, Discoverers and Inventors*

Explorers:

Venetian who explored Asia	Marco Polo
Norse explorer who first reached Greenland	Eric the Red
Norse explorer of northeast North America, Eric the Red's son	Leif Erickson
Flemish cartographer	Mercator
Portuguese navigation instructor	Henry the Navigator
First to go around the Cape of Good Hope	Bartolomeu Dias
Discoverer of the New World	Christopher Columbus
Italian map maker/explorer who coined the term "New World"	Amerigo Vespucci
Portuguese explorer and first to reach India	Vasco da Gama
First to see the Pacific Ocean	Vasco Nuñez de Balboa
Aztec conqueror	Hernando Cortez
Incan Conqueror and explorer of Peru	Francisco Pizarro
Explorer of American southwest; searched for 7 cities of Cibola	Francisco de Coronado
First to set foot on U.S. mainland (Florida)	Ponce de Leon
Italian explorer who discovered Newfoundland	John Cabot
John Cabot's son who explored the Rio de la Plata	Sebastian Cabot
Frenchman who founded Montreal and charted St. Lawrence River	Jacques Cartier
Portuguese discoverer of Brazil	Pedro Cabral
Portuguese discoverer of California	Juan Cabrillo
Frenchman who explored the southern Mississippi River	Sieur de la Salle
Frenchmen who explored the length of Mississippi River	Marquette & Joliet
First to sail into New York Harbor	Giovanni da Verrazano
Spaniard who discovered the Mississippi River	Hernando de Soto
The Father of New France, founded Quebec	Samuel de Champlain
German naturalist who explored the Orinoco	Friedrich Humboldt
Explorer of the Gambia and Niger rivers	Mungo Park
First person given credit for sailing around the world	Ferdinand Magellan
First Englishman to sail around the world	Sir Francis Drake
Dutchman who explored the Pacific	Able Tasman
Norwegian who first navigated Northwest Passage	Roald Amundsen
Englishman who discovered Australia and Hawaii	James Cook
First Englishman to reach Australia	William Dampier
Danish discoverer of Alaska and namesake strait	Vitus Bering
Explorer of northwest Canada	Alexander Mackenzie
Discovered the Great Salt Lake	Jim Bridger

Englishman who discovered world's 5th largest island .... William Baffin
Englishman who discovered source of the Nile (disputed) John Speke
Speke's colleague, who spoke 29 languages .... Sir Richard Burton
First to reach North Pole, 1909 .... Robert Peary & Matthew Henson
First to reach South Pole, 1911 .... Roald Amundsen
Competitor of Amundsen, died after reaching South Pole Robert Scott
First to fly over North Pole .... Richard Byrd & Floyd Bennett
First to fly over South Pole .... Richard Byrd
British explorer of Antarctic .... James Ross
Scottish medical missionary to Africa .... David Livingstone
Man who found Livingstone .... Henry Stanley
Machu Picchu discoverer .... Hiram Bingham
Explored northern Louisiana Purchase territory .... Lewis and Clark
Explored southern Louisiana Purchase territory .... Zebulon Pike

Discoverers:

Oral polio vaccine .... Albert Sabin
Polio vaccine .... Jonas Salk
Photo-electric effect .... Albert Einstein
Hydrostatics .... Archimedes
Fermentation .... Louis Pasteur
DNA .... Francis Crick & James Watson
Neptune .... Johann Galle
Uranus .... Sir William Herschel
Pluto .... Clyde Tombaugh
Moons of Jupiter .... Galileo
Expanding Universe .... Edwin Hubble
Theory of relativity .... Albert Einstein
X-ray imaging .... Wilhelm Roentgen
Radium .... Marie and Pierre Curie
Penicillin .... Alexander Fleming
Cells .... Robert Hooke
Bacteria .... Anton van Leeuwenhoek
Oxygen .... Joseph Priestly
Speech center of the brain .... Paul Broca
Cause of tuberculosis and cholera .... Robert Koch
Antibodies .... Louis Pasteur
Cause of syphilis .... August von Wassermann
Cure for smallpox .... Edward Jenner
Cause of yellow fever .... Walter Reed
Laws of genetics .... Gregor Mendel
Insulin .... Banting and Best
Electromagnetic or radio waves .... Heinrich Hertz
Electrical resistance laws .... George Ohm
Rabies vaccine .... Louis Pasteur

21   *Explorers, Discoverers, and Inventors*

Nucleus of the atom .... Ernest Rutherford
Structure of the atom .... Neils Bohr

Inventors:

AC generator .... Nicoli Tesla
Adding machine .... Blaise Pascal
Air brakes .... George Westinghouse
Air conditioner .... Willis Carrier
Airplane .... Wright brothers
Alternator .... Chrysler Corporation
Aqua-lung.. Jacques Cousteau
Artificial heart .... Robert Jarvik
Barometer .... Evangelista Torricelli
Bifocal lens .... Ben Franklin
Blind reading system .... Louis Braille
Calculus... Sir Isaac Newton
Contact lenses .... Frick
Compression-ignition engine .... Rudolf Diesel
Computer conceiver .... Charles Babbage
Cotton gin .... Eli Whitney
Cyclotron .... Ernest O. Laurence
Cylinder locks.. Linus Yale
Dirigible airship .... Ferdinand von Zeppelin
Dynamite .... Alfred Nobel
Dynamo .... Michael Faraday
Earthquake intensity device .... Charles Richter
Electric toaster .... General Electric labs
Electric lamp .... Thomas Edison
Electric razor .... Jacob Schick
Electric coil... Stanley
Electric motor.. Michael Faraday
Elevator .... Elisha Otis
English derby hat.. Bowler
Eye Chart .... Snellen
Fountain pen .... Lewis Waterman
Food freezing .... Clarence Birdseye
Gas burner .... Robert Bunsen
Geometry .... Euclid
Grape juice .... Thomas Welch
Gyroscope.. Leon Foucault
Hamburger .... Salisbury
Helicopter (single rotor) .... Igor Sikorsky
Hot air balloon .... Montgolfier brothers
Hybrid popcorn.. Orville Redenbacher
Ink blot test .... Herman Rorschach

Instant (Polaroid) camera	Edwin Land
IQ test	Alfred Binet
Kodak camera (hand-held)	George Eastman
Lightning rod	Ben Franklin
Liquid-fueled rocket	Robert Goddard
Loom	Joseph Marie Jacquard
Machine gun	Richard Gatling
Magnifying glass	Roger Bacon
Mechanical grain reaper	Cyrus McCormick
Microscope (compound)	Zacharias Janssen
Microscope (electron)	Vladimir Zworykin
Mimeograph	A. B. Dick
Motion picture machine	Thomas Edison
Motion picture camera	Lumiere brothers
Movable type	Johann Gutenberg
Neon lights	George Claude
Outboard engine	Ole Evinrude
Pacemaker (cardiac)	Wilson Greatbatch
Paper	Cai Lun
Phonograph	Thomas Edison
Photographic film	George Eastman
Railroad sleeping car	George Pullman
Refrigerator car	Gustavis Swift
Revolver	Samuel Colt
Rotary engine	Felix Wankel
Safety razor	King Gillette
Scissors	Leonardo da Vinci
Screw	Archimedes
Sewing machine	Elias Howe
Spark plug	Albert Champion
Steam engine	James Watt
Steel making process	Sir Henry Bessemer
Storage battery	Alessandro Volta
Submachine gun	John Thompson
Telegraph	Samuel Morse
Telephone	Alexander Graham Bell
Telescope	Hans Lippershey
Telescope (astronomical)	Galileo
Telescope (reflecting)	Sir Isaac Newton
Television iconoscope	Vladimir Zworykin
Thermometer (open column)	Galileo
Thermometer (mercury)	Gabriel Fahrenheit
Transistor	Bell Telephone labs
Vulcanized rubber	Charles Goodyear
Wireless	Guglielmo Marconi
Zipper	Whitcomb Judson

22 *Famous Names*

Greek philosopher/statesman, poisoned by hemlock .... Socrates
Greek philosopher, Academy founder, and student of Socrates .... Plato
Greek philosopher and scientist, teacher of Alexander the Great ..... Aristotle
Greek who sought an honest man .... Diogenes
Greek mathematician and founder of the science of hydrostatics .... Archimedes
Greek historian .... Herodotus
Greek historian and biographer .... Plutarch
Greek mathematician and geometry innovator .... Euclid
Greek mathematician famous for his theorem .... Pythagoras
Greek famous as being first actor .... Thespis
Greek with sword hanging over his head .... Damocles
Greek physician, doctor's oath is named for him .... Hippocrates
Greek physician who promoted the work of Hippocrates .... Galen
Roman orator and statesman .... Cicero
Founder of the Persian Empire .... Cyrus the Great
Man who conquered the world's largest land empire .... Genghis Khan
Genghis Khan's grandson .... Kubla Khan
First Christian Roman emperor .... Constantine
Man crowned Holy Roman Emperor on Christmas Day in 800 AD
.... Charlemagne
The Paladin (knight) of Charlemagne .... Orlando
Charlemagne's father .... Pepin the Short
Pepin the Short's father, founder of Carolingian dynasty .... Charles Martel
Founder of the Capetian dynasty in France, 987 AD .... Hugh Capet
The "Scourge of God" .... Attila (The Hun)
Carthaginian who crossed the Alps with 37 elephants .... Hannibal
First king of all the English .... Alfred the Great
Muslim defender of Jerusalem, 1189-91 .... Saladin
Crusader king who fought Saladin .... Richard the Lionhearted
"Recluse" crusader king .... Peter the Hermit
"Magnificent" Ottoman ruler .... Suleyman (the Magnificent)
Red bearded crusader .... Frederick Barbarosa
"The Maid of Orleans" .... Joan of Arc
"Magnificent" Florence dictator .... Lorenzo de Medici
16th century Italian sculptor, painter and poet .... Michelangelo
16th century Dutch humanist .... Erasmus
Subject of T.S. Eliot's *Murder in the Cathedral* .... Thomas A. Becket
Lord Chancellor beheaded by Henry VIII .... Sir Thomas More
17th century English philosopher and statesman .... Francis Bacon
Man who started Protestant Reformation with "95 theses" .... Martin Luther
Swiss-French reformist .... John Calvin
Scottish reformist .... John Knox

French queen regent implicated in St. Bartholomew's day massacre
.... Catherine de Medici
Cesare Borgia's infamous sister and patron of the arts .... Lucretia Borgia
French mistress to Louis XV .... Madame de Pompadour
Violin maker family from Cremora, Italy .... Amati
Violin maker who learned his craft from the Amatis .... Antonio Stradivarius
17th century French mathematician .... Blaise Pascal
He led the mutiny on the Bounty .... Fletcher Christian
Italian adventurer and lover .... Giacomo Casanova
French cardinal who fought the Huguenots .... Cardinal Richelieu
17th century French philosopher and mathematician .... René Descartes
The Angelic Doctor .... St. Thomas Aquinas
Man who overthrew Charles I of England .... Oliver Cromwell
Zulu leader .... Shaka
"The Little Corporal" .... Napoleon Bonaparte
He defeated Napoleon at Waterloo .... The Duke of Wellington
"The Lady with the Lamp" .... Florence Nightingale
"Gentle Pirate" who aided in Battle of New Orleans .... Jean Lafitte
English pirate hung at Old Baily, 1701 .... Captain Kid
Pirate Ed Teach a.k.a. .... Blackbeard
Frederick Barbarosa .... Redbeard
Cook who led the mutiny on the Hispaniola .... Long John Silver
Famous female pirates .... Ann Bonnie and Mary Reed
South American revolutionary born in Caracas .... Simon Bolivar
Fidel Castro's revolutionary friend .... Che Guevara
Mexican bandit who raided U.S. border towns .... Pancho Villa
Italian leader of the Red Shirts .... Garibaldi
First chancellor of the German Empire, 1871 .... Otto von Bismarck
Chinese provisional president, 1912 .... Sun Yat-Sen
Man who established Chinese government on Taiwan .... Chiang Kai-Shek
Chinese Communist Party head who died in 1997 .... Deng Xiaoping
Sir Edmund Hillary's Himalayan Sherpa guide .... Tensing Norgay
19th century shipping magnate .... Cornelius Vanderbilt
19th century banking magnet/philanthropist .... J.P. (John Pierpont) Morgan
20th century Greek shipping magnate .... Aristotle Onassis
Steel magnate and philanthropist .... Andrew Carnegie
British tea magnate .... Sir Thomas Lipton
Billionaire who disappeared from his yacht in 1991 .... Robert Maxwell
Philosopher who asked, "Is man a blunder of God?" .... Friedrich Nietzsche
Cambridge mathematician-philosopher .... Bertrand Russell
Jean Paul Sartre's philosopher friend .... Simone de Beauvoir
Man who first received an artificial heart .... Barney Clark
Doctor who preformed Barney Clark's heart transplant .... William DeVries
K Paul's chef .... Paul Prudhomme
"The Galloping Gourmet" .... Graham Kerr
"Favorites from New York Times" chef .... Craig Claiborne

22　*Famous Names*

Chinese celebrity chef .... Wolfgang Puck
She wrote the Boston Cook Book .... Fannie Farmer
Lawyer for the Creationists at Scopes trial .... William Jennings Bryan
Lawyer for the Darwinists at the Scopes trial .... Clarence Darrow
Female prosecutor in the O.J. Simpson trial .... Marcia Clark
Leopold and Loeb's defense attorney .... Clarence Darrow
Claus von Bulow's defense attorney .... Alan Dershowitz
He defended the Boston Strangler .... F. Lee Bailey
Charles Manson's prosecutor .... Vincent Bugliosi
"King of Torts" who died in 1996 .... Melvin Belli
He founded DeBeers .... Cecil Rhodes
Famous oil well fire fighter .... Red Adair
He planted apple trees in the Ohio Valley .... Johnny Appleseed
Famous 19th century furrier .... John Jacob Astor
19th century American lithographers .... Currier and Ives
Scottish clock maker .... Seth Thomas
He blazed the Wilderness Road .... Daniel Boone
"Life is worth living" speaker .... Bishop Sheen
Inspiration for *Citizen Kane* .... William Randolph Hearst
19th century British travel agent .... Thomas Cook
French lexicographer .... Pierre Larousse
American lexicographer .... Noah Webster
English lexicographer .... Samuel Johnson
French economist .... Jean Baptiste Say
Scottish economist .... Adam Smith
American economist, 1920's .... John Maynard Keynes
Canadian-born American economist and Harvard Professor of Economics
 .... John Kenneth Galbraith
French mathematician famous for his "last theorem" .... Pierre de Fermat
The Fugitive series is based on his life .... Sam Sheppard
Man who built the Erie Canal .... De Witt Clinton
American winner of Tchaikovsky music competition, 1958 .... Van Cliburn
Scottish philanthropist and Lord Rector .... Andrew Carnegie
Late finance magazine tycoon .... Malcolm Forbes
Army surgeon who found the cause of yellow fever .... Walter Reed
Newspaper editor and South sympathizer .... Horace Greeley
President's brother who was president of Johns Hopkins .... Milton Eisenhower
PLO leader .... Yasser Arafat
Spanish tenor whose name means "peaceful Sunday" .... Placido Domingo
Presidential brother who had a beer named for him .... Billy Carter
Pair who died in a light plane crash in Point Barrow, Alaska
 .... Will Rogers and Wiley Post
Gay '90's financier and philanthropist .... Diamond Jim Brady
Train engineer killed in head-on collision, 1900 .... Casey Jones
Boys Town founder, 1917 .... Father Edward Flanagan
"The Father of Science Fiction" .... Jules Verne

"The American Leonardo" .... Samuel Morse
"The American Caesar" .... Douglas MacArthur
"America's handyman" .... Bob Vila
"American ornithologist" .... John James Audubon
"New England Orator" .... Daniel Webster
"Virginia Orator" .... Thomas Paine
"The Lone Eagle" .... Charles Lindbergh
"The Great Profile" .... John Barrymore
"The Great Dissenter" .... Oliver Wendell Holmes
"The Great Commoner" .... William Jennings Bryan
"The Great Compromiser" or "The Great Pacificator" .... Henry Clay
"The Little Flower" .... Fiorello La Guardia
"The Great Communicator" .... Ronald Reagan
"The Wizard of Menlo Park" .... Thomas Edison
"Satchmo" .... Louis Armstrong
"The King of Ragtime" .... Scott Joplin
"The Little Tramp" .... Charlie Chaplin
"The Man of a Thousand Voices" .... Mel Blanc
"The Prince of Humbugs" .... P.T. Barnum
"The Chairman of the Board" .... Frank Sinatra
"The Lord of San Simeon" .... William Randolph Hearst
"The Peoples Lawyer" .... Ralph Nader
America's cowboy-philosopher .... Will Rogers
Philadelphia publisher and philanthropist .... Walter Annenberg
Baltimore critic .... H. L. Mencken
Father of American public education .... Horace Mann
He made stainless steel cars in Ireland .... John DeLorean
Pilot who landed in Europe instead of California, 1938 .... "Wrong Way" Corrigan
He broke the sound barrier in 1947 .... Chuck Yeager
Chairs astrophysics department, Cambridge University .... Stephen Hawking
MIT linguistic scholar .... Noam Chomsky
1960's Harvard psychologist; recreational drug advocate .... Timothy Leary
Yosemite photographer .... Ansel Adams
The original Siamese twins .... Chang and Eng
Man who found King Tut's tomb .... Howard Carter
American satirical comedian, imprisoned for obscenity, 1962 .... Lenny Bruce
Pro clown with his own postage stamp .... Lou Jacobs
Las Vegas magicians who work with big cats .... Siegfried and Roy
Famous tight rope walking family .... Wallendas
Canadian quintuplets .... Dionnes
American septuplets .... McCaugheys

23 *Familiar Quotes*

"When you have fears, do not fear to abandon them."
.... -Confucius

"The unexamined life is not worth living." .... -Socrates

"A soft answer turns away wrath." .... -Solomon

"Man does not live by bread alone." .... -Moses, repeated by Jesus Christ

"The meek shall inherit the Earth." .... -Jesus Christ

"Patriotism is the last refuge of a scoundrel." .... -Samuel Johnson

"A jug of wine, a loaf a bread and thou." .... -Omar Khayyam (from *The Rubaiyat*)

"Give the devil his due." .... -Miguel de Cervantes

"The proof of the pudding is in the eating." .... -Miguel de Cervantes

"Uneasy is the head that wears the crown." .... -William Shakespeare

"Fools rush in where angels fear to tread." .... -Alexander Pope

"A little learning is a dangerous thing." .... -Alexander Pope

"Hope springs eternal in the human breast."
.... -Alexander Pope (repeated in *Casey at the Bat*)

"In Xanadu did Kubla Khan a stately pleasure dome decree."
.... -Samuel Taylor Coleridge

"Water, water everywhere, but not a drop to drink."
.... -Samuel Taylor Coleridge

"Knowledge is power." .... - Francis Bacon

"Time and tide wait for no man." .... -Unknown

"They also serve who only stand and wait." .... -John Milton

"Slow but steady wins the race." .... -Aesop

"When you have eliminated the impossible, whatever remains must be the truth."
.... -Sherlock Holmes

"It was the best of times, it was the worst of times."
.... -Charles Dickens (first sentence from *A Tale of Two Cities*)

"It is a far, far better thing I do than I have ever done."
.... -Charles Dickens (from *A Tale of Two Cities*)

"It is better to have loved and lost than never to have loved at all."
.... -Alfred Lord Tennyson

"Stone walls do not a prison make, nor iron bars a cage."
.... -Richard Lovelace

"If God did not exist, it would be necessary to invent him."
.... Voltaire

"Man is born free and everywhere he is in chains." -Jean Jacques Rousseau

"I think, therefore I am." .... -Rene Descartes

"L'etat c'est moi" (I am the state). .... -Louis XIV

"Never complain and never explain." .... -Benjamin Disraeli

"I have not yet begun to fight." .... -John Paul Jones

"Don't fire until you see the whites of their eyes."
.... -William Prescott (Battle of Bunker Hill)

"We have met the enemy and they are ours."
....-Oliver Hazzard Perry (about the Battle of Lake Erie)

"Gridley, you may fire when ready." .... -Commodore Dewey

"Damn the torpedoes, full speed ahead!" .... -Admiral David Farragut
(at the Battle of Mobile Bay)

"War is cruelty, you cannot refine it." .... -William Tecumseh Sherman

"An army marches on its stomach." .... -Napoleon

"From the sublime to the ridiculous is but a step." ... -Napoleon

"Eternal vigilance is the price of liberty." .... -John Curran

23 *Familiar Quotes*

"These are the times that try men's souls." .... -Thomas Paine

"I know not what course others may take, as for me , give me liberty, or give me death!" .... -Patrick Henry

"I regret that I have but one life to give for my country." ......-Nathan Hale

"If winter comes, can spring be far behind?" .... -Percy Bysshe Shelly

"Hail to thee, Blythe Spirit." .... -Percy Bysshe Shelly

"Beauty without grace is like a fish hook without bait."
.... -Ralph Waldo Emerson

"Hitch your wagon to a star." .... -Ralph Waldo Emerson

"Music has charms to soothe the savage beast." .... -William Congreve

"God is in His Heaven, all's right with the world." .. -Robert Browning

"Come grow old with me, the best is yet to be." .... -Robert Browning

"Whosoever loves, believes the impossible." .... -Elizabeth Barrett Browning

"The mass of men live lives of quiet desperation." ... .-Henry David Thoreau (from *Walden*)

"Success is counted sweetest by those who never succeed."
.... -Emily Dickinson

"Because I could not stop for death, he stopped for me."
.... -Emily Dickinson

"Hope is the thing that perches in the soul and sings the tune without words."
.... -Emily Dickinson

"A thing of beauty is a joy forever." .... -John Keats

"Truth is beauty." .... -John Keats

"A rose is a rose, is a rose, is a rose." .... -Gertrude Stein

"I have promises to keep and miles to go before I sleep."   -Robert Frost

"Good fences make good neighbors." .... -Robert Frost

"East is east and west is west and never the twain shall meet."
.... -Rudyard Kipling

"Religion is the opium of the people." .... -Karl Marx

"From each according to his abilities, for each according to his needs."
.... -Karl Marx

"How can the consent of the governed be given, if the right to vote be denied?"
.... -Susan B Anthony

"We need religion for religion's sake, morality for morality's sake and art for art's sake."
.... -Victor Cousins

"All power tends to corrupt, absolute power corrupts absolutely."
.... -John Acton

"Early to bed and early to rise makes a man healthy, wealthy, and wise."
.... -Benjamin Franklin

"Little strokes fell great oaks." .... -Benjamin Franklin

"Nothing is certain but death and taxes." .... -Benjamin Franklin

"There is a sucker born every minute." .... -P. T. Barnum

"I never met a man I didn't like." .... -Will Rogers

"Genius is 99 percent perspiration and 1 percent inspiration."
.... -Thomas Edison

"Men never make passes at girls who wear glasses." .. -Dorothy Parker

"What happens to a dream deferred, does it dry up like a raisin in the sun?"
.... -Langston Hughes

"Go west, young man." .... -Horace Greeley

"There, but for the grace of God, go I." .... -John Bradford

"Libery and union, now and forever, one and inseparable."
.... -Daniel Webster

"A house divided against itself cannot stand." .... -Abraham Lincoln

"We need to make the world safe for democracy." .... -Woodrow Wilson

"There is no right to strike against the public safety by anyone, anywhere, anytime."
.... -Calvin Coolidge (about the Boston Police strike)

23 *Familiar Quotes*

"The business of America is business." .... -Calvin Coolidge

"The buck stops here." .... -Harry S Truman

"I don't get ulcers, I give them." .... -Lyndon Baines Johnson

"I would give anything not to be standing here today."
.... -Lyndon Baines Johnson

"An iron curtain has fallen over eastern Europe." ..... -Winston Churchill

"We are in a cold peace." .... -Trygve Lie

"The customer is always right." .... -Marshall Field

"The public be damned." .... -Cornelius Vanderbilt

"The medium is the message." .... -Marshall McLuhan

"Television is a vast waistland." .... -Newton Minow

"When the going gets tough, the tough get going." . -Knute Rockne

"The game ain't over 'til it's over." .... -Yogi Berra

"Nice guys finish last." .... -Leo Durocher

"It not whether you win or lose, but how you play the game."
.... -Grantland Rice

"Everyone is famous for fifteen minutes." .... -Andy Warhol

"History is bunk." .... -Henry Ford

"Flower power." .... -Allen Ginsberg

"There is no such thing as a free lunch." .... -Milton Freedman

"God does not play dice with the universe." .... -Albert Einstein

"Our smile is for people who have forgotten how to smile."
.... -Mother Teresa

"In this age of materialism, the single most important thing
we can give our children is our time." .... -Steven J. Ferrill

Fashion 24

East Indian dress	Sari
Sari sash	Obi
Tuxedo sash	Cummerbund
Hernia supporter	Truss
Rump padding	Bustle
Tight bottom shirt	Hobble shirt
Hawaiian shirt	Aloha shirt
Printed African shirt	Dashiqiao
Matador jacket	Bolero
Suit with vertical stripes	Seersucker
1940's "hepcat" suit style	Zoot Suit
Bridal skullcap	Juliet
Basque cap	Beret
Central American hat	Panama hat
Sherlock Holmes hat (double billed)	Deerstalker
Inverness coat attachment	Cape
Fabric with 22 wales per inch	Corduroy
Plaid pattern	Tartan
Scottish material	Tweed
Scottish tartan sock pattern	Argyle
Worsted fabric	Wool
Fabric made from flax	Linen
Canvas fabric	Cotton
Wedding veil fabric	Tulle
Flag material	Bunting
Fine natural fiber from south Asia	Cashmere
Angora goat fabric	Mohair

24 *Fashion*

Book cover fabric	Muslin
Thin crinkly fabric	Crepe
Tobacco cloth	Cheese cloth
See-through woven fabric	Gauze
Glazed cotton fabric	Chintz
Small bit of metal on an outfit	Sequin
Metallic thread material	Lamé
Woman's slip on shoe	Pump
French female pants designer	Coco Channel
DFV fashion designer	Diane von Firstenburg
DKNY fashion designer	Donna Karan
He had Polo line	Ralph Lauren
Iman's fashion designer	Claude Montana
"New Look" and "Y" Line designer	Christian Dior
Chief designer for Christian Dior, 1957	Yves Saint Laurent
Designer with trademark red, white, and blue nautical flag	Tommy Hilfiger
Russian-Italian fashion designer	Oleg Cassini
He designed Italian Air Force uniforms	Georgio Armini
Pancake makeup maker	Max Factor
18th century English fashion authority	Beau Brummell
She designed sports attire for women in the 1850's	Amelia Bloomer
Revolutionary War seamstress	Betsy Ross
Fashion designer who won 8 Oscars	Edith Head
She initiated the "waif look"	Twiggy
London designer of the miniskirt	Mary Quant
Fashion designer slain, 1997	Gianni Versace
Hollywood fashion street	Rodeo Drive
London fashion street	Carnaby Street
High fashion in France	Haute couture

Food 25

Hungarian meat stew	Goulash
Indian relish	Chutney
Russian beet soup	Borscht
Russian beef and sour cream dish	Beef stroganoff
Polish or Yugoslavian sausage	Kielbasa
Italian corn meal pudding	Polenta
Italian "little tongue" noodles	Linguini
Italian "little worm" noodles	Vermicelli
Italian Custard	Zabaglione
Italian Sausage	Salami
Italian veal and ham dish	Saltimbocca
Italian dish using thin cut of veal	Scallopini
Italian sauce with pine nuts	Pesto
Italian "springtime" pasta	Pasta primavera
Italian "before meal" appetizer	Antipasto
Italian ice cream	Gelato
German popular veal dish	Wiener Schnitzel
German cherry soup	Kirsch
German sausage	Knockwurst
German cabbage dish	Sauerkraut
German pot roast marinated in vinegar	Sauerbraten
German pastry with apples, cherries and cheese	Strudel
German peppery rabbit stew	Hasenpfeffer
French salad containing greens, olives, tuna & potatoes	Salade Nicoise
French molded gelatin salad	Aspic
French leek and potato soup	Vichysoisse
French chowder with several kinds of fish	Bouillabasse
French beef tenderloin, made for two	Chateaubriand
French paste with goose liver	Paté de fois gras
French relish from eggplant	Ratatouille
French egg and bacon pie	Quiche Lorraine
French sauce with egg yolk, mustard, and tabasco	Hollandaise sauce
Hollandaise sauce with tarragon and vinegar added	Bearnaise sauce
French orange flaming dish	Crepes Suzette
Roast beef covered with paté de fois gras	Beef Wellington
Greek lamb dish	Souvlaki
Greek popular beef sandwich	Gyro
Greek dish with eggplant	Moussaka
Japanese meat and vegetable dish	Sukiyaki
Japanese mushroom	Shiitake
Japanese beef	Kobe
Japanese noodles	Soba

25 *Food*

Jewish meat pie	Canis
Jewish stuffed egg pancake	Blintze
Mid-east processed wheat found in tabbouleh	Bulgur (wheat berries)
Mid-eastern Bulgur wheat salad	Tabrile
Mid-eastern paste with sesame seeds	Tahini
Mid-east thin sliced dough	Phyllo
Algerian or North African steamed dish	Couscous
Mediterranean honey dessert	Baklava
English "modest" pie	Humble pie
English popover	Yorkshire pudding
Scottish tea treat	Scone
Scottish dish of sheep innards and oatmeal	Haggis
Spanish cold tomato soup	Gazpacho
Mexican sausage	Chorizo
Mexican spicy chocolate sauce	Molé
Mexican tripe soup	Minuto
Cheese on toast	Welsh rarebit
Baked ice cream and sponge cake dessert	Baked Alaska
Pennsylvania Dutch apple dessert	Apple pan dowdy
Pennsylvania Dutch treat	Funnel cakes
Hawaiian taro root dish	Poi
Corn served with the hull and germ removed	Hominy
Cajun stew with ham	Jambalaya
Creole stew	Gumbo
Louisiana spicy crawfish tails	Cajun popcorn
Chinese cabbage	Bok choy
Marzipan paste nut	Almond
Hazel nuts	Filberts
Triangular Amazon nut	Brazil nut
Praline nut	Pecan
Chickpeas aka	Garbonzo beans
Beans with most fiber	Pinto beans
Soy milk or soybean curd	Tofu
Tofu legume	Soy bean
Cooking banana	Plantain
Lens shaped legumes, high in protein	Lentils
Pig intestines	Chitlins (chitterlings)
Corned beef and lima beans dish	Succotash
Beef soup made from the tail	Ox tail soup
Brunswick stew meat	Squirrel
Turkey gravy or turkey innards	Giblets
Pumpernickel grain	Rye
Tapioca root	Casaba
Fried Squid	Calamari
Source of caviar	Sturgeon
"Elastic" protein found in wheat	Gluten

Raw material for chocolate .... Cacao bean
Combined coffee and chocolate flavor .... Mocha
Course ground grain of Durham wheat .... Semolina
Nondigestible food .... Fiber
Pickled beef .... Corned beef
Controversial fat substitute .... Olestra
Red-leaf salad ingredient .... Radicchio
Ricotta liquid .... Whey
Jelly thickener .... Pectin
Scientific name for sugar .... Sucrose
Fruit sugar .... Fructose
Milk sugar .... Lactose
Black strap sweetener .... Molasses
Fruit and nut cereal introduced in 1910 .... Muslix
Dutch cheese with wax coating .... Gouda
English blue cheese .... Stilton
French cream cheese .... Neufchatel
Greek salad cheese .... Feta
"King of cheeses" .... Brie
Pizza cheese used as string cheese .... Mozzarella

Herbs and Spices:

Expensive yellow-orange spice .... Saffron
"Tasty" spice .... Savory
Quill spice or red spice from evergreen tree .... Cinnamon
Egg nog topper .... Nutmeg
Nutmeg coat spice .... Mace
Tobacco spice from Madagascar used for toothaches .... Cloves
"Master spice" .... Pepper
East Indian spice .... Curry
Hungarian spice .... Paprika
Jamaican multi-flavored spice .... Allspice
Licorice-flavored seeds .... Anise
Grasslike herb used to top potatoes .... Chives
Laurel tree food flavoring.. Bay leaf
Chinese parsley or coriander leaves .... Cilantro
Italian sausage flavoring .... Fennel
Flavoring sold in cloves .... Garlic
Rye bread herb .... Caraway
Symbol of remembrance, needle shaped spice .... Rosemary
Source of digitalis .... Foxglove
Indian bitter orange spice .... Turmeric
Marjoram.. Oregano
Clam chowder spice... Thyme
"Sweet" annual aromatic herb .... Basil
Spice and French Guiana capital .... Cayenne

26 *Geology*

Gems:

World's hardest mineral .... Diamond
Diamond material .... Carbon
Green beryl gem .... Emerald
"Mutton fat" nephrite .... Jade
Yellow or golden gem .... Topaz
Purple quartz .... Amethyst
Gem named after a tsarina .... Alexandrite
Gem found in Tanzania .... Tanzanite
Green chalcedony spotted with red jasper .... Bloodstone
Reddish-brown gem .... Garnet
Black organic gem .... Jet
Opaque blue or azure gemstone (sometimes flecked) .... Lapis lazuli
Purple corundum .... Sapphire
Red corundum .... Ruby
Kashmir Blue type of gem .... Sapphire
Star of India type of gem .... Ruby
95.5 carat diamond in the Smithsonian .... Hope Diamond
Diamond in *Titanic* .... Heart of the Ocean

Birth stones:

January .... Garnet
February .... Amethyst
March .... Aquamarine
April .... Diamond
May .... Emerald
June .... Pearl
July .... Ruby
August .... Peridot
September .... Sapphire
October .... Opal
November .... Topaz
December .... Turquoise

Other Facts:

Study of Earth's physical properties .... Geophysics
Study of the motion of Earth's plates .... Tectonics
Study of rocks .... Petrology
Earth's age .... 4.5 billions years
Earth's outer layer .... Crust

Earth's layer below the crust	Mantle
Current geologic period	Quaternary
Current geologic epoch	Holocene
Current geologic era	Cenozoic (recent life)
Middle geologic era	Mesozoic (middle life)
Early geologic era	Paleozoic (ancient life)
Ancient super continent, 240 million years ago	Pangaea
Nouthern super continent, 120 million years ago	Lauasia
Southern super continent, 120 million years ago	Gongwana
Earth's energy	Geothermal
Ocean surrounded by volcanic "ring of fire"	Pacific
Large volcanic crater	Caldera
Scale measuring earthquake intensity	Richter scale
Tidal wave caused by an earthquake	Tsunami
Fool's gold	Iron pyrite
Uranium and radium ore	Pitchblend
Aluminum ore	Bauxite
Mercury ore	Cinnabar
Copper ore	Cuprite
Lead ore	Galena
Hard carbon	Diamond
Soft carbon	Graphite
Hard coal	Anthracite
Soft coal	Bituminous
Brown coal	Lignite
Deep black lignite	Jet
Dense rock formed from cooling lava	Basalt
Glass formed from cooling lava	Obsidian
Three types of rock	Igneous, sedimentary, metamorphic
Earth's crust most abundant rock	Igneous
Most common igneous rock	Granite
Soft igneous rock	Pumice
Course grain rock	Gneiss
Translucent gypsum	Alabaster
Shale rock type	Sedimentary
Cave ceiling fixtures	Stalactites
Cave floor fixtures	Stalagmites
Stalactite and stalagmite combination	Column
Scale measuring mineral hardness	Mhos scale
Diamond rating on mhos scale	Ten
Ruby rating on mhos scale	Nine
Talc rating on mhos scale	One
Large California fault line	San Andreas Fault
Large east Africa fault line	Great Rift Valley

27 *Holidays and Observances*

Third Monday in January .... Martin Luther King Day

January 15 .... Martin Luther King's birthday

February 2 .... Groundhog Day

February 12 .... Lincoln's birthday

February 14 .... St. Valentine's Day

Third Monday in February .... President's Day

February 22 .... Washington's birthday

May 5 .... Cinco de Mayo

March 17 .... St. Patrick's Day

April 22 .... Earth Day

Wednesday of the last full week of April .... Secretary's Day

Last Friday in April .... Arbor Day

Second Sunday of May .... Mother's Day

Third Saturday in May .... Armed Forces Day

Last Monday in May .... Memorial Day

June 14 .... Flag Day

Third Sunday of June .... Father's Day

July 1 .... Canada Day

July 4 .... Independence Day

July 14 .... Bastille Day (France)

July 20 .... Moon (landing) Day

Second Sunday in September .... Grandparent's Day

September 17 .... Constitution Day

First Monday in September .... Labor Day

First Tuesday after first Monday in November .... Election Day

Second Monday in October .... Columbus Day

October 12 .... Original Columbus Day

October 24 .... United Nation's Day

October 31 .... Halloween

November 1 .... All Saint's Day

November 2 .... All Soul's Day

November 3 .... Guy Fawkes Day (England)

First Tuesday after first Monday in November .... Election Day

November 11 .... Veteran's Day (Armistice Day)

Fourth Thursday in November .... Thanksgiving

Sunday closest to November 30 .... Advent

December 25 .... Christmas

December 26 .... Boxing Day (Canada and Britain)

December 25 to January 1 .... Kwanzaa

Holiday formerly known as Dominion Day .... Canada Day

Holiday represented with 44 candles .... Hanukkah

Eight-day Jewish holidays .... Passover and Hanukkah

Holiday celebrating the end of WW I .... Armistice Day

First Sunday, after the first full moon, after the Spring equinox
.... Easter

Friday before Easter .... Good Friday

Sixth Sunday of Lent, Sunday before Easter .... Palm Sunday

First day of Lent .... Ash Wednesday

Day before Ash Wednesday .... Mardi Gras (Shrove Tuesday)

Mardi Gras in Europe and South America .... Carnival

End of Easter celebration .... Pentecost

Holiday about the 12 days of Christmas .... Epiphany

Holiday Anna Jarvis founded .... Mother's Day

Children collect money for UNICEF on this holiday Halloween

State holiday of Alaska .... Seward's Day

State holiday of Massachusetts .... Patriot's Day

28 *The Human Body*

Number of bones in the adult human body 206

Number of vertebrae in the spine 33

Three bones of the inner ear .... Hammer, anvil, stirrup

Body's smallest bone .... Hammer (stapes)

Wrist bones .... Carpels

Shoulder bone .... Scapula

Upper jaw bone .... Maxilla

Lower jaw bone .... Mandible

Collar bone .... Clavicle

Shoulder blade .... Scapula

Bone ribs are attached to .... Sternum (breastbone)

Upper arm bone .... Humerus

Lower arm bones .... Radius and ulna

Body's longest bone .... Femur (upper leg)

Shin bone .... Tibia

Smaller bone that runs next to the tibia .... Fibula

Shoulder bone and collar bone .... Pectoral girdle

Between the talus and tibia .... Ankle

Tail bone .... Coccyx

Hallux .... Big toe

Minnimus .... Little toe

Tissue that connects bones .... Ligaments

Central knee ligament .... ACL

Fiberous structure at the end of most muscles .... Tendon

Largest tendon in the body .... Achillies tendon

Material that attaches tendons to bones .... Cartilage

Science of skeletal muscles .... Orthopedics

Shoulder muscles .... Deltoids

Front upper arm muscle .... Biceps

Back upper arm muscle .... Triceps

Front thigh muscle .... Quadriceps

Inhalation muscle .... Diaphragm

Rectus femoris muscle .... Thigh

Group of nerves .... Plexus

Body's longest nerve .... Sciatic

Sense of smell nerve .... Olfactory nerve

Nerves at back of abdomen .... Solar plexus

Number of chambers in the heart .... Four

Heart's upper chambers .... Left and right atrium

Heart's lower chambers .... Left and right ventricles

Sac surrounding heart .... Pericardium

Blood type "factor" (measured in positive and negative) .... Rh factor

Blood type of a "universal donor" .... Type O negative

Watery part of blood .... Plasma

Where blood is produced .... Bone marrow

Disc-shaped blood cell .... Platelet

What leukocytes carry .... White blood cells

What erythrocytes carry .... Red blood cells

Blood protein .... Globulin

What makes blood clot .... Fibrin

Body's largest artery .... Aorta

Largest artery in leg .... Femoral artery

Large artery in the neck .... Carotid artery

Artery supplying the heart muscle .... Pulmonary artery

Body's largest vein .... Vena cava (major)

Large vein in neck .... Jugular vein

These join to form veins .... Venules

These join arteries and veins .... Capillaries

Where insulin is produced .... Pancreas

Renal cortex gland .... Kidney

Gland "on the kidney" .... Adrenal

Master gland (at base of brain) .... Pituitary

Gland that regulates metabolism .... Thyroid

Gland that aids in development of the immune system .... Thymus

Female sex hormone .... Estrogen

28 | *The Human Body*

Male sex hormone	Testosterone
Tear glands	Lacrimal
Where vocal chords are located	Larynx
Tube traveling from mouth to lungs	Trachea
Tubes that connect trachea to lungs	Bronchi
Protrusions that transfer oxygen in lungs	Alveoli
Hard outside layer of teeth	Enamel
Soft center part of teeth	Pulp
Calcified tissue surrounding the pulp	Dentin
Normal number of adult teeth	32
Gingiva	Gums
Gustatory organs	Taste buds
Flesh that hangs from soft palate	Uvula
Four tastes the tongue is capable of	Sweet, salty, sour and bitter
Tube traveling to stomach	Esophagus
Tube from nose to esophagus	Pharynx
Stomach acid	Hydrochloric
Blood purifying organ below the stomach	Spleen
Largest organ in the body	Skin
Skin's outer layer	Epidermis
Skin protein	Keratin
Skin pigmentation provider	Melanin
Digestive canal	Alimentary
Where bile is made, largest internal organ	Liver
Where bile is stored	Gallbladder
Colored part of the eye	Iris
Movable part of the eye controlled by the iris	Pupil
Blood vessel in the eye	Retina
Transparent layer of the outer eye	Cornea
Eye "jelly"	Vitreous humor
Two types of light receptors in the eye	Rods and cones
Nerve connecting eye to brain	Optic nerve
Where Graafian follicles are located	Ovaries
Tubes connecting ovaries to womb	Fallopian tubes
This organ removes glucose from the blood	Liver

Where islets of langerhans are located .... Pancreas

Three parts of brain .... Cerebrum, cerebellum,
                                                                             medulla oblongata (brain stem)

Outer membrane of the brain .... Dura mater

Speech lobe of brain .... Frontal lobe

Hemisphere of brain containing musical, artistic aptitudes ...... Right hemisphere

Brain's nerve cells .... Neurons

Fiber that transmit nerve impulses to neurons .... Axons

Brain chemicals that move nerve impulses .... Neurotransmitters

Neurotransmitters "jump" these spaces between cells .... Synapses

Sensory, motor, and associative covering layer of the brain .... Cerebral cortex

Joints connecting skull plates .... Suture joints

Largest joint in the body .... Knee

Tube traveling from the throat to inner ear .... Eustachian tube

Tympanic membrane .... Ear drum

Spiral passages of the ear .... Cochlea

Loop-shaped ear canals that help control balance .... Semicircular canals

Hair pocket .... Follicle

Hair follicle gland .... Subacial gland

Fibrous protein that makes up hair and nails .... Keratin

Fertilized egg .... Zygote

These unite to form zygote .... Gametes

Fluid in womb .... Amniotic fluid

This controls the body's temperature .... Hypothalamus

Rise in basal body temperature indicates this .... Ovulation

Cell division .... Mitosis

Cell division which cuts chromosomes in half.......................... Meiosis

Free-moving cell .... Corpuscle

Helical structure material .... DNA

Outer layer of skin .... Epidermis

Proteins that combat foreign proteins .... Antibodies

Thread-like bodies in cell nuclei .... Chromosomes

Normal number of human chromosomes .... 46 (23 pairs)

The soft spot on a baby's head .... Fontanel

29 *Languages*

World's Most Widely Spoken Languages:

1. Mandarin Chinese
2. English
3. Hindi
4. Russian*
5. Spanish*

Bangladesh language	Bengali
Pakistani language	Urdu
Sri Lanka language	Singhalese
Classic Hindu language	Sanskrit
Artificial language	Esperanto
Hong Kong Chinese	Cantonese
North China language	Mandarin
Philippines language	Tagalog
Old Testament language	Hebrew
Language of Jesus Christ	Aramaic
Northern Belgian language	Flemish
Northeast Spain dialect	Catalan
Non-romantic language of northern Spain	Basque
Hungarian language	Magyar
Persian or Iranian	Farsi
"Vulgar" Latin	Sardinian
Boer language	Afrikaans
"High and low" language	German
French derivitive spoken in Haiti	Creole
Most widely spoken language in Africa	Swahili
Swahili is from this group	Bantu
Magna Carta and Book of Kells language	Latin
Family of Welsh, Irish, and Gaelic	Celtic
Scottish language	Gaelic
Irish Celt language	Erse
Language of the Koran	Arabic
Family of languages, including Hebrew, Arabic and Maltese	Semitic
Canada's official languages	English and French
Kenya's official languages	Swahili and English
International court languages	English and French

* Some sources list Spanish fourth and Russian fifth

Latin Phrases **30**

Always faithful .... Semper Fidelis (Marine motto)

Always ready .... Semper Paratus (Coast Guard motto)

Thus ever to tyrants .... Sic semper tyrannis (Virginia motto)

Higher, faster, stronger................................... Citius, altius, fortius (Olympic motto)

Something for something (fair exchange) ...... Quid pro quo

Time flies .... Tempus fugit

Method of operation..................................... Modus operandi

A god out of a machine .... Deux ex machina

Nurturing mother.. Alma mater

Lamb of God .... Agnus Dei

Seize the day .... Carpe diem

I think, therefore I am .... Cogito ergo sum

No contest .... Nolo contendere

Friend of the court.. Amicus curiae

Court order.. Habeas corpus

Not of sound mind .... Non compos mentis

Under penalty .... Subpoena

It does not follow.. Non sequitur

In wine, truth .... In vino, veritas

From many, one.. E pluribus, unum

Entirely .... En toto

Go on without limit .... Ad infinitum

Good faith .... Bona fide

As such .... Per se

Buyer beware .... Caveat emptor

Not present.. In absentia

On the first face .... Prima facie

For example .... Exempli gratia (e.g.)

That is .... Id est (i.e.)

In matter of .... In re

By the fact .... Ipso facto

From the fact .... De facto

30 *Latin Phrases*

After the fact	Ex post facto
For all	Omnibus
For the moment	Ex tempore
Oh, the time, oh, the morals	O tempora, O mores
Roman peace	Pax Romana
Even you, Brutus	Et tu Brute
Under the voice	Sotto voce
Someone not welcome	Persona non grata
Without a fee	Pro bono
For this purpose	Ad hoc
Before the war	Ante bellum
With great praise	Magna cum laude
In good faith	Bona fide
Behold the man	Ecce homo
Solid Earth	Terra firma
Unknown territory	Terra incognita
In the middle level	Mezzanine
In the middle age	Mesozoic
Racecourse	Curriculum
Make alike	Facsimile
Almost an island	Peninsula
Elsewhere	Alibi
Up the ladder	Escalator
Sound	Sonata
Listen	Audi
Sweet song	Dulcimer
Servant	Valet
Talking alone	Soliloquy
Handwritten	Manuscript
Little hand	Manacle
Leaf	Folio
Little worm	Vermillion
Bearlike	Orson

Literature **31**

The best selling book of all time	*The Bible*
Second-best selling book of all time	*Quotations of Mao Tse Tung*
Best selling continously updated book of all time	The Guinness Book of Records
The best selling novel of all time	*Valley of the Dolls*
Virgil writes that this man is the ancestor of all Romans	Aeneas
5th or 6th century Saxon saga	*Beowulf*
Beowulf monster	Grendel
8th century Anglo-Saxon monk and translator	Venerable Bede
Classic medieval morality play	*Everyman*
14th century "Father of English Literature"	Geoffrey Chaucer
Crystal City is in this work	*Pilgrim's Progress*
1653 book on fishing	*The Compleat Angler*
Dante's love	Beatrice
Milton work about the fall of Satan	*Paradise Lost*
Mephistopheles is the devil in this work	*Dr. Faustus*
Vlad the Impaler is the basis for this character	Count Dracula
Cyrano de Bergerac's love	Roxanne
Sir Galahad's father	Lancelot
King Arthur's island	Avalon
King Arthur's sword	Excaliber
Edmond Dantes is this man	*The Count of Monte Cristo*
Don Quixote's squire	Sancho Panza
Count Vronsky's love	Anna Karenina
Land in *Lost Horizon*	Shangri-La
Subject of *The Agony and the Ecstasy*	Michelangelo
Baroness Orczy's hero	The Scarlet Pimpernel
Oscar Wilde's never aging murderer	Dorian Grey
C. S. Forester's naval hero	Captain Horatio Hornblower
Jules Verne's captain	Captain Nemo
Captain Nemo's submarine	Nautilus
Phileas Fogg is in this novel	*Around the World in 80 Days*
Fogg's sidekick	Passepartout
Creator of the character Jean Valjean	Victor Hugo
Main character in *The Hunchback of Notre Dame*	Quasimodo
Quasimodo's love	Esmeralda
Character Oliver Mellors was known as	*Lady Chatterley's Lover*
Philip Nolan is this title character	*The Man Without a Country*
19th century writer of dime novels	Ned Buntline
James Fenimore Cooper's hometown	Cooperstown, NY
Cooper's five-novel tales	*The Leather-Stocking Tales*
The first Leather-Stocking tale	*The Pioneers*
Cooper's scout in *The Pathfinder* and *The Deerslayer*	Natty Bumppo

31   *Literature*

Natty Bumppo's nickname .... Hawkeye
Cooper's last Mohican .... Uncas
Sauk Center, Minnesota author .... Sinclair Lewis
Town in *Our Town* .... Grover's Corners
Sinclair Lewis' Vermont doctor character .... Arrowsmith
Sinclair Lewis' real estate agent character.............. Babbitt
Sinclair Lewis novel of European travels .... *Dodsworth*
John Steinbeck's fish factory tale............................. *Cannery Row*
Steinbeck's poodle tale.. *Travels With Charlie*
Adam Trask appears in this novel............................ *East of Eden*
First American man of letters, from Tarrytown, NY .... Washington Irving
Irving's Sleepy Hollow rider .... The Headless Horseman
Mountains where Rip Van Winkle slept for 20 years .... The Catskills
Louisa May Alcott's literary alter ego .... Jo March
Salem, Massachusetts author .... Nathaniel Hawthorne
She wore the scarlet letter .... Hester Prynne
Hester Prynne's daughter .... Pearl
Vanity Fair lady .... Becky Sharp
Albany, NY author .... Herman Melville
Melville's award-winning short story .... *Billy Budd*
Moby-Dick captain.. Captain Ahab
Moby-Dick story teller and sole survivor .... Ishmael
First female writer in U.S. Writer's Hall of Fame.............. Harriet Beecher Stowe
Uncle Tom's Cabin villain .... Simon Legree
Little girl from *Uncle Tom's Cabin* .... Little Eva
Sherlock Holmes' address .... 221B Baker Street
Sherlock Holmes' sidekick .... Dr. Watson
Sherlock Holmes' arch villain...................................... Professor Moriarty
Author and anthropologist raised in Samoa .... Margaret Mead
Scottish author from Edinburgh .... Sir Walter Scott
Scottish "Robin Hood" .... *Rob Roy*
Irish author who used "stream of consciousness" technique
.... James Joyce
Ulysses main character .... Stephen Daedalus
Big Brother watched Winston Smith in this novel *1984*
Alexander Selkirk's life is the basis for this novel............. *Robinson Crusoe*
Author who saw the Alaska gold rush .... Jack London
Call of the Wild dog.. Buck
Novel in which Wolf Larson appears .... *The Sea Wolf*
Scottish author who lived in Samoa .... Robert Lewis Stevenson
Boy in *Treasure Island* .... Jack Hawkins
Treasure Island peg-legged pirate .... Long John Silver
Author from Hannibal, Missouri .... Mark Twain
Mark Twain title lawyer .... Pudd'nhead Wilson
Tom Sawyer's girlfriend .... Becky Thatcher
Tom Sawyer's Aunt .... Aunt Polly

Huckleberry Finn's black friend	Jim
Mark Twain worked for this author	Bret Harte
Charles Dickens's unfinished novel	*The Mystery of Edwin Drood*
The two cities in *A Tale of Two Cities*	London and Paris
Oliver Twist thief	Uriah Heep
Ebeneezer Scrooge's deceased partner	Jacob Marley (first ghost)
Bob Cratchit's son	Tiny Tim
Lucy Manett is in this novel	*A Tale of Two Cities*
Nicknamed "Papa," he committed suicide in Idaho	Ernest Hemingway
Hemingway's novel of the Spanish Civil War	*For Whom the Bell Tolls*
Hemingway novel about 1920's Europe and the lost generation	*The Sun Also Rises*
Hemingway's novel of Bullfighting	*Death in the Afternoon*
Hemingway's novel of WW I in Italy	*A Farewell to Arms*
Character in *The Old Man and the Sea*	Santiago
Deer Park author	Norman Mailer
Norman Mailer novel set in WW II	*The Naked and the Dead*
After the Fall was about her	Marilyn Monroe
Taos, New Mexico author	E. M. Forster
E.M. Forster's country home	Howard's End
Lifelong friend of Gertrude Stein	Alice B. Toklas
Mansion in *Rebecca*	Manderly
Mansion in *Jane Eyre*	Thornfield Hall
Wuthering Heights lad	Heathcliff
The Little House on the Prairie family	Ingalls
Novel in which "Scout" Finch appeared	*To Kill a Mockingbird*
Novel in which Willie Stark appeared	*All the King's Men*
Novel in which Billie Pilgrim appeared	*Slaughterhouse Five*
Ed McBain's precinct	87th Precinct
Salesman in *Death of a Salesman*	Willy Loman
Poe's *Rue Morgue* and *Purloined Letter* detective	C. August Dupain
Jeeve's creator	P. G. Wodehouse
Nero Wolfe creator	Rex Stout
Father Brown creator	G. K. Chesterton
Lord Peter Wimsey creator	Dorothy Sayer
Kay Scarpetta creator	Patricia Cornwell
Kinsey Millhone creator	Sue Grafton
V.I. Warshawski creator	Sara Paretsky
Doctor Fu Manchu creator	Sax Rohmer
Mr. Moto creator	John Marquand
Charlie Chan creator	Earl Derr Biggers
Perry Mason creator	Erle Stanley Gardner
Nathan Zuckerman creator	Phillip Roth
Mike Hammer's creator	Mickey Spillane
Phillip Marlow's creator	Raymond Chandler
Sam Spade creator	Dashiell Hammett

31 *Literature*

Travis McGee creator	John MacDonald
Adam Daglish creator	P. D. James
Harry Lime creator	Dashiell Hammett
Harry Potter creator	J. K. Rowling
"The Working author"	Studs Terkel
"Lincoln biographer"	Carl Sandburg
"The Queen of Suspence"	Mary Higgins Clark
Pygmalion professor	Henry Higgins
Lady in *A Portrait of a Lady*	Isabel Archer
Lord Jim and *Heart of Darkness* narrator	Marlow
F. Scott Fitzgerald's namesake	Francis Scott Key
Salesman in *The Great Gatsby*	Nick Carroway
The Great Gatsby's love	Daisy Buchanan
Main character in *The Natural*	Roy Hobbs
Hero of *Catcher in the Rye*	Holden Caulfield
Winnie the Pooh's human friend	Christopher Robin
The "lady" in *A Streetcar Named Desire*	Blanche Dubois
Leading man in *A Streetcar Named Desire*	Stanley Kowalski
French-born American diarist	Anaïs Nin
King of the Techno-thriller	Tom Clancy
Tom Clancy's government agent	Jack Ryan
Writer and LA policeman for 14 years	Joseph Wambaugh
Castle Rock or Maine author	Stephen King
French short story writer	Guy de Maupassant
Creator of Nick and Nora Charles	Dashiell Hammett
Winner of the first U.S. Nobel Prize for Literature	Eugene O'Neill
2001: A Space Odyssey computer	HAL-9000

Books and Authors:

1984	George Orwell
2001: A Space Odyssey	Arthur C. Clarke
87ᵗʰ Precinct	Ed McBain
Absalom, Absalom	William Faulkner
Acceptable Risk	Robin Cook
Accidental Tourist, The	Anne Tyler
Adam Bede	George Eliot
Adonis	Percy Bysshe Shelly
Admirable Crichton, The	James Barrie
Advancement of Learning, The	Francis Bacon
Adventures of Huckleberry Finn, The	Mark Twain
Adventures of Tom Sawyer, The	Mark Twain
Advise and Consent	Allen Drury (Pulitzer)
Aerowan	Samuel Butler
Aeneid, The	Virgil
African Queen, The	C. S. Forester
Age of Innocence, The	Edith Wharton (Pulitzer)

Age of Reason, The	Jean-Paul Sartre
Ageless Body, Timeless Mind	Deepak Chopra
Agony and the Ecstasy, The	Irving Stone
Airport	Arthur Hailey
Alaska	James Michener
Alexandrian's Geography	Ptolemy
Alhambra, The	Washington Irving
Alice Adams	Booth Tarkington (Pulitzer)
Alice in Wonderland	Lewis Carroll
Alice Through the Looking Glass	Lewis Carroll
All Quiet on the Western Front	Erich Maria Remarque
All the King's Men	Robert Penn Warren
Alphabet mysteries	Sue Grafton
Ambassadors, The	Henry James
Americans, The	Henry James
American Crisis, The	Thomas Paine
American Dictionary, The	Noah Webster
American Language, The	H. L. Mencken
American Tragedy, An	Theodore Dreiser
Analects	Confucius
Andersonville	MacKinlan Kantor (Pulitzer)
And Quiet Flows the Don	Mikhail Sholokhov
Andromeda Strain, The	Michael Crichton
Angela's Ashes	Frank McCourt
Anne of Green Gables	L. M. Montgomery
Anna and the King of Siam	Margaret Landon
Anna Karenina	Leo Tolstoy
Anne of a Thousand Days	Maxwell Anderson
Answered Prayers	Truman Capote
Antigone	Sophocles
Any Woman's Blues	Erica Jong
Apocalypse Watch	Robert Ludlum
Armies of the Night	Norman Mailer
Around the World in Eighty Days	Jules Verne
Arrowsmith	Sinclair Lewis (Pulitzer)
Art of Happiness, The	Dalai Lama
As I Lay Dying	William Faulkner
Ascent of Man, The	Jacob Bronowski
Atlas Shrugged	Ayn Rand
Autobiography of Alice B. Toklas, The	Gertrude Stein
Awake and Sing!	Clifford Odets
Bad Seed, The	Maxwell Anderson
Bald Soprano, The	Eugene Ionesco
Ball Four	Jim Bouton
Barchester Towers	Anthony Trollope
Barry Lyndon	William Makepeace Thackeray

| 31 | *Literature* |

Basketball Diaries, The	Jim Carroll
Battlefield Earth	L. Ron Hubbard
Be My Guest	Conrad Hilton
Beast	Peter Benchley
Beautiful and Damned, The	F. Scott Fitzgerald
Being There	Jerzy Kosinski
Being and Nothingness	Jean-Paul Sartre
Bell Jar, The	Sylvia Plath
Bellefleur	Joyce Carol Oates
Beloved	Toni Morrison (Pulitzer)
Ben-Hur	General Lew Wallace
Bestseller	Oliver Goldsmith
Betsy, The	Harold Robbins
Beyond Good and Evil	Friedrich Nietzsche
Big Sleep, The	Raymond Chandler
Billions and Billions	Carl Sagan
Billy Bathgate	E. L. Doctorow
Billy Budd	Herman Melville
Birds of America, The	John J. Audubon
Birds, The (modern)	Daphne du Maurier
Birds, The (ancient)	Aristophanes
Black Beauty	Anna Sewell
Black Stallion, The	Walter Farley
Bleak House	Charles Dickens
Blue Back Speller	Noah Webster
Bluebeard	Kurt Vonnegut, Jr.
Bonfire of the Vanities, The	Thomas Wolfe
Book of Common Prayer, A	Joan Didion
Book of Virtues	William J. Bennett
Boris Godunov	Alexander Pushkin
Border, The (trilogy)	Cormac McCarthey
Born Free	Joy Adamson
Boston Cooking School Cook Book	Fannie Farmer
Bostonians, The	Henry James
Boys of Summer, The	Roger Kahn
Boys from Brazil, The	Ira Levin
Brain	Robin Cook
Brave New World	Aldous Huxley
Breakfast at Tiffany's	Truman Capote
Breakfast of Champions	Kurt Vonnegut, Jr.
Breathing Lessons	Anne Tyler (Pulitzer)
Brideshead Revisited	Evelyn Waugh
Bridge of San Luis Rey, The	Thornton Wilder (Pulitzer)
Bridge on the River Kwai, The	Pierre Boulle
Bridges of Madison County, The	James Waller
Bridges at Toko-Ri, The	James Michener

Brief History of Time, A	Stephen Hawking
Bronze Horseman, The	Alexander Pushkin
Brothers Karamazov, The	Fyodor Dostoyevsky
Burden of Proof, The	Scott Turow
Bus Stop	William Inge
Butterfield 8	John O'Hara
Caballero's Way, The	O. Henry
Caesar	Coleen McCullough
Caine Mutiny, The	Herman Wouk (Pulitzer)
Call for the Dead	John Le Carré
Call of the Wild, The	Jack London
Camera Never Blinks, The	Dan Rather
Camille	Alexandre Dumas (fils)
Cancer Ward	Aleksandr Solzhenitsyn
Candide	Voltaire
Cannery Row	John Steinbeck
Canterbury Tales, The	Geoffrey Chaucer
Captain Horatio Hornblower	C. S. Forester
Captains Courageous	Rudyard Kipling
Cardinal Sins	Andrew Greeley
Cardinal of the Kremlin, The	Tom Clancy
Caribbean	James Michener
Carpetbaggers, The	Harold Robbins
Carrie	Stephen King
Cask of Amontillado, The	Edgar Allan Poe
Catbird Seat, The	James Thurber
Cat in the Hat, The	Dr. Seuss
Cat Stories	James Herriot
Catch-22	Joseph Heller
Catcher in the Rye, The	J. D. Salinger
Cat's Cradle	Kurt Vonnegut, Jr.
Celebrated Jumping Frog of Calaveras County, The	Mark Twain
Centaur, The	John Updike
Centennial	James Michener
Century, The	Peter Jennings
Chamber, The	John Grisham
Charlie and the Chocolate Factory	Roald Dahl
Charlotte's Web	E. B. White
Chesapeake	James Michener
Child's Christmas in Wales, A	Dylan Thomas
Chitty Chitty Bang Bang	Ian Fleming
Christine	Stephen King
Christmas Carol, The	Charles Dickens
Chronicles of Narnia, The	C. S. Lewis
Cider House Rules, The	John Irving
Cimmaron	Edna Ferber

31   *Literature*

Circle of Friends	Maeve Binchy
Civil Disobedience	Henry David Thoreau
Clear and Present Danger, A	Tom Clancy
Client, The	John Grisham
Clockwork Orange, A	Anthony Burgess
Close Encounters of the Third Kind	Stephen Spielberg
Color Purple, The	Alice Walker
Coma	Robin Cook
Coming of Age in Samoa	Margaret Mead
Common Sense	Thomas Paine
Communist Manifesto, The (complete works)	Karl Marx
Complete Book of Running, The	Jim Fixx
Compleat Angler, The	Izaak Walton
Confessions of Nat Turner, The	William Styron (Pulitzer)
Congo	Michael Crichton
Connecticut Yankee in King Arthur's Court, A	Mark Twain
Constant Reader	Dorothy Parker
Corsair, The	Lord Byron
Cosmos	Carl Sagan
Count of Monte Cristo, The	Alexandre Dumas
Country Girl, The	Clifford Odets
Covenant, The	James Michener
Cover Her Face	P. D. James
Cradle Will Fall, The	Mary Higgins Clark
Crime and Punishment	Fyodor Dostoyevsky
Crimes of the Heart	Beth Henley
Crimson Tide	Tom Clancy
Crossing the Threshold of Hope	Pope John Paul II
Cry in the Night, A	Mary Higgins Clark
Cry the Beloved Country	Alan Payton
Crystal Cave, The	Mary Stewart
Cujo	Stephen King
Cyrano de Bergerac	Edmond Rostand
Daisy Miller	Henry James
Dandelion Wine	Ray Bradbury
Darkness at Noon	Arthur Koestler
Das Kapital	Karl Marx
David Copperfield	Charles Dickens
Day of the Locust, The	Nathanael West
Day of the Jackal, The	Frederick Forsyth
Dazzle	Judith Krantz
Dead Souls	Nikolai Gogol
Death in Venice	Thomas Mann
Death on the Nile	Agatha Christie
Death in the Afternoon	Ernest Hemingway
Death in the Family	James Agee

Death Trap	Ira Levin
Decameron	Giovanni Boccaccio
Declaration of Independence, The	Thomas Jefferson
Decline and Fall of the Roman Empire	Edward Gibbon
Deerslayer, The	James Fenimore Cooper
Deliverance	James Dickey
Demon Box	Ken Kesey
Devil and Daniel Webster, The	Stephen Vincent Benet
Devil's Dictionary, The	Ambrose Bierce
Dialogues	Plato
Diary of Ann Frank, The	Anne Frank
Dictionary of the English Language, A	Samuel Johnson
Disclosure	Michael Crichton
Divine Comedy, The	Dante Alighieri
Dodsworth	Sinclair Lewis
Dog Training My Way	Barbara Woodhouse
Dogs of War, The	Frederick Forsyth
Doll's House, A	Henrik Ibsen
Dolores Claiborne	Stephen King
Dombey and Son	Charles Dickens
Don Juan	Lord Byron
Don Quixote	Miguel de Cervantes
Dr. Dolittle (The Story of Dr. Dolittle)	Hugh Lofting
Dr. Jekyll and Mr. Hyde	Robert Louis Stevenson
Doctor Faustus	Thomas Mann
Doctor Zhivago	Boris Pasternak
Double Indemnity	James M. Cain
Dracula	Bram Stoker
Dragon's Teeth	Upton Sinclair (Pulitzer)
Dubliners	James Joyce
Dune	Frank Herbert
Dunwich Horror, The	H. P. Lovecraft
East of Eden	John Steinbeck
Eclectic Readers, The	William McGuffey
Ego and the Id	Sigmund Freud
Elements, The	Euclid
Elmer Gantry	Sinclair Lewis
Enfants Terrible, Les	Jean Cocteau
Elvis and Me	Priscilla Presley
Embraced by the Light	Betty J. Eadie
Emma	Jane Austen
English Patient, The	Michael Andajie
Entertaining	Martha Stewart
Equus	Peter Schaefer
Erewhon	Samuel Butler
Essays	Ralph Waldo Emerson

31 *Literature*

Ethan Frome	Edith Wharton
Eugene Onegin	Aleksandr Pushkin
Even Cowgirls Get the Blues	Tom Robbins
Every Night, Josephine	Jacqueline Susann
Everything I Need to Know, I Learned in Kindergarten	Robert Fulghum
Executioner's Song, The	Norman Mailer (Pulitzer)
Executive Orders	Tom Clancy
Exile, The	Pearl Buck
Exodus	Leon Uris
Exorcist, The	William Blatty
Eye of the Needle	Ken Follet
Fable, A	William Faulkner (Pulitzer)
Faerie Queene, The	Edmund Spenser
Fahrenheit 451	Ray Bradbury
Fall of the House of Usher, The	Edgar Allan Poe
Fallen Man, The	Tony Hillerman
Familiar Quotations	James Bartlett
Fanshawe	Nathaniel Hawthorne
Far From the Madding Crowd	Thomas Hardy
Farewell to Arms, A	Ernest Hemingway
Farewell, My Lovely	Raymond Chandler
Fatherhood	Bill Cosby
Fathers and Sons	Ivan Turgenev
Faust	Johann von Goethe
Fear of Flying	Erica Jong
Federalist Papers, The	Alexander Hamilton
Female Eunuch, The	Germaine Greer
Feminine Mystique, The	Betty Frieden
Fighting Angel	Pearl Buck
Finnegan's Wake	James Joyce
Firestarter	Stephen King
Firm, The	John Grisham
First Wives' Club, The	Oliver Goldsmith
Fixer, The	Bernard Malamud (Pulitzer)
Flappers and Philosophers	F. Scott Fitzgerald
Foucault's Pendulum	Umberto Eco
For the Record	Donald Regan
For Whom the Bell Tolls	Ernest Hemingway
Forest Gump	Winston Groom
Forsyte Saga, The	John Galsworthy
Foundation's Edge	Isaac Asimov
Fountainhead, The	Ayn Rand
Four Past Midnight	Stephen King
Frankenstein	Mary Shelley
French Lieutenant's Woman, The	John Fowles
Frogs	Aristophanes

From Here to Eternity	James Jones
Gambler, The	Fyodor Dostoyevsky
Gargantua	Francois Rabelais
Gentleman from Indiana, The	Booth Tarkington
Gentlemen Prefer Blondes	Anita Loos
Getting Even	Woody Allen
Ghosts	Henrik Ibsen
Giant	Edna Ferber
Gift of the Magi, The	O. Henry
Gigi	Colette
Glory	Herman Wouk
Go Tell It on the Mountain	James Baldwin
Godfather, The	Mario Puzo
God's Little Acre	Erskine Caldwell
Gold Bug, The	Edgar Allan Poe
Gone With the Wind	Margaret Mitchell (Pulitzer)
Good Earth, The	Pearl Buck (Pulitzer)
Good Soldier, The	Ford Madox Ford
Goodbye Columbus	Phillip Roth
Good-bye, Mr. Chips	James Hilton
Goodbye to Berlin	Christopher Isherwood
Gorillas in the Mist	Diane Fosse
Goose Bumps series	R. L. Stein
Gorky Park	Martin Cruise Smith
Grapes of Wrath, The	John Steinbeck (Pulitzer)
Grasshopper and the Ant, The	Aesop
Gravity's Rainbow	Thomas Pynchon
Great Expectations	Charles Dickens
Great Gatsby, The	F. Scott Fitzgerald
Green Hills of Africa	Ernest Hemingway
Gremlins, The	Roald Dahl
Grossology	Silvia Branzei
Group of Noble Dames, A	Thomas Hardy
Growing Up	Russell Baker
Gulag Archipelago, The	Aleksandr Solzhenitsyn
Gulliver's Travels	Jonathan Swift
Hajj, The	Leon Uris
Handmaid's Tale, A	Margaret Atwood
Hansel and Gretel	Brothers Grimm
Hardy Boys mysteries	Franklin W. Dixon
Harriet the Spy	Louise Fitzhugh
Haunting of Hill House, The	Shirley Jackson
Having Our Say, the First 100 Years	The Delaney Sisters
Hawaii	James Michener
Hay Fever	Noel Coward
Heart of Darkness	Joseph Conrad

31 *Literature*

Heart is a Lonely Hunter, The	Carson McCullers
Heart of Midothian, The	Sir Walter Scott
Heaven and Hell	John Jakes
Heidi	Johanna Spyri
Herzog	Saul Bellow
Hiroshima	John Hersey
History of the English Speaking People, The	Winston Churchill
History of Tom Jones, The	Henry Fielding
Hitchhiker's Guide to the Galaxy, The	Douglas Adams
Hobbit, The	J. R. R. Tolkien
Hollywood Wives	Jackie Collins
Homecoming, The	Harold Pinter
Hondo	Louis L'Amour
Hope, The	James Michener
Hope	Herman Wouk
Hostage, The	Brendan Behan
Hotel New Hampshire, The	John Irving
Hotel	Arthur Hailey
Hound of the Baskervilles, The	Sir Arthur Conan Doyle
House of Earth trilogy	Pearl Buck
House of Mirth	Edith Wharton
House of Seven Gables, The	Nathaniel Hawthorne
House of Spirits, The	Isabel Allende
How the Grinch Stole Christmas	Dr. Seuss
How the West Was Won	Louis L'Amour
How to Argue and Win Every Time	Jerry Spence
How to Make an American Quilt	Whitney Otto
How to Win Friends and Influence People	Dale Carnegie
Howard's End	E. M. Forster
Howl	Allen Ginsberg
Human Comedy, The	William Saroyan
Human Comedy, The (French)	Honore de Balzac
Human Sexual Response	Masters and Johnson
Humbold's Gift	Saul Bellow (Pulitzer)
Hunch-Back of Norte Dame, The	Victor Hugo
Hundred Secret Senses, The	Amy Tan
Hunt for Red October, The	Tom Clancy
Hunting of the Snark, The	Lewis Carroll
Hustler, The	Walter Tevis
I am a Camera	John Van Druten
I Ching	Confucius
I, Claudius	Robert Graves
I, The Jury	Mickey Spillane
I, Robot	Isaac Asimov
Iberia	James Michener
Idiot, The	Fyodor Dostoyevsky

Idylls of the King	Alfred Lord Tennyson
Iliad	Homer
Illustrated Man, The	Ray Bradbury
Importance of Being Earnest, The	Oscar Wilde
In Cold Blood	Truman Capote
Inca Gold	Clive Cussler
Infinite Jest	David Foster Wallace
Innocents Abroad, The	Mark Twain
Inside the Third Reich	Albert Speer
Insomnia	Stephen King
Interpretation of Dreams, The	Sigmund Freud
Interview With the Vampire	Anne Rice
Invasion	Robin Cook
Invisible Man, The	H.G. Wells
Invisible Man	Ralph Ellison
Ipcress File, The	Len Deighton
Ironweed	William Kennedy (Pulitzer)
Island of the Day Before, The	Umberto Eco
Islands in the Stream	Ernest Hemingway
It	Stephen King
It's Good to be Alive	Roy Campenella
It Takes a Village	Hillary Clinton
Ivanhoe	Sir Walter Scott
J'Accuse	Émile Zola
Jacob's Room	Virginia Woolf
James Bond novels	Ian Fleming
James and the Giant Peach	Roald Dahl
Jane Eyre	Charlotte Brontë
Jaws	Peter Benchley
Jazz Age, The	F. Scott Fitzgerald
Jewels and Fine Things	Danielle Steele
John Brown's Body	Stephen Vincent Benet
Jonathan Livingstone Seagull	Richard Bach
Journey to the Center of the Earth, A	Jules Verne
Joy Luck Club, The	Amy Tan
Jude the Obscure	Thomas Hardy
July's People	Nadine Gordimer
Jungle Book, The	Rudyard Kipling
Jungle, The	Upton Sinclair
Jurassic Park	Michael Crichton
Just as I Am	Billy Graham
Just So Stories	Rudyard Kipling
Kenilworth	Sir Walter Scott
Kidnapped	Robert Louis Stevenson
Kim	Rudyard Kipling
King Rat	James Clavell

31   *Literature*

King Solomon's Mines	H. Rider Haggard
Kiss the Girls	James Patterson
L.A. Confidential	James Elroy
Labyrinthe, The	Jorge Luis Borges
Lady Chatterley's Lover	D. H. Lawrence
Lake Wobegon Days	Garrison Keillor
Lassie Come Home	Eric Knight
Last Don, The	Mario Puzo
Last Days of Pompeii, The	Edward Buliver-Litton
Last of the Mohicans, The	James Fenimore Cooper
Last Picture Show, The	Lar.y McMurtry
Last Tycoon, The	F. Scott Fitzgerald
Late George Apley, The	John Marquand (Pulitzer)
Lays of Ancient Rome	Thomas Macaulay
Legend of Sleepy Hollow, The	Washington Irving
Life of Johnson, The	James Boswell
Life of Heidi Abromiwitz, The	Joan Rivers
Like Water for Chocolate	Laura Esquaval
Little Yellow Dog, A	P. D. James
Little Foxes	Lillian Hellman
Little House in the Big Woods	Laura Ingalls (Wilder)
Little House on the Prairie	Laura Ingalls (Wilder)
Little Lord Fauntleroy	Frances Hodgson Burnett
Little Men	Louisa May Alcott
Little Prince, The	Antoine de Saint-Exupery
Little Red Book, The	Mao Tse-tung
Little Women	Louisa May Alcott
Lonesome Dove	Larry McMurtry (Pulitzer)
Long Hot Summer, The	William Faulkner
Long Good-bye, The	Raymond Chandler
Look Back in Anger	John Osborne
Look Homeward Angel	Thomas Wolfe
Looking for Mr. Goodbar	Judith Rossner
Lord of the Rings, The	J. R. R. Tolkien
Lorna Doone	R. D. Blackmore
Lord Jim	Joseph Conrad
Lord of the Flies	William Golding
Lost Horizon	James Hilton
Lottery, The	Shirley Jackson
Loved One, The	Evelyn Waugh
Love Machine, The	Jacqueline Susann
Love Song of J. Alfred Prufrock, The	T. S. Eliot
Love Story	Erich Segal
Luck of Roaring Camp, The	Bret Harte
Lucky Jim	Kingsley Amis
Lust for Life	Irving Stone

Lysistrata	Aristophanes
L'Education Sentimental	Gustave Flaubert
L'Etranger (The Stranger)	Albert Camus
Madame Bovary	Gustave Flaubert
Made in America	Sam Walton
Magnificent Ambersons, The	Booth Tarkington (Pulitzer)
Main Street	Sinclair Lewis
Maine Woods, The	Henry David Thoreau
Magic Mountain, The	Thomas Mann
Making of the President, 1960, The	Theodore White (Pulitzer)
Maltese Falcon, The	Dashiell Hammett
Mammoth Hunters, The	Jane Auel
Man in Full, A	Tom Wolfe
Man in the Iron Mask, The	Alexandre Dumas
Man of Property, The	John Galsworthy
Man Without a Country, A	Edward Everett Hale
Mansion, The	William Faulkner
Manchurian Candidate, The	Richard Condon
Manuscript Found in a Bottle	Edgar Allen Poe
Martian Chronicles, The	Ray Bradbury
Martin Chuzzlewit	Charles Dickens
Mary Poppins	P. L. Travers
Masque of the Red Death	Edgar Allan Poe
Mayor of Casterbridge, The	Thomas Hardy
Medium is the Message, The	Marshall McLuhan
Mein Kampf	Adolf Hitler
Metamorphosis (ancient)	Ovid
Metamorphosis, The (modern)	Franz Kafka
Mexico	James Michener
Middlemarch	George Eliot
Midnight in the Garden of Good and Evil	John Berendt
Mila 18	Leon Uris
Mildred Pierce	James M. Cain
Mill on the Floss, The	George Eliot
Mirror Crack'd, The	Agatha Christie
Misérables, Les	Victor Hugo
Miss Julie	August Strindberg
Moby-Dick	Herman Melville
Moll Flanders	Daniel Defoe
Month in the Country, A	Ivan Turgenev
Moon and Sixpence, The	Somerset Maugham
Moonstone, The	Wilkie Collins
Morte D'Arthur, Le	Thomas Malory
Mosses from an Old Manse	Nathaniel Hawthorne
Mourning Becomes Electra	Eugene O'Neill
Mouse and the Motorcycle, The	Beverly Cleary

31   *Literature*

Mousetrap, The	Agatha Christie
Mrs. Tittlemouse	Beatrix Potter
Murder in the Cathedral	T.S. Eliot
Murder at the National Gallery	Margaret Truman
Murder on the Orient Express	Agatha Christie
Murders in the Rue Morgue, The	Edgar Allan Poe
Murder Under Blue Skies	Willard Scott
My Ántonia	Willa Cather
My Son's Story	Nadine Gordimer
My American Journey	Colin Powell
My Wicked, Wicked Ways	Errol Flynn
Mysterious Island, The	Jules Verne
Mystery of Edwin Drood, The	Charles Dickens
Naked and the Dead, The	Norman Mailer
Name of the Rose, The	Umberto Eco
Nancy Drew series	Carolyn Keene
National Velvet	Enid Bagnold
Native Son	Richard Wright
Natural History	Pliny the Elder
Natural, The	Bernard Malamud
Nature	Ralph Waldo Emerson
Nausea	Jean-Paul Sartre
Needful Things	Stephen King
New Centurions, The	Joseph Wambaugh
Nicholas Nickleby	Charles Dickens
Nick Adams stories	Ernest Hemingway
No Exit	Jean-Paul Sartre
Noble House	James Clavell
North and South	John Jakes
Northanger Abbey	Jane Austen
Nostromo	Joseph Conrad
Notes on Nursing	Florence Nightingale
Octopus, The	Frank Norris
Odessa File, The	Frederick Forsyth
Odyssey	Homer
Oedipus at Colonus	Sophocles
Oedipus Rex	Sophocles
Of Human Bondage	W. Somerset Maugham
Of Mice and Men	John Steinbeck
Old Possum's Book of Practical Cats	T. S. Eliot
Old Curiosity Shop, The	Charles Dickens
Old Man and the Sea, The	Ernest Hemingway (Pulitzer)
Oldest Living Confederate Widow	Allen Gurgamus
Old Yeller	Fred Gibson
Oliver Twist	Charles Dickens
Omoo	Herman Melville

One of Ours	Willa Cather (Pulitzer)
On the Road	Jack Kerouac
Once and Future King, The	T. H. White
One Day in the Life of Ivan Denisovich	Alexandr Solzhenitsyn
One Hundred Years of Solitude	Gabriel Marquez
Onion Field, The	Joseph Wambaugh
O Pioneers!	Willa Cather
Optimist's Daughter, The	Eudora Welty (Pulitzer)
Optics	Euclid
Origin of Species, The	Charles Darwin
Orlando	Virginia Woolf
Other Side of Midnight, The	Sidney Sheldon
Other, The	Thomas Tryon
Our Man in Havana	Graham Greene
Outbreak	Robin Cook
Out of Africa	Isak Dinesen
Outcasts of Poker Flat, The	Bret Harte
Owl and the Pussy-cat, The	Edward Lear
Pale Horse, Pale Rider	Katherine Anne Porter
Pantagruel	Francois Rabelais
Paradise	Toni Morrison
Parallel Lives	Plutarch
Paris in the 20th Century	Jules Verne
Parsifal Mosaic	Robert Ludlum
Passage to India, A	E. M. Forster
Path to Love, The	Deepak Chopra
Patriot Games	Tom Clancy
Pearl, The	John Steinbeck
Pelican Brief, The	John Grisham
Pendennis	William Makepeace Thackeray
Penrod	Booth Tarkington
Perfect Storm, The	Sebastian Junger
Perry Mason mysteries	Erle Stanley Gardner
Peter Principal, The	Lawrence Peter
Pet Sematary	Stephen King
Peter Pan	James Barrie
Peyton Place	Grace Metalious
Philadelphia Story, The	Phillip Barry
Physics (ancient)	Aristotle
Pickwick Papers, The	Charles Dickens
Picture of Dorian Gray, The	Oscar Wilde
Pilgrim's Progress	John Bunyan
The Pilot	James Fenimore Cooper
Pippi Longstocking	Astrid Lindgren
Pisan Cantos, The	Ezra Pound
Pit and the Pendulum, The	Edgar Allan Poe

31 *Literature*

Plague, The	Albert Camus
Playboy of the Western World, The	John Millington Synge
Poisonwood Bible, The	Barbara Kingsolver
Poland	James Michener
Politics	Aristotle
Pollyanna	Eleanor Porter
Poor Richard's Almanac	Benjamin Franklin
Portnoy's Complaint	Philip Roth
Portrait of a Lady, The	Henry James
Poseidon Adventure, The	Paul Gallico
Postcards From the Edge	Carrie Fisher
Postman Always Rings Twice, The	James M. Cain
Power of Positive Thinking, The	Norman Vincent Peale
Prairie Town Boy, A	Carl Sandburg
Prairie, The	James Fenimore Cooper
Prayer for Owen Meany, A	John Irving
Premature Burial	Edgar Allan Poe
Presumed Innocent	Scott Turow
Pride and Prejudice	Jane Austen
Primary Colors	Joe Kline
Prime of Miss Jean Brodie, The	Muriel Spark
Prince and the Pauper, The	Mark Twain
Prince of Tides, The	Pat Conroy
Prince, The	Niccolò Machiavelli
Princess and the Pea, The	Hans Christian Andersen
Princess Daisy	Judith Krantz
Principia Mathematica	Sir Isaac Newton
Prisoner of Zenda	Anthony Hope
Prizzi's Honor	William Condon
Prophet, The	Khalil Gibran
Prometheus Bound	Aeschylus
Prometheus Unbound	Percy Bysshe Shelley
Purloined Letter, The	Edgar Allan Poe
Rabbit is Rich	John Updike (Pulitzer)
Rabbit Run	John Updike
Rabbit at Rest	John Updike (Pulitzer)
Ragged Dick	Horatio Alger
Rainbow Six	Tom Clancy
Ragtime	E. L. Doctorow
Rainmaker, The	John Grisham
Ramona	Helen Hunt Jackson
Rap on Race, A	Margaret Mead
Rapunzel	Brothers Grimm
Ravers, The	William Faulkner
Razor's Edge, The	W. Somerset Maugham
Reading Dynamics	Evelyn Wood

Rebecca	Daphne du Maurier
Red and the Black, The	Stendahl
Red Badge of Courage, The	Stephen Crane
Red Pony, The	John Steinbeck
Red Storm Rising	Tom Clancy
Remembrance of Things Past	Marcel Proust
Reivers, The	William Faulkner (Pulitzer)
Republic, The	Plato
Requiem for a Heavyweight	Rod Serling
Return of the Native, The	Thomas Hardy
Reve, Le (The Dream)	Émile Zola
Rhinoceros	Eugéne Ionesco
Rhumba is My Life	Xavier Cougat
Rich Man, Poor Man	Irwin Shaw
Riders of the Purple Sage	Zane Grey
Right Stuff, The	Tom Wolfe
Riki-Tivi-Tavi	Rudyard Kipling
Rip Van Winkle	Washington Irving
Rising Sun	Michael Crichton
Rob Roy	Sir Walter Scott
Robinson Crusoe	Daniel Defoe
Roman Spring of Mrs. Stone, The	Tennessee Williams
Room of One's Own, A	Virginia Woolf
Room With a View, A	E. M. Forster
Roots	Alex Haley
Rosencrantz and Guildenstern Are Dead	Tom Stoffard
Roughing It	Mark Twain
Rubáiyát	Omar Khayyam
Rumblefish	S. E. Hinton
Runaway Jury, The	John Grisham
R.U.R.	Karel Capek
Russia House, The	John LeCarré
Sacket sagas	Louis L'Amour
Sahara	Clive Cussler
Salem's Lot	Stephen King
Salomé	Oscar Wilde
Salvador	Joan Didion
Saint Joan	George Bernard Shaw
Sartoris	William Faulkner
Satanic Verses, The	Salman Rushdie
Saving the Queen	William Buckley
Scarlet Letter, The	Nathaniel Hawthorne
Scarlett	Alexandra Ripley
School for Scandal, The	Richard Brinsley Sheridan
Science and Human Behavior	B. F. Skinner
Scruples	Judith Krantz

31 *Literature*

Sea-Wolf, The	Jack London
Secret Life of Walter Mitty, The	James Thurber
Secret Garden, The	Frances Hodgson Burnett
Self-Reliance	Ralph Waldo Emerson
Separate Peace, A	John Knowles
Sense and Sensibility	Jane Austin
Seven Against Thebes	Aeschylus
Seven Percent Solution, The	Nicholas Meyer
Seven Pillars of Wisdom, The	T. E. Lawrence (of Arabia)
Seven Spiritual Laws, The	Deepak Chopra
Sex and the Single Girl	Helen Gurley Brown
Sexual Personae	Camille Paglia
She Walks in Beauty	Lord Byron
She's Come Undone	Wally Lamb
She Stoops to Conquer	Oliver Goldsmith
Sheltering Sky, The	Paul Bowles
Sherlock Holmes mysteries	Sir Arthur Conan Doyle
Shining, The	Stephen King
Ship of Fools, A	Katherine Anne Porter
Shogun	James Clavell
Short Happy Life of Francis Macomber, The	Ernest Hemingway
Show Boat	Edna Ferber
Shropshire Lad, A	A. E. Housman
Silas Marner	George Eliot
Silent Night	Mary Higgins Clark
Silence of the Lambs	Thomas Harris
Silent Spring	Rachel Carson
Sister Carrie	Theodore Dreiser
Sisters Rosensweig, The	Wendy Wasserstein
Six Crises	Richard Nixon
Sketchbook, The	Washington Irving
Sketches by Boz	Charles Dickens
Slaughterhouse Five	Kurt Vonnegut, Jr.
Sleepers	Lorenzo Carcatera
Sly Old Cat, The	Beatrix Potter
Smoke and Steel	Carl Sandburg
Snows of Kilimanjaro, The	Ernest Hemingway
Social Contract, The	Jean-Jacques Rousseau
Son of the Circus, A	John Irving
Song of Myself	Walt Whitman
Song of Solomon	Toni Morrison
Sons and Lovers	D. H. Lawrence
Sophie's Choice	William Styron
Sorrows of Young Werther, The	Johann von Goethe
Sound and the Fury, The	William Faulkner
Source, The	James Michener

Southern Cross	Patricia Cornwell
Space	James Michener
Spandau	Albert Speer
Special Theory of Relativity, The	Albert Einstein
Sphinx	Robin Cook
Spoon River Anthology	Edgar Lee Masters
Spy Who Came in from the Cold, The	John Le Carré
Spy, The	James Fenimore Cooper
Stand, The	Stephen King
Steppenwolf	Herman Hesse
Stewart Little	E.B. White
Stillness at Appomattox, A	Bruce Catton
Story of Civilization, The	Will and Ariel Durant
Stranger in a Strange Land	Robert Heinlein
Stranger, The	Albert Camus
Street Lawyer, The	John Grisham
Studs Lonigan trilogy	James Farrell
Study in Scarlet, A	Sir Arthur Conan Doyle
Summa Theologia	St. Thomas Aquinas
Summer Sisters	Judy Bloom
Sun Also Rises, The	Ernest Hemingway
Sword of Homer trilogy	Evelyn Waugh
Tai-Pan	James Clavell
Tek War	William Shatner
Tale of Peter Rabbit, The	Beatrix Potter
Tale of Two Cities, A	Charles Dickens
Tales of a Traveler, The	Nathaniel Hawthorne
Tales of the South Pacific	James Michener (Pulitzer)
Talisman, The	Sir Walter Scott
Tam o'Shanter	Robert Burns
Tamburlaine the Great	Christopher Marlowe
Taming the Star Runner	S. E. Hinton
Tanglewood Tales for Girls and Boys	Nathaniel Hawthorne
Tara Road	Maeve Binchy
Tarzan of the Apes	Edgar Rice Burroughs
Taste for Death, A	P.D. James
Tattered Tom	Horatio Alger
Tell-Tale Heart, The	Edgar Allan Poe
Temple of My Familiar, The	Alice Walker
Ten Days That Shook the World	John Reed
Tender is the Night	F. Scott Fitzgerald
Terms of Endearment	Larry McMurtry
Tess of the D'Urbervilles	Thomas Hardy
Testament, The	John Grisham
Texas	James Michener
Thin Red Line, The	James Jones

31 *Literature*

Thin Man, The	Dashiell Hammett
Third Man, The	Graham Green
This Side of Paradise	F. Scott Fitzgerald
Thorn Birds, The	Colleen McCullough
Three Musketeers, The	Alexander Dumas
Through the Looking Glass	Lewis Carroll
Thus Spake Zarathustra	Freidrich Nietzsche
Timeline	Michael Crichton
Time Machine, The	H.G. Wells
Time of Your Life, The	William Saroyan
Time to Kill, A	John Grisham
Tin Drum, The	Günter Grass
Tinker, Taylor, Soldier, Spy	John Le Carré
Tintern Abby	William Wordsworth
To Kill a Mockingbird	Harper Lee (Pulitzer)
To Have and Have Not	Ernest Hemingway
To Hell and Back	Audie Murphy
To the Lighthouse	Virginia Woolf
Tobacco Road	Erskine Caldwell
Tom Jones	Henry Fielding
Tommyknockers, The	Stephen King
Topaz	Leon Uris
Tortilla Flat	John Steinbeck
Tragedy of Pudd'nhead Wilson, The	Mark Twain
Travels with Charlie	John Steinbeck
Travis McGee mysteries	John MacDonald
Treasure Island	Robert Louis Stevenson
Tree Grows in Brooklyn, A	Betty Smith
Trial, The	Franz Kafka
Tristam Shandy	Laurence Sterne
Tropic of Cancer	Henry Miller
Tropic of Capricorn	Henry Miller
Tuesdays With Morrie	Mitch Albom
Turn of the Screw, The	Henry James
Twenty Thousand Leagues Under the Sea	Jules Verne
Two Mrs. Greenvilles, The	Dominick Dunne
Two Years Before the Mast	Richard Dana
Typee	Herman Melville
Ugly Duckling, The	Hans Christian Andersen
Ulysses	James Joyce
Uncle Tom's Cabin	Harriet Beecher Stowe
Uncle Remus and His Friends	Joel Chandler Harris
Under Milkwood	Dylan Thomas
Under the Volcano	Malcolm Lowry
Unsafe at Any Speed	Ralph Nader
Up From Slavery	Booker T. Washington

USA Trilogy	John Dos Passos
Utopia	Sir Thomas More
Valley of the Dolls	Jacqueline Susann
Valpone	Ben Johnson
Vampire Chronicles	Ann Rice
Vector	Robin Cook
Veteran, The	Stephen Crane
Vicar of Wakefield, The	Oliver Goldsmith
Vitamin C and the Common Cold	Linus Pauling
Waiting to Exhale	Terry MacMillan
Walden	Henry David Thoreau
Walrus and the Carpenter	Lewis Carroll
Wanderlust	Danielle Steele
War of the Worlds, The	H. G. Wells
War and Remembrance	Herman Wouk
War and Peace	Count Leo Tolstoy
Wasps	Aristophanes
Waste Land, The	T. S. Eliot
Watcher	Dean Koontz
Waverley series	Sir Walter Scott
Way of All Flesh, The	Samuel Butler
Wuthering Heights	Emily Brontë
Watership Down	Richard Adams
Wealth of Nations, The	Adam Smith
What Dreams May Come	Richard Matheson
What Makes Sammy Run	Budd Schulberg
Where the Wild Things Are	Maurice Sendak
White Fang	Jack London
William Tell	Friedrich von Schiller
Wind in the Willows, The	Kenneth Grahame
Winds of War, The	Herman Wouk
Winnie-the-Pooh	A. A. Milne
Winning Bridge Made Easy	Charles Goren
Winter of Our Discontent, The	John Steinbeck
Winterset	Maxwell Anderson
Witches of Eastwick, The	John Updike
Without a Doubt	Marcia Clark
Witness Tree, A	Robert Frost
Witness for the Prosecution	Agatha Christie
Wizard of Oz, The	L. Frank Baum
Women in Love	D.H. Lawrence
Women, Mortality and Birth Control	Margaret Sanger
World According to Garp, The	John Irving
Yearling, The	Marjorie Kinnan Rawlings (Pulitzer)
Yentl	Isaac Bashevis Singer
You Can't Go Home Again	Thomas Wolfe

32 *Music*

Musical Terms:

Slow tempo .... Adagio
Lively and fast tempo .... Allegro
Slow pace .... Lento
Moderate pace .... Andante
Fast pace .... Presto
Obligatory accompaniment .... Obligato
Highest female voice .... Soprano
Lowest female voice .... Contralto
Male form of female contralto .... Alto
Highest male voice .... Tenor
Middle-range male voice .... Baritone
Lowest male voice .... Basso profundo
Artificial form of singing .... Falsetto
Falsetto voice (higher than tenor) .... Countertenor
Solo in an opera .... Aria
Work for a solo instrument with an orchestra .... Concerto
Light music played in the evening .... Serenade
Combination of two or more notes .... Chord
Study or solo instrument piece .... Etude
Songs for solo voice or piano .... Lieder
Night piece .... Nocturne
Piece written for the outdoors .... Pastoral
Sacred musical composition .... Oratorio
Main female singer .... Prima Donna
Music by a soloist .... Recital

Artist and Their Instrument:

Louis Armstrong .... Trumpet (jazz)
Jack Benny .... Violin
Dave Brubeck .... Piano
Pablo Casals .... Cello
Harry Connick, Jr .... Piano
Chick Corea .... Piano
Van Cliburn .... Piano
John Coltrain .... (Soprano) Saxophone
Miles Davis .... Trumpet
Jacqueline Du Pre .... Cello
Maynard Ferguson .... Trumpet
Benny Goodman .... Clarinet
Lionel Hampton .... Vibraphone

David Helfgott (from the movie *Shine*) .... Piano
Jimi Hendrix .... Fender Stratocaster guitar
Woody Herman .... Clarinet
Buddy Rich .... Drums
Vladimir Horowitz (won 20 Grammys) .... Piano
Harry James .... Trumpet
Thomas Jefferson .... Violin
Scott Joplin .... Piano
Kenny G .... Saxophone
Liberace .... Piano
Franz Liszt .... Piano
Chuck Mangione .... Flugelhorn
Wynton Marsalis .... Trumpet
Midori .... Violin
Ignace Paderewski .... Piano
Niccolo Paganini .... Violin
Itzhak Perlman .... Violin
Andres Segovia .... Guitar
Doc Severinsen .... Trumpet
Isaac Stern .... Violin
Lawrence Welk .... Accordion
Yo Yo Ma .... Cello

Song and Artist:

Banana Boat Song .... Harry Belafonte
In the Mood .... Glenn Miller
This Land is Your Land .... Woody Guthrie
Boogie Woogie Bugle Boy .... Andrews Sisters
Alice's Restaurant .... Arlo Guthrie
Johnny Angel .... Shelly Fabares
Chances Are .... Johnny Mathis
Unchained Melody (original) .... Righteous Brothers
Tennessee Waltz .... Patti Page
When I Fall in Love .... Nat King Cole
Take the A Train .... Duke Ellington
Crazy .... Patsy Cline
Okie From Muskogee .... Merle Haggard
Walking the Floor Over You .... Ernest Tubb
Sixteen Tons .... Tennessee Ernie Ford
Big Bad John .... Jimmy Dean
Earth Angel .... Penguins
Big Girls Don't Cry .... The Four Seasons
Georgia on my Mind .... Ray Charles
Rock Around the Clock. .... Bill Haley and the Comets
Woolly Bully .... Sam the Sham and the Pharaohs

La Bamba (original)	Richie Valens
La Bamba (remake)	Los Lobos
Sherry	The Four Seasons
Blue Velvet	Bobby Vinton
Sixteen Candles	The Crests
Its My Party	Leslie Gore
This Guy is in Love With You	Herb Alpert
Downtown	Petula Clark
To Sir With Love	Lulu
El Paso	Marty Robbins
My Girl	The Temptations
Just My Imagination	The Temptations
Light My Fire (original)	Doors
Light My Fire (remake)	Jose Feliciano
MacArthur Park	Richard Harris
In the Year 2525	Zager and Evens
Convoy	C. W. McCall
Stand By Your Man	Tammy Wynette
Only the Lonely	Roy Orbison
Pretty Woman (original)	Roy Orbison
Pretty Woman (remake)	Van Halen
Paper Roses	Marie Osmond
Wild Thing	The Trogs
Theme for *Shaft*	Isaac Hayes
Constant Craving	k.d. lang
Venus (original)	Shocking Blue
Venus (remake)	Bananarama
Bette Davis Eyes	Kim Carnes
Rhythm is Gonna Get You	Gloria Estefan
Vision of Love	Mariah Carey
Achy Breaky Heart	Billy Ray Cyrus
My Maria	Brooks and Dunn
All I Want To Do	Sheryl Crow

Albums:

Dark Side of the Moon (longest on the charts, 741 weeks)	Pink Floyd
Thriller (47 million copies)	Michael Jackson
The Chronic Album (top selling rap album)	Dr. Dre
Physical	Olivia Newton John
Fresh Horses	Garth Brooks
Music Box	Mariah Carey
Rumours	Fleetwood Mac
Blues Summit	B.B. King
Tapestry	Carole King
Born in the USA	Bruce Springsteen

Unplugged .... Eric Clapton
Pieces of You (on the charts for 100 weeks) .... Jewel
Bob Dylan bootleg album, 1966 .... *Bob Dylan Live*

Song Writers:

Stardust .... Hoagy Carmichael
I Dream of Jeannie .... Stephen Foster
St. Louis Blues .... W. C. Handy
Night and Day .... Cole Porter
Unforgettable .... Nat King Cole
I'm Just Wild About Harry .... Eubie Blake
Raindrops Keep Falling on My Head .... Bert Bacharach & Hal David
Theme From Star Wars .... John Williams
Theme From Pink Panther .... Henry Mancini

Conductors:

Berlin Philharmonic conductor .... Herbert von Karajan
Boston Symphony conductor .... Seiji Ozawa
Renowned Boston Pops conductor .... Arthur Fiedler
Fantasia conductor .... Leopold Stokowski
New York Philharmonic conductor .... Leonard Bernstein
Philadelphia Symphony conductor .... Eugene Ormandy
National Symphony .... Leonard Slatkin
NBC Symphony conductor .... ArturoToscanini
Chicago Symphony conductor .... George Solti (31 Grammys)

Lead Singers: *

Rolling Stones .... Mick Jagger
Big Brother and the Holding Company .... Janice Joplin
The Stone Ponies .... Linda Ronstadt
Cream .... Eric Clapton
The Animals .... Eric Burton
Jethro Tull .... Ian Anderson
Jefferson Airplane/Starship .... Grace Slick
Miami Sound Machine .... Gloria Estefan
The Doors .... Jim Morrison
Faces .... Rod Stewart
Sex Pistols .... Sid Vicious
Blondie .... Debbie Harry
Genesis .... Phil Collins
The Commodores .... Lionel Richie
Aerosmith .... Steve Tyler
The Boomtown Rats .... Bob Geldoff
Eurythmics .... Annie Lennox
Queen .... Freddie Mercury

The Police .... Sting
U2 .... Bono
Guns and Roses .... Axl Rose
10,000 Maniacs .... Natalie Merchant
Nirvana .... Kurt Cobain
REM .... Michael Stipe
Nine Inch Nails .... Trent Reznor
Dire Straits .... Mark Knoffler

* Other singers have led some of these bands, the one mentioned is the most established.

Other facts:

Top selling single of all time .... *English Rose* by Elton John
Second top selling single of all time .... *White Christmas* by Bing Crosby
Single #1 on the charts the longest (16 weeks) .... *One Sweet Today* by Maria Carey and Boyz II Men
Elvis Presley's first #1 single .... *Heartbreak Hotel*
Top selling album of all time .... *The Eagles Greatest Hits*
Female with the most number one hits .... Mariah Carey (15)
The Three Tenors .... José Carreras, Placido Domingo, Luciano Pavarotti
Foreign songs to hit #1 .... *Volare, Sukiyaki, Dominique*
Rockers killed in 1959 plane crash (the day the music died)
.... Buddy Holly, The Big Bopper, Richie Valens
A&M Records founders .... Herb Alpert and Jerry Moss
Jamaican Reggae singer .... Bob Marley
Grateful Dead guitarist .... Jerry Garcia
The fifth Beatle .... Stu Sutcliff
Beatles original drummer .... Pete Best
Beatles original name .... Johnny and the Moondogs
The King of Swing .... Benny Goodman
The First Lady of Song .... Ella Fitzgerald
Lady Day .... Billie Holiday
Empress of the Blues .... Bessie Smith
Bubbles .... Beverly Sills
The Father of Country Music .... Jimmie Rogers
The Father of Bluegrass .... Bill Monroe
The Silver Fox .... Charlie Rich
The Dust Bowl Balladeer .... Woody Guthrie
The Texas Troubadour .... Ernest Tubb
The Man in Black .... Johnny Cash
Killer .... Jerry Lee Lewis
Coke Time Crooner .... Eddie Fisher
The Velvet Fog .... Mel Torme
The Godfather of Soul .... James Brown
First rap group on American Bandstand .... Run DMC

First white performer on Soul Train .... Elton John
Icelandic pop group .... Bjork
Swedish pop group .... Abba
Triangular Russian instrument .... Balalaika
Licorice stick.. Clarinet
Xylophone's Latin cousin .... Marimba
Side-blown flute .... Fife
Helicon instrument .... Tuba
Bells instrument.. Glockenspiel
"Sweet Potato" .... Ocarina
Hexagonal accordion-like instrument .... Concertina
African Xylophone....................................... Marimba
Bellows instrument .... Bag Pipes
"Bull Fiddle" .... Double Bass
Dried gourd instrument.................................. Maracas
Plucked keyboard instrument .... Harpsichord
Number of keys on a piano 88
B.B. King's guitar.. Lucille
"New Trend" music .... Bossa Nova
Sailors' work song .... Chanty
Swiss jazz festival city .... Montreux
California jazz festival city .... Monterey
Berkshire Music Festival city .... Tanglewood, MA
Rhode Island jazz festival city .... Newport
Richard Wagner Music Festival city .... Bayreuth, Germany

Musicals by:

Irving Berlin .... *Annie Get Your Gun*
Leonard Bernstein.. *West Side Story*
.... *On the Town*
Bob Fosse.. *Cabaret*
Gilbert and Sullivan.................................... *Yeoman of the Guard*
.... *Thespis*
.... *The Mikado*
George and Ira Gershwin .... *Porgy and Bess*
Marvin Hamlisch....................................... *A Chorus Line*
Jerome Kern... *Showboat*
Rogers and Hammerstein .... *Carousel*
.... *Oklahoma!*
.... *The King and I*
.... *The Sound of Music*
.... *South Pacific*
Victor Herbert .... *Babes in Toyland*
Jerry Herman .... *Mame*
.... *Hello Dolly*
.... *La Cage aux Folles*

Jonathan Larson .... *Rent*
Lerner and Loewe .... *Brigadoon*
.... *Paint Your Wagon*
.... *My Fair Lady*
.... *Camelot*
.... *Gigi*
Frank Loesser .... *Guys and Dolls*
....*How to Succeed in Business Without Really Trying*
Cole Porter .... *Anything Goes*
.... *Kiss Me Kate*
Stephen Sondheim .... *A Little Night Music*
Meredith Wilson .... *The Music Man*
Andrew Lloyd Webber .... *Cats*
.... *Sunset Boulevard*
.... *Evita*
.... *Jesus Christ Superstar*
....*Joseph and His Amazing Technicolor Dream Coat*
.... *Starlight Express*
.... *Phantom of the Opera*

Other Facts about Musicals:

Musical based on *La Boheme* .... *Rent*

Musical based on *Pygmalion* .... *My Fair Lady*

Musical based on *I Am a Camera* .... *Cabaret*

Musical based on *The Taming of the Shrew* .... *Kiss Me Kate*

Musical based on *The Once and Future King* .... *Camelot*

Musical based on *The Matcher* .... *Hello Dolly*

Broadway's longest-running musical .... *Cats*

Broadway's second longest-running musical .... *A Chorus Line*

Roller skating musical .... *Starlight Express*

Blanche Dubois is a character in this play .... *A Streetcar Named Desire*

Norma Desmond is a character in this play .... *Sunset Boulevard*

1953 musical set in Bagdad .... *Kismet*

Medieval play of good and evil .... Morality play

Unconventional theater .... Theater of the Absurd

London Theater built by Gilbert and Sullivan .... The Savoy

London theater on Drury Lane .... Royal Theater

Milan theater .... Piccolo Teatro

World's largest indoor theater .... Radio City Music Hall

Mythology 33

Greek Mythology:

Chief of the gods	Zeus
Zeus' wife	Hera
Zeus' father	Cronus
Zeus' mother	Rhea
Cronus' father, god of the sky	Uranus
Uranus' wife, goddess of the Earth	Gaea
Zeus' brother, god of the underworld	Hades
Zeus' brother, god of the sea	Poseidon
Zeus' son, god of music, poetry and games	Apollo
Zeus' mortal son, who performed twelve labors	Hercules
God of love	Eros
God of war	Aries
God of fire	Hephaestus
God of the sun	Helios
Goddess of beauty and love	Aphrodite
Goddess of wisdom	Athena (Athena Pallas)
Goddess of the hunt and Apollo's twin	Artemis
Goddess of fertility	Persephone
God of shepherds and their flocks	Pan
Goddess of agriculture	Demeter
Goddess of the hunt	Artemis
Goddess of wine and fertility	Dionysius
Goddess of the moon	Selena
Goddess of victory	Nike
Messenger of the gods	Hermes
God of the west wind	Zephyr
God of dreams	Morpheus
Sons of Heaven and Earth	Gigantes
Home of the gods	Mt. Olympus
Food of the gods	Ambrosia
Greek warrior with vulnerable heel	Achilles
Trojan warrior killed by Achilles	Hector
The "second bravest" Greek warrior who committed suicide	Ajax
Wisest Greek in Trojan War	Nestor
Trojan prince who fled to Rome after the Trojan War	Aeneas
Man who kidnaped Helen	Paris
Helen's husband	Menelaus
Paris' father, king of Troy	Priam
Wife of Priam	Hecuba

33 *Mythology*

Man who wandered for ten years after Trojan War	Odysseus (Roman name-Ulysses)
Odysseus' wife	Penelope
Odysseus' son	Telemachus
Greek leader in the Trojan War	Agamemnon
Agamemnon's wife, who killed him	Clytemnestra
Agamemnon's son, who avenged his death	Orestes
Agamemnon's daughter	Electra
Name of Cyclops who held Odysseus prisoner	Polyphemus
Enchantress who turned Odysseus' men into swine	Circe
Nymph who held Odysseus prisoner for seven years	Calypso
Monster and whirlpool who threatened Odysseus' ship	Scylla and Charybdis
Goddesses whose song lured men to their deaths	Sirens
Builder of the labyrinth	Daedalus
Daedalus' son, who flew too close to the sun	Icarus
Daedalus built the labyrinth for this king of Crete	Minos
Beast kept in the labyrinth	Minotaur
King of Athens who slew the Minotaur	Theseus
She helped Theseus through the labyrinth	Ariadne
Female warriors who cut off one breast	Amazons
Theseus married this queen of the Amazons	Hippolyta
Man who sought the Golden Fleece	Jason
Jason's ship	Argo
Jason's crew	Argonauts
Sorceress who helped Jason	Medea
He drowned swimming the Hellespont	Leander
Leander was swimming to meet this lover	Hero
River of Hades	Styx
Ferryman on the River Styx	Charon
She was abducted into the underworld	Persephone
The first woman, Hephaestus molded her from clay	Pandora
The only thing left in Pandora's box	Hope
Zeus had her turnied into a heifer	Io
Goddess who is the personification of the soul	Psyche
He sculpted Galatea	Pygmalion
She was turned into a laurel tree	Daphne
King of Thebes who solved the riddle of the Sphinx	Oedipus
Oedipus' mother and lover	Jocasta
Daughter of Oedipus and Jocasta	Antigone
He slew Medusa	Perseus
Perseus saved her from the Titan	Andromeda
Youth who fell in love with his own reflection	Narcissus
She loved Narcissus	Echo
Hunter slain by Artemis	Orion
King with the golden touch	Midas
Pyramus' lover	Thisbe

She beat Athena in a weaving contest .... Arachne
Nymphs who guarded the golden apple .... Hesperides
She stopped to pick up the golden apple .... Atalanta
He mastered the lyre given to him by his father Apollo .... Orpheus
Orpheus' wife; he lost her when he looked back to see her .... Euridice
He had to roll a stone up a hill forever .... Sisyphus
She had the gift of prophesy, but no one believed her .... Cassandra
Titan who stole fire from heaven .... Prometheus
Titan who holds up the sky .... Atlas
The daughters of Atlas .... Pleiades (The Seven
.... Sisters)
Goddesses who controlled human destiny .... Fates
Goddess of the rainbow .... Iris
God of the flock .... Pan
The daughters of Zeus, goddesses of charm and beauty .... Graces
Three sisters who had snakes for hair .... Gorgons
Gorgon that Perseus slew .... Medusa
Avenging spirits .... Furies
The children of Uranus and Gaea .... Titans
The daughters of Zeus, goddesses of arts and learning .... Muses
Muse of love poetry .... Erato
Muse of epic poetry .... Calliope
Muse of astronomy .... Urania
Muse of song and dance .... Terpsichore
Muse of history .... Clio
Muse of music .... Euterpe
Half eagle, half lion .... Griffin
Half man, half lion, mythical riddler .... Sphinx
Half man, half bull .... Minotaur
Half man, half goat who chased nymphs .... Satyr
Half man, half horse .... Centaur
Half woman, half bird .... Harpy
Flying horse who sprung for Medusa's head .... Pegasus
Three-headed dog that guarded Hades .... Cerberus
One hundred-eyed giant .... Argus
Nine-headed monster slain by Hercules .... Hydra

Roman Mythology:

Chief god .... Jupiter
Queen of the gods .... Juno
God of the sun, music, and poetry .... Apollo
Goddess of the moon and the hunt .... Diana
God of war .... Mars
God of the hearth .... Vesta
Goddess of love and beauty .... Venus

Mythology

God of the underworld .... Pluto
God of the sea .... Neptune
God of love .... Cupid
God of fire .... Vulcan
God of the harvest .... Saturn
God of wine and fertility .... Bacchus
God of agriculture .... Ceres
Goddess of wisdom .... Minerva
Goddess of love .... Amor
Goddess of the moon .... Luna
Messenger of the gods .... Mercury
Founders of Rome .... Romulus and Remus

Norse Mythology:

Father of the gods .... Odin (Woton)
Odin's wife, queen of the gods .... Frigg
Son of Odin and Frigg, god of beauty .... Balder
God of thunder or the sky .... Thor
Mischievous god .... Loki
Home of the gods .... Asgard
Norse dragon .... Fafnir
Bifrost bridge .... Rainbow
A hall in Asgard where dead heroes go .... Valhalla
Female spirits who bring dead warriors to Valhalla .... Valkyries

Egyptian Mythology:

Chief god who cheated death .... Osiris
Osiris' wife, queen of the gods .... Isis
Osiris and Isis' son .... Horace (or Seth)
Sun god .... Ra (or Re)
Jackal god, god of the dead .... Anubis
Divine animal .... Cat

Other Facts:

Babylonian fertility god .... Baal
Lustful Babylonian god .... Ishtar
Chief Aztec god .... Quetzaquadl
Polynesian god who created Hawaii .... Maui
Polynesian volcano god .... Pelee

Native Americans 34

Pawtucket chief (welcomed Pilgrims) .... Squanto

Chief who befriended Plymouth Colony .... Massasoit

Shawnee chief .... Tecumseh

Sauk chief .... Blackhawk

The Lakota belonged to this tribe .... Sioux

Teton Sioux chief .... Sitting Bull

Oglala Sioux chief .... Crazy Horse

Site where Sitting Bull and Crazy Horse massacred Custer's men, 1876
.... Little Big Horn, Montana

Site where the Sioux were massacred, 1890 .... Wounded Knee, SD

Chiricahua and Kiowa tribe .... Apache

Apache chief 1860's .... Cochise

Chiricahua Apache, captured 1886 .... Geronimo

Nez Perce chief .... Chief Joseph

Squamish chief .... Chief Seattle

Delaware Indian and New York hall .... Tammany

Indians of southern Florida .... Semiloles

Seminole chief .... Osceola

Ottawa Indian chief .... Pontiac

She married Jamestown settler John Rolfe .... Pocahontas

Pocahontas' father .... Powhatan

Pocahontas' English name .... Rebecca

Lewis and Clark's guide .... Sacajawea

"Trail of Tears" Indians .... Cherokee

Cherokee language developer .... Sequoya

New Mexico tribe, "Ancient Ones" .... Anasazi

Alaskan Eskimos .... Inuits

Cliff dwellers of Arizona .... Pueblo

Pueblo dolls .... Kachina Dolls

Pueblo Indians of northeast Arizona .... Hopi

"Long Walk" tribe, largest in US .... Navajo

34 *Native Americans*

Navajo dwelling	Hogan
Mississippi Indians	Creek
Honduras-Nicaragua Indians	Mosquito
Sculptors of Middle America	Olmecs
Indians of Central Mexico	Aztecs
Aztec capital	Tenochtitlan
Aztec leader	Montezuma
Aztecs over ran them, 1100 A.D.	Toltecs
Astronomers of South Mexico	Maya
Indians of Peru	Inca
Incan capital	Cuzco
Incan city in the Andes	Machu Picchu
Indians of Lesser Antilles	Carib Indians
1520 Indian confederacy	Iroquois League
Iroquois League founder	Hiawatha
Hiawatha's mate	Minihaha
Iroquois house	Long House
Five original Iroqouis League tribes	Mohawk, Seneca, Onondaga, Oneida, Cayuga
The five civilized tribes	Cherokee, Chickasaw Choctaw, Creek, Seminoles
Olympic hero, 1912	Jim Thorp
Native American in anti-pollution commercials	"Iron Eyes" Cody
Tonto portrayer	Jay Silverheels
She turned down Marlon Brando's Oscar in 1972	Sasheen Littlefeather
Colorado senator	Ben Nighthorse Campbell
Indian corn	Maize
Indian conference	Pow wow
Indian money	Wampum
State with largest Indian population	Oklahoma
State with the most Indian land	Arizona

Newspapers and *Magazines* 35

Major Cities and Their Newspapers:

Arlington .... *USA Today*
Atlanta .... *Constitution*
Baltimore .... *Sun*
Boston .... *Globe*
.... *Herald*
.... *Christian Science Monitor*
Chicago .... *Tribune* (Illinois' largest)
.... *Sun Times*
Cincinnati .... *Inquirer*
Cleveland .... *Plain Dealer*
Columbus .... *Dispatch*
Dallas.. *Morning News*
Denver .... *Post*
.... *Rocky Mountain News*
Des Moines .... *Register*
Detroit.. *Free Press*
Hartford .... *Courant*
Houston.. *Chronicle*
Indianapolis .... *Star*
Kansas City .... *Star*
London .... *Times*
.... *Daily Telegraph*
Los Angeles .... *Times* (largest Sunday circulation)
.... *Daily News*
Manchester .... *Guardian*
Miami .... *Herald*
Minneapolis .... *Star Tribune*
New Orleans .... *Times-Picayune*
New York .... *Post*
.... *Times*
.... *Daily News*
.... *Village Voice*
.... *Wall Street Journal*
.... *Amsterdam News*
.... *Tribune*
Oakland .... *Tribune*
Paris.. *La Monde*
Philadelphia .... *Inquirer*
Portland .... *Oregonian*
Sacramento .... *Bee*

35 *Newspapers and Magazines*

San Francisco	*Examiner*
	Chronicle
St. Louis	*St. Louis Post-Dispatch*
Seattle	*Times*
Toronto	*Star* (Canada's largest)
Washington	*Post*

Other Facts:

Daily Mirror founder	William Randolph Hearst
Christian Science Monitor founder	Mary Baker Eddy
New York Tribune founder	Horace Greeley
Katherine Graham's newspaper	*Washington Post*
New Jersey's oldest newspaper	*Elizabethan Daily Journal*
"The Nation's Newspaper"	*USA Today*
Daily with largest circulation	*The Wall Street Journal*
Established in 1877 as voice of Democratic Party	*Washington Post*
Phoenix's Native American newspaper	*Cherokee*
Daily newspaper for military personnel	*Stars and Stripes*
It's "All the business news you need"	*The Wall Street Journal*
It's "All the news that's fit to print"	*New York Times (The "Gray Lady", newspaper with most Pulitzers)*
"Dewey defeats Truman" newspaper	*Chicago Tribune*
Newspaper that broke Watergate story	*Washington Post*
Hollywood's newspaper	*Variety*
Dave Berry works for this newspaper	*Miami Herald*
World's largest news service	Associated Press
Former British humor magazine	*Punch*
"The Magazine for Women Over Forty"	*Lear*
"Magazine From Our Nations Attic"	*Smithsonian*
Magazine for the Library of Congress	*Civilization*
Jann Wenner's magazine	*Rolling Stone*
Magazine with "Dubious Achievement Award"	*Esquire*
Popular magazine from 1937-71	*Look*
AARP's magazine (highest U.S. circulation)	*Modern Maturity*
Magazine with column "Final Analysis"	*Physiology*
Magazine for "free minds and free markets"	*Reason*
Magazine for black women	*Essence*
Women's magazine formerly called *Queen*	*McCalls*
Women's magazine that debuted in 1884	*Ladies Home Journal*
Andy Warhol founded this magazine	*Interview*
Consumer's Union test rating magazine	*Consumer Reports*
John F. Kennedy, Jr. founded this magazine	*George*
Magazine that contains the "Index"	*Harpers*
Dewitt and Lila Wallace founded this magazine	*Reader's Digest*
The Luces started this magazine	*Life*
Harvard's humor magazine	*Harvard Lampoon*

American Heart Association magazine .... *Hypertension*
Boy Scout's magazine .... *Boy's Life*
The first editor of *Cosmopolitan* .... Helen Gurley Brown
National Review founder .... William F. Buckley
Playboy founder.. Hugh Hefner
"Talk of the Town" writer for *New Yorker*........... E. B. White
New Yorker columnist, 1931 .... Dorothy Parker
New Yorker staff photographer, 1992 .... Richard Avedon
She founded *Ms.* Magazine .... Gloria Steinem
Muscle and Fitness founder...................................... Joe Weider
TV Guide and *Seventeen* founder........................... Walter Annenberg
He bought the *Washington Post* in 1976 .... Rupert Murdoch
Public Citizen founder .... Ralph Nader
Where the crossword puzzle debuted, 1913 .... *New York World*
Poor Richard's last name .... Saunders
First person on the cover of *Rolling Stone* .... John Lennon
First person on the cover of *TV Guide* .... Little Rickie (Ricardo)
First person on the cover of *People* .... Mia Farrow
First person on the cover of *George* .... Cindy Crawford
Demi Moore appeared pregnant and nude on its cover
.... *Vanity Fair*
Person most often on the cover of *People* .... Diana (Spencer)
Person most often on the cover of *Time* .... Richard Nixon
Woman most often on the cover of *Time* .... The Virgin Mary

Comic Strips and Creator:

Dennis the Menace .... Hank Ketcham
Beetle Bailey .... Mort Walker
Doonesbury .... G.B (Garry) Trudeau
The Far Side.. Gary Larson
Calvin and Hobbes... Bill Watterman
Dilbert .... Scott Adams
Garfield .... Jim Davis
Peanuts .... Charles Schultz
Pogo .... Walt Kelly
Shoe... Jeff MacNeally
Dick Tracy .... Chester Gould
L'il Abner... Al Capp
The Family Circus .... Bill Keane
Cathy .... Cathy Guisewite
Steve Canyon .... Milton Caniff
Creator of the "comics contraptions" .... Rube Goldberg
Pop artist who used "comics" style .... Roy Liechtenstein
U.S. longest continuous running comic strip .... The Katzenjammer Kids
Creator of the Republican elephant and Democratic donkey political cartoons
.... Thomas Nast

36 *Notorious People*

Medieval Romanian impaler	Vlad the Impaler
Fall River, MA woman accused of ax murders, 1892	Lizzie Borden
Sheriff Pat Garrett killed him	Billy the Kid (William Bonny)
Missouri gang shot up in Northfield, Minnesota	James Gang
Brothers who were cohorts of the James Gang	The Youngers
Gang shot up in Coffeyville, Kansas	Dalton Gang
The Wild Bunch leaders	Butch Cassidy and The Sundance Kid
The Wild Bunch's hideout	Hole in the wall
Jack McCall shot this man	Wild Bill Hickock
Hickock was holding this poker hand	Aces and eights (Dead man's hand)
London killer of seven prostitutes, 1888	Jack the Ripper
Matriarch killed by G-men, 1935	Ma Barker
Meyer Lansky's group	Murder, Inc.
First public enemy #1	John Dillinger
Mobster nicknamed "Machine gun"	Machine Gun Kelly
Mobster who built the Flamingo Hilton	"Bugsy" Siegel
"Lucky" crime boss	"Lucky" Luciano
Chicago mobster jailed for tax evasion, a.k.a. "Scarface"	Al Capone
Day "Bugs" Moran's gang was killed	St. Valentine's Day, 1929
Mobster who testified before the Senate, 1951	Frank Costello
Couple gunned down by police in Louisiana, 1934	Bonnie Parker and Clyde Barrow
Man executed in 1936 for kidnapping Lindbergh baby	Bruno Hauptmann
1950 robbery from a Boston garage ($2,775,000 stolen)	Brinks robbery
Pair imprisoned for kidnapping Bobby Franks	Leopold and Loeb
Italian immigrants executed for murder in 1927	Sacco and Vanzetti
Couple executed in 1951 for selling A-bomb secrets	Ethel and Julius Rosenberg
Nebraska garbage man and mass murderer	Carl Starkweather
He shot JFK	Lee Harvey Oswald

He shot Lee Harvey Oswald .... Jack Ruby

He shot Robert Kennedy .... Sirhan Sirhan

He shot Martin Luther King, Jr. .... James Earl Ray

Killer and cannibalizer of 17 men in Milwaukee .... Jeffrey Dahmer

Killer of 30 young women executed in Florida, 1989 .... Ted Bundy

He was court-martialed for the My Lai massacre .... Lt. William Calley

First American executed after 10 year hiatus, in 1977 .... Gary Gilmore (firing
                                                                                                                           squad in Utah)

Nickname for .44 Caliber Killer David Berkowitz .... Son of Sam (after his dog)

Nickname of Ilich Arthur Sanchez .... Carlos the Jackal

The Boston Strangler .... Albert Desalvo

The Hillside Strangler .... Kenneth Bianchi

The Night Stalker .... Richard Ramirez

The Unibomber .... Theodore Kazinsky

The Bird Man of Alcatraz .... Robert Stroud

The Long Island Lolita .... Amy Fischer

Skyjacker who parachuted from a 727 in 1971 .... D.B. Cooper

Fake Howard Hughes biographer .... Clifford Irving

Mustachioed Chinese arch-fiend .... Fu Manchu

Head of the Gambino crime family, "The Teflon Don" .... John Gotti

The People's Temple suicide leader, 1978 .... Jim Jones

Branch Davidian leader in Waco, TX, 1993 .... David Koresh

Navy spy family caught in 1985 .... The Walkers

Man convicted in Oklahoma City bombing .... Timothy McVeigh

Exxon Valdez captain .... Capt. Joseph Hazelwood

He shot Ronald Reagan and James Brady .... John Hinkley, Jr.

He shot John Lennon .... Mark David Chapman

Cult leader and killer of nine in Los Angeles, 1968 .... Charles Manson

Terrorist wanted for bombing of U.S. embassies .... Osama bin Laden

He had millions put to death in Cambodia .... Pol Pot

She shot J. R. Ewing on TV's *Dallas* .... Kristin Shepard

37 *Organizations*

19th Century English Socialist Society .... Fabian Society

League of Women Voters founder .... Carrie Chapman Catt

Boy Scouts founder .... Lord Baden-Powell

Girl Scouts founder .... Juliette Low

Salvation Army founder .... William Booth

Sierra Club founder .... John Muir

March of Dimes founder .... Franklin Roosevelt

Planned Parenthood founder .... Margaret Sanger

Hull House founder .... Jane Addams

John Birch Society founder .... Robert Welch

National Organization for Women founder .... Betty Friedan

Red Cross founder .... Clara Barton

International Red Cross founder .... Will Durant

Special Olympics founder .... Eunice Shriver

First Peace Corps director .... Sargent Shriver

Defense organization founded April 4, 1949 .... NATO

Location of NATO headquarters .... Brussels, Belgium

Organization founded in Bogota in 1948 .... OAS

Organization founded by 33 scientists in 1888 .... National Geographic Society

Famine relief fund raiser .... Live Aid

"Rainbow Warriors" organization .... Greenpeace

Organization founded to aid political prisoners, 1961

.... Amnesty International

Animal protection group .... ASPCA

Group that teaches employment skills to youth .... Job Corps

Organization that teaches economics to youth .... Junior Achievement

National youth service created in 1993 .... Americorps

"We do by learning" organizaion 4H

Civil rights organization founded in 1909 .... NAACP

Organization founded by Carolyn Scott Harrison .... DAR

United Nation's children's aid organization .... UNICEF

Location of Interpol headquarters .... Paris

Cartel founded in Baghdad in 1960 .... OPEC

Latin American economic cooperation organization ..... OAS

Western European organization establised to promote free trade, 1957

.... EEC

George Bernard Shaw's socialist society .... Fabian Society

America's largest veteran's organization .... American Legion

Organization established for overseas veterans .... VFW

League founded in 1910 to help blacks migrate .... Urban League

Organization trying to unite Africa .... Pan Africa

Largest teachers union ....American Federation of Teachers

19th century female union leader .... Mother Jones

American Railway Union founder, 1893 .... Eugene Debs

United Mine Workers leader (1920-60) .... John L. Lewis

United Farm workers founder .... Caesar Chavez

Detroit-based union .... United Auto Workers

UAW president .... Walter Ruether

Akron-based union .... United Rubber Workers

Teamsters leader, 1957-71 .... Jimmy Riddle Hoffa

Teamsters president, 1991- .... Ron Carey

AFL founder .... Samuel Gompers

AFL-CIO leader, 1955-79 .... George Meany

AFL-CIO leader following Meany .... Joseph Lane Kirkland

Railroad car manufacturer's strike, 1894 .... Pullman Strike

Union that had a major strike in 1959 .... Steelworkers

U.S. Department of Labor safety and health agency

.... OSHA

Organization of World's Leading Industrial Nations

....G-7 (Group of 7, somtimes Russia is

included and then it becomes the Group of 8)

38 *The Plant Kingdom*

Plants and Trees:

Oldest living tree	Bristle Cone Pine (5,100 years)
World's tallest tree	California Redwood
World's most massive tree	Giant Sequoia
Largest hickory tree	Pecan tree
Tree with many supporting roots and trunks	Banyan tree
Banyan tree fruit	Fig
Black and English type tree	Walnut
"Bald" Everglades tree	Cypress
Tree turpentine comes from	Pine
Bowling pin wood	Maple
Baseball bat wood	Ash
"Quaking" tree	Aspen
Tree on Lebanon's flag	Cedar
Blue gum tree	Eucalyptus
Canoe wood	Birch
Silk cotton tree	Kapok
Florida tree with stilt-like roots	Mangrove
Kon Tiki raft material	Balsa
Tree that the *Bounty* sought	Breadfruit tree
An oak's main root	Tap root
Largest single family of succulents	Cacti (Cactus)
Cactus fruit	Prickly pear
Tallest cactus	Saguaro
Hawaiian root crop	Taro
Violet dye plant	Indigo
Red dye plant	Henna
Linseed oil is from this plant	Flax
Long moss of American south	Spanish moss
Rope fiber plant	Hemp
Vine that grows 4 inches per day	Kudzu
Fastest growing grass	Bamboo
Russian thistle	Tumbleweed
"Stinging" plant	Stinging nettles
Algae and fungus living as a single unit	Lichen
Digitalis source	Foxglove
Rye and wheat hybrid	Tritacale
Leaf openings	Stomata
Evaporation of water from leaves	Transpiration
Non-flowering plant	Gymnosperm
Flowering plant	Angiosperm
Plant that lives for one year	Annual

Plant that lives for two years .... Biennial
Plant that lives for many years .... Perennial
A plant's male organ .... Stamen
Pollen producer at the end of the stamen .... Anther
A plant's female organ .... Pistil
Trees that do not shed leaves .... Coniferous
Tree that sheds its leaves annually .... Deciduous
Term for how deciduous trees lose their leaves .... Abscession
A plant's fertilized ovule .... Seed
Plant that tolerates salt .... Halophyte

Flowers:

Cymbidium, the flower of Thailand .... Orchid
Japanese flower .... Chrysanthemum
King Alfred Narcissus type .... Daffodil
Madonna type .... Lily
Common name for the yellow daisy .... Black-eyed Susan
Common name for Helianthus .... Sunflower
Purple flower of Scotland .... Heather
Man in the Moon or Cape type .... Marigold
Sword lily type .... Gladiola
Traditional Mother's Day flower .... Carnation
Sacred flower of Buddhism .... Lotus
Flower used in Codeine and Morphine .... Poppy
"Shasta" flower .... Daisy
Tall flower grown for seeds .... Sunflower
Vanilla-flavoring flower .... Orchid
Crocus and gladiola family .... Iris
Carnation family .... Pink
Rochester New York festival .... Lilac Festival

Fruits and Vegetables:

Star fruit .... Carambola
Morello, marasca, maraschino .... Cherries
Winesap, Baldwin and Northern Spy .... Apples
Chutney relish fruit, "the peach of the tropics" .... Mango
Seedless grape .... Thompson's
Cooking banana .... Plantain
Damson or greengage fruit .... Plum
Fruit used in peach Melba sauce .... Raspberry
Bigarade fruit .... Orange
Adriatic fruit .... Fig
Tiny Chinese orange .... Kumquat
"Fuzzy" New Zealand fruit .... Kiwi
Tropical fruit from which papain is obtained .... Papaya

38   *The Plant Kingdom*

Tropical fruit with five-pound seeds .... Mango
Tropical pumpkin-shaped melon .... Casaba
Pomelo relative .... Grapefruit
Raspberry and blackberry hybrid .... Loganberry
Tangerine and grapefruit hybrid .... Tangelo
Alligator pear .... Avocado
Lisbon fruit .... Lemon
Clingstone and freestone fruit .... Peach
Small golden fruit .... Apricot
Yellow pear shaped fruit .... Guava
Fertility symbol .... Pomegranate
Fruit named for Moroccan city .... Tangerine
Fruit measured in hands .... Banana
Greening fruit .... Apple
Rose family fruit .... Quince
Linzer tort fruit .... Raspberry
Jelly grape .... Concord
French "la prune" .... Plum
French "la raison" .... Grape
French currant .... Raisin
Chick peas a.k.a. .... Garbanzo beans
Hubbards' butternut or acorn vegetable .... Squash
Chinese cabbage .... Bok Choy
Chinese fruit related to longan .... Lichi nut
"A la Florentine" vegetable .... Spinach
Yukon gold vegetable .... Potato
Heading vegetable .... Broccoli
Savoy or collard vegetable .... Cabbage
Pascal vegetable .... Celery
Lens shaped vegetable, highest in protien .... Lentil
Yellow turnip .... Rutabaga
European aubergine .... Eggplant
Red-stalked vegetable .... Rhubarb
Vichysoisse vegetables .... Leeks and potatoes
Gumbo vegetable .... Okra
Jerusalem vegetable .... Artichoke
White carrot .... Parsnip
Chicken Divan vegetable .... Broccoli
Mexican potato .... Jicama
Miniature cabbage from Belgium .... Brussels sprouts
Chicory vegetable .... Radish
Kentucky hybrid lettuce pioneer .... Bibb
Botanist who developed the spineless cactus .... Luther Burbank
Man who developed dozens of uses for peanuts .... George Washington Carver
Man who planted apple trees throughout Ohio Valley
.... Johnny Appleseed

Plays and Playwrights 39

After the Fall	Arthur Miller
All's Well That Ends Well	William Shakespeare
Amadeus	Peter Shaffer
Androcles and the Lion	George Bernard Shaw
Anna Christie	Eugene O'Neill
Anthony and Cleopatra	William Shakespeare
Antigone	Sophocles
Armies of the Night	Norman Mailer
Autumn Garden, The	Lillian Hellman
Awake and Sing!	Clifford Odets
Barefoot in the Park	Neil Simon
Bear, The	Anton Chekhov
Biloxi Blues	Neil Simon
Birthday Party, The	Harold Pinter
Blithe Spirit	Noel Coward
Bourgeois Gentlehomme, Le	Moliere
Brighton Beach Memoirs	Neil Simon
Broadway Bound	Neil Simon
Buried Child	Sam Shepard
California Suite	Neil Simon
Candida	George Bernard Shaw
Casino Real	Tennessee Williams
Cat on a Hot Tin Roof	Tennessee Williams
Cherry Orchard, The	Anton Chekhov
Children's Hour, The	Lillian Hellman
Come Back, Little Sheba	William Inge
Country Girl, The	Clifford Odets
Crucible, The	Arthur Miller
Death of a Salesman	Arthur Miller
Delicate Balance, A	Edward Albee
Desire Under the Elms	Eugene O'Neill
Doll's House, A	Henrik Ibsen
Emperor Jones	Eugene O'Neill
Equus	Peter Shaffer
Fences	August Wilson
Fool for Love	Sam Shepard
Ghosts	Henrik Ibsen
Glass Menagerie, The	Tennessee Williams
Glengarry Glen Ross	David Mamet
Golden Boy	Clifford Odets
Hairy Ape, The	Eugene O'Neill
Hamlet	William Shakespeare

39   *Plays and Playwrights*

Heartbreak Kid, The	Neil Simon
Hay Fever	Noel Coward
Heartbreak House	George Bernard Shaw
Hedda Gabler	Henrik Ibsen
Heidi Chronicles, The	Wendy Wasserstein
Henry V	William Shakespeare
Henry VIII	William Shakespeare
Homecoming, The	Harold Pinter
Iceman Cometh, The	Eugene O'Neill
Imaginary Invalid, The	Moliére
Importance of Being Ernest, The	Oscar Wilde
Jew of Malta, The	Christopher Marlowe
Julius Caesar	William Shakespeare
Juno and the Paycock	Sean O'Casey
King Lear	William Shakespeare
King John	William Shakespeare
Lady Windermere's Fan	Oscar Wilde
Little Foxes, The	Lillian Hellman
Long Day's Journey into Night	Eugene O'Neill
Look Back in Anger	John Osborne
Lost in Yonkers	Neil Simon
Love's Labours Lost	William Shakespeare
Lower Depths, The	Maxim Gorki
Macbeth	William Shakespeare
Major Barbara	George Bernard Shaw
Man and Superman	George Bernard Shaw
Merchant of Venice, The	William Shakespeare
Merchant of Yonkers, The	Thornton Wilder
Merry Wives of Windsor, The	William Shakespeare
Midsummer Night's Dream, A	William Shakespeare
Misanthrope	Moliére
Misfits, The (screenplay)	Arthur Miller
Miss Julie	August Strindberg
Moon for the Misbegotten, A	Eugene O'Neill
Mourning Becomes Electra	Eugene O'Neill
Murder in the Cathedral	T.S. Eliot
Night of the Iguana, The	Tennessee Williams
Odd Couple, The	Neil Simon
Orpheus Descending	Tennessee Williams
Othello	William Shakespeare
Our Town	Thornton Wilder
Piano Lesson, The	August Wilson
Picnic	William Inge
Peer Gynt	Henrik Ibsen
Player, The (screenplay)	Robert Altman
Plaza Suite	Neil Simon

Plow and the Stars, The	Sean O'Casey
Private Lives	Noel Coward
Pygmalion	George Bernard Shaw
Raisin in the Sun, A	Lorraine Hansberry
Rent	Jonathan Larson
Richard III	William Shakespeare
Roman Spring of Mrs. Stone, The	Tennessee Williams
Romeo and Juliet	William Shakespeare
Rose Tatoo, The	Tennessee Williams
Seagull, The	Anton Chekhov
School for Scandal	Oliver Goldsmith
Seascape	Edward Albee
Seven Against Thebes	Aeschylus
She Stoops to Conquer	Oliver Goldsmith
Sisters Rosenzweig, The	Wendy Wasserstein
Skin of Our Teeth, The	Thornton Wilder
Strange Interlude	Eugene O'Neill
Streetcar Named Desire, A	Tennessee Williams
Summer and Smoke	Tennessee Williams
Sunshine Boys, The	Neil Simon
Sweet Bird of Youth	Tennessee Williams
Tamberlaine the Great	Christopher Marlowe
Taming of the Shrew, The	William Shakespeare
Tartuffe	Moliere
Three Penny Opera, The	Bertolt Brecht
Three Sisters	Anton Chekhov
Three Tall Women	Edward Albee
Tiny Alice	Edward Albee
Torch Song Trilogy	Harvey Fierstein
Toys in the Attic	Lillian Hellman
Troilus and Cressida	William Shakespeare
Trojan Women, The	Euripides
True West	Sam Shepard
Twelfth Night	William Shakespeare
Two Gentlemen of Verona, The	William Shakespeare
Uncle Vanya	Anton Chekhov
Valpone	Ben Johnson
View From the Bridge, A	Arthur Miller
Waiting for Godot	Samuel Beckett
Waiting for Lefty	Clifford Odets
Watch on the Rhine	Lillian Hellman
Way of the World, The	William Congreve
Who's Afraid of Virginia Woolf?	Edward Albee
Winterset	Maxwell Anderson
Winter's Tale, The	William Shakespeare
Zoo Story	Edward Albee

40 *Poets and Poetry*

America the Beautiful	Kathy Lee Bates
Annabell Lee	Edgar Allen Poe
Ariel	Percy Bysshe Shelly
Assurance	Emily Dickinson
Arsenal at Springfield, The	Henry Wadsworth Longfellow
Auld Lang Syne	Robert Burns
Aurora Leigh	Elizabeth Barrett Browning
Battle Hymn of the Republic	Julia Ward Howe
Belle Dame Sans Merci, La	John Keats
Bells, The	Edgar Allan Poe
Bells and Pomegranates	Robert Browning
Casey at the Bat	Ernest Thayer
Chambered Nautilus, The	Oliver Wendell Holmes
Charge of the Light Brigade	Alfred Lord Tennyson
Chicago Poems	Carl Sandburg
Concord Hymn, The	Ralph Waldo Emerson
Courtship of Miles Standish, The	Henry Wadsworth Longfellow
Crossing the Bar	Alfred Lord Tennyson
Crossing the Brooklyn Ferry	Walt Whitman
Daffodils	William Wordsworth
Death Be Not Proud	John Donne
Don Juan	Lord Byron
Do Not Go Gentle into that Good Night	Dylan Thomas
Endymion	John Keats
Elegy Written in a Country Churchyard	Thomas Grey
Evangeline	Henry Wadsworth Longfellow
Faerie Queen, The	Edmund Spencer
Fog	Carl Sandberg
Gunga Din	Rudyard Kipling
Harp Weaver, The	Edna St. Vincent Millay
Howl	Allen Ginsberg
If	Rudyard Kipling
I Know Why the Caged Bird Sings	Maya Angelou
I Never Saw a Moor	Emily Dickinson
Idylls of the King	Alfred Lord Tennyson
Jabberwocky	Lewis Carroll
John Brown's Body	Stephen Vincent Benet
Kubla Khan	Samuel Taylor Coleridge
Lady of the Lake	Sir Walter Scott
Lake Isle at Innisfree, The	William Butler Yeats
Lays of Ancient Rome, The	Thomas Macaulay
Leaves of Grass	Walt Whitman

Little Boy Blue	Eugene Field
Love Letter to Her Husband, A	Anne Bradstreet
Love Songs	Sara Teasdale
Lyrical Ballads	William Wordsworth and Samuel Tayor Colerdidge
Mending Wall	Robert Frost
Midnight Ride of Paul Revere, The	Henry Wadsworth Longfellow
My Last Duchess	Robert Browning
New Colossus, The	Emma Lazarus
No Man is an Island	John Donne
O Captain, My Captain	Walt Whitman
Ode to a Nightingale	John Keats
Ode on a Grecian Urn	John Keats
Ode on Melancholy	John Keats
Ode to the West Wind	Percy Bysshe Shelly
Old Ironsides	Oliver Wendell Holmes
On His Blindness	John Milton
Pied Piper of Hamelin, The	Robert Browning
Pippa Passes	Robert Browning
Pisan Cantos, The	Ezra Pound
Prometheus Unbound	Percey Bysshe Shelley
Rape of the Lock, The	Alexander Pope
Raven, The	Edgar Allan Poe
Rime of the Ancient Mariner, The	Samuel Taylor Coleridge
Road Not Taken, The	Robert Frost
Road to Mandalay, The	Rudyard Kipling
Rubaiyat	Omar Khayyam
She Walks in Beauty	Lord Byron
Snowbound	John Greenleaf Whittier
Song of Hiawatha, The	Henry Wadsworth Longfellow
Song of Myself	Walt Whitman
Songs of Experience	William Blake
Songs of Innocence	William Blake
Sonnets from the Portuguese	Elizabeth Barrett Browning
Spoon River Anthology	Edgar Lee Masters
Stopping by the Woods on a Snowy Evening	Robert Frost
Strange Victory	Sara Teasdale
Tales of Wayside Inn	Henry Wadsworth Longfellow
Tamberlane	Edgar Allan Poe
Tam o'Shanter	Robert Burns
Thanatopsis	William Cullen Bryant
There Will Come Soft Rains	Sara Teasdale
Trees	Joyce Kilmer
Tinturn Abbey	William Wordsworth
To a Mouse	Robert Burns
To a Louse	Robert Burns

40   *Poets and Poetry*

To a Skylark	Percy Bysshe Shelly
To Helen	Edgar Allan Poe
Tyger, The	William Blake
Under Milkwood	Dylan Thomas
Village Blacksmith, The	Henry Wadsworth Longfellow
Visit From St. Nicholas, A	Clement Moore
Walrus and the Carpenter, The	Lewis Carroll
Waste Land, The	T. S. Eliot
What's O'Clock	Amy Lowell
When the Frost is on the Punkin	James Whitcomb Riley
Wild Swans at Coole, The	William Butler Yeats
Wreck of the Hesperus, The	Henry W. Longfellow

Other Facts:

Earliest known poem, 3rd millennium, B.C. Mesopotamia	*The Epic of Gilgamesh*
Persian poet (11th century)	Omar Khayyam
"A Second Johnson"	Samuel Taylor Coleridge
American colonies first female poet	Anne Bradstreet
"Old 'Possum"	T. S. Eliot
The Ode poet	John Keats
Plowman Poet or The Scottish Poet	Robert Burns
Lake Poet	William Wordsworth
Mussolini friend who died in an asylum	Ezra Pound
The Lincoln Poet	Carl Sandburg
New Hampshire or New England Poet	Robert Frost
Quaker Poet	John Greenleaf Whittier
Welsh Poet	Dylan Thomas
Limerick writer, 1870's	Edward Lear
Limerick writer for *The New Yorker*	Ogden Nash
The Harlem Poet	Langston Hughes
The Alter Poet	George Herbert
The Belle of Amherst	Emily Dickinson
U.S. poet of the beat generation	Allen Ginsberg
Poet who read at JFK's inauguration	Robert Frost
Poet who read at Clinton's inauguration	Maya Angelou
Perceval Lowell's sister	Amy Lowell
Poet who used only lower case letters	e. e. cummings
English poet who drowned at the age of 25	John Keats
First U.S. poet laureate	Robert Penn Warren
Poets buried in same Roman cemetery	John Keats and P.B. Shelly
Canadian poet's school	School of Montreal
Number of lines in a sonnet	Fourteen
Edda poetry comes from this country	Iceland

Potent Potables **41**

Drink invented at Raffels Hotel in Singapore	Singapore Sling
Drink invented by oil workers who stirred it with this tool	Screwdriver
Spanish fortified wine, brown and sweet	Sherry
Fortified wine from Oporto, Portugal	Port
Greek licorice-flavored liquor	Ouzo
Licorice-flavored liquor made from wormwood	Absinthe
Liquor made from distilled wine	Brandy
French fine brandy	Cognac
Kirsch brandy is made from this fruit	Cherries
Mirabelle brandy is made from this fruit	Plums
Framboise brandy is made from this fruit	Raspberries
Brandy, cointreau and lemon juice	Sidecar
Dom Perignon's sparkling wine	Champagne
Champagne and orange juice	Mimosa
Alcohol made with juniper or blackthorn berries	Gin
Gin, lemon, and powdered sugar	Tom Collins
White wine flavored with herbs	Vermouth
Gin and dry vermouth	Martini
Martini with an onion	Gibson
Almond-flavored liquor	Amaretto
Drink made from fermented honey	Mead
Blue liquor	Curaçao
Liquor made from mezcal	Tequila
Tequila, triple sec, and lime juice	Margarita
Tequila, grenadine and orange juice	Tequila sunrise
Mexican coffee-flavored liquor	Kahlua
Jamaican coffee-flavored liquor	Tia Maria
Peach flavored bourbon	Southern Comfort
Bourbon grain	Corn
Liquor from sugar cane	Rum

41 *Potent Potables*

Rum, coconut, and pineapple	Piña colada
Rum diluted	Grog
Russian liquor make from wheat	Vodka
Vodka, triple sec, and lime juice	Kamikaze
Vodka, galliano, and orange juice	Harvey Wallbanger
Fine Finnish vodka	Absolute
Vodka and Kahlua	Black Russian
Vodka and cranberry juice	Cape Cod Coddler
Vodka and orange juice	Screwdriver
Liquor distilled from grain	Whiskey
Whiskey, mint and sugar	Mint Julep
Whiskey, bitters and sugar	Old fashioned
Whiskey, vermouth and bitters	Manhattan
Manhattan with scotch	Rob Roy
Drink served before a meal	Aperitif
Drink served after a meal	Digestif
Guinness port	Stout
Where Guinness is brewed	Ireland
Drambuie is made here	Scotland
Bacardi is made on this island	Puerto Rico
V.O. whiskey maker	Seagram's (Canada)
Where Tuborg is brewed	Denmark
Where Lowenbrau is brewed	Germany
Where Corona is brewed	Mexico
Where Fosters is brewed	Australia
Japanese rice wine	Sake
Drink of the Kentucky Derby	Mint Julep
Edgar Allen Poe' sherry	Amontillado
Brandy glass	Snifter
Champagne glass	Flute
These remove the acid from a drink	Bitters
VSOP	Very Special Old Pale

Presidents, Vice Presidents and First Ladies **42**

1. George Washington 1789-97 (The Father of His Country)
- Political Party: Federalist
- Vice President: John Adams
- First Lady: Martha (Custis, nee Dandridge) Washington
- State: Virginia (retired to Mount Vernon in Va.)
- George Washington was a major player in the French & Indian War of 1754-63. He fought with the American Colonists on the side of the British and gained valuable experience as a soldier, leader, and knowledge of British war tactics.
- He was the only president to not live in the White House.
- He was the only president to have a state named after him.
- He was the only president elected by unanimous electoral vote.
- He had no natural children.

2. John Adams 1797-1801 (The Duke of Braintree)
- Political Party: Federalist
- Vice President: Thomas Jefferson
- First Lady: Abigail Adams
- State: Massachusetts (Braintree)
- John Adams graduated from Harvard University.
- He opposed the Stamp Act.
- He was delegate to first Continental Congress.
- He is the first president alphabetically.
- He is the father of John Quincy Adams.

3. Thomas Jefferson 1801-09 (The Sage of Monticello)
- Political Party: Democratic-Republican
- Vice Presidents: Aaron Burr (killed Alexander Hamilton in a duel)
                          George Clinton
- First Lady: none (his wife Martha died before he took office)
- State: Virginia (Monticello)
- Thomas Jefferson was elected to his first term by the House of Representatives because he was tied with Aaron Burr and did not receive a majority of electoral votes in the general election.
- He wrote the Declaration of Independence.
- He was the first president inaugurated in Washington D.C.
- He made the Louisiana Purchase from Napoleon in 1803.
- He founded The University of Virginia.
- He fathered one and probably several children by slave Sally Hemmings.
- He played the violin.

42   *Presidents, Vice Presidents and First Ladies*

4. *James Madison 1809-17 (The Father of the Constitution, The Sage of Montpelier)*
- Political Party: Democratic-Republican
- Vice Presidents: George Clinton
  Elbridge Gerry (the term Gerrymandering was named after him for rearranging voting districts for political purposes)
- First Lady: Dolley Madison (noted for her being a great hostess in the White House)
- State: Virginia (Montpelier)
- James Madison was president during the War of 1812.
- He is credited with writing the Bill of Rights.
- He was the shortest president at 5', 4".

5. *James Monroe 1817-25*
- Political Party: Democratic-Republican
- Vice President: Daniel Tompkins
- First Lady: Eliza Monroe
- State: Virginia (Ash Lawn)
- James Monroe fought as a major in the American revolution and was wounded in the battle of Trenton.
- He served in the cabinet of Thomas Jefferson and as governor of Virginia.
- In 1820 he ran unopposed for president.
- He established Monroe Doctrine in 1823 that opposed European intervention in the affairs of the Western Hemisphere.
- He presided over "The Era of Good Feelings."
- Monrovia, the capital of Liberia, is named for him.
- His picture is on the $5,000 bill.

6. *John Quincy Adams 1825-29 (Old Man Eloquent)*
- Political Party: National-Republican
- Vice President: John C. Calhoun
- First Lady: Louise (Johnson) Adams
- State: Massachusetts (Braintree)
- John Quincy Adams won the election of 1824 over Andrew Jackson by decision of the House of Representatives.
- He returned to the House of Representatives after being president.
- He was the attorney for the slaves of the mutiny ship *Amistad.*
- He was the son of John Adams.

7. *Andrew Jackson 1829-37 (Old Hickory)*
- Political Party: Democrat
- Vice Presidents: John C. Calhoun (first V.P. to resign), Martin Van Buren
- First Lady: Rachel Jackson
- State: Tennessee (The Hermitage)
- Andrew Jackson led the American troops in the Battle of New Orleans.
- His wife Rachael died seven weeks into his first term.
- His cabinet was nicknamed the "Kitchen Cabinet"
- He was the first president from a state west of the Appalachians.

- He withdrew all funds from the Bank of the United States.
- He adopted the "spoils system" of appointing political supporters to government positions.
- He was the first president involved in an assassination attempt.
- He was the first president born in a log cabin.
- He defeated the Creek Indians in Alabama.

8. Martin Van Buren 1837-41 (The Sage of Kinderhook)
- Political Party: Democrat
- Vice President: Richard Johnson
- First Lady: none (wife died in 1819, never remarried)
- State: New York
- Martin Van Buren was of Dutch descent.
- He served as governor of New York.
- He served in the cabinet of Andrew Jackson as Secretary of State.
- He was the first president born in the USA.
- He was beaten decisively by W. H. Harrison in the 1840 election, mainly because of a depression during his administration.

9. William Henry Harrison 1841 (Old Tippecanoe)
- Political Party: Whig
- Vice President: John Tyler
- William Henry Harrison was the first president to die in office.
- He gave a 3.5 hour inauguration speech in the cold and rain, caught pneumonia and died 32 days later.
- He was grandfather of President Benjamin Harrison.

10. John Tyler 1841-45
- Political Party: Whig
- Vice president: none
- First Lady: Julia Tyler (married while president)
- State: Virginia
- Secretary of State: Daniel Webster
- John Tyler served as governor of Virginia.
- He was the first VP to succeed to presidency upon the death of a president.
- He served briefly in the Confederate Congress.
- He was the president with the most children. (15)

11. James Knox Polk 1845-49 (First Dark Horse, Young Hickory)
- Political Party: Democrat
- Vice president: George M. Dallas (Dallas, TX namesake)
- First Lady: Sarah (Childress) Polk
- State: Tennessee
- James K. Polk served as governor of Tennessee and as Speaker of the House of Representatives.

Presidents, Vice Presidents and First Ladies

- His administration fought and won the war with Mexico, annexing Texas and a vast amount of land west of the Rocky Mountains.
- He was a ran on the platform of "Manifest Destiny", i.e., all land west to the Pacific Ocean should become part of the United States.

12. Zachary Taylor 1849-50 (Old Rough and Ready)
- Political Party: Whig
- Vice president: Millard Fillmore
- State: Virginia
- First Lady: Margaret (Smith) Taylor
- Zachary Taylor was a general in the Mexican-American War.
- He won the Battle of Buena Vista, defeating Mexican general Santa Anna.
- He was the second president to die in office July 9, 1850.
- He was Jefferson Davis' father in law.

13. Millard Fillmore 1850-53
- Political party: Whig
- Vice president: none
- First Lady: Abigail Fillmore
- State: New York
- Millard Fillmore became president upon the death of Zachary Taylor.
- He established the first trade talks with Japan.
- He was the last Whig president.

14. Franklin Pierce 1853-57 (Handsome Frank)
- Political party: Democrat
- Vice president: William Rufus King
- First Lady: Jane (Appleton) Pierce
- State: New Hampshire (only New Hampshire president)
- Franklin Pierce graduated from Bowdoin College.
- He served in the Mexican-American War.
- He made Gadsden Purchase from Mexico.
- He was the first president to have a full time bodyguard.

15. James Buchanan 1857-61 (The Bachelor President)
- Political party: Democrat
- Vice President: John C. Breckinridge (youngest V.P.)
- First Lady: none
- State: Pennsylvania (Wheatland)
- James Buchanan was James Polk's Secretary of State.
- He was the only president to never marry.
- He retired to his Wheatland estate in Lancaster, PA.

16. Abraham Lincoln 1861-65 (Honest Abe)
- Political Party: Republican
- Vice presidents: Hannibal Hamlin, Andrew Johnson

- First Lady: Mary Todd Lincoln (spoke French and died in mental ward)
- State: Illinois
- Abraham Lincoln was born in Kentucky.
- He fought in The Blackhawk War.
- He participated in Lincoln-Douglas debates.
- He was the first Republican president.
- He was the tallest president.
- He enacted Emancipation Proclamation. (He called it his greatest achievement).
- He was shot by John Wilkes Booth while attending the play *Our American Cousin* at Ford's Theater.
- Son Robert Lincoln was Secretary of War under Chester Arthur.

17. Andrew Johnson 1865-69
- Political Party: Republican
- Vice president: none
- State: Tennessee
- Andrew Johnson served as governor of Tennessee.
- He was impeached and tried during his tenure. (won trial by one vote)
- He was the only president to return to the Senate after his presidency.

18. Ulysses Simpson Grant 1869-77 (The Galena Tanner)
- Political party: Republican
- Vice Presidents: Schuyler Colfax (involved in the Credit Mobilier scandal)
  Henry Wilson
- First Lady: Julia (Dent) Grant
- State: Ohio
- Ulysses S. Grant graduated from West Point Military Academy.
- He served under Zachary Taylor in the Mexican-American War.
- He captured Vicksburg and Chattanooga in the Civil War.
- He became commander of the Union Armies toward the end of the Civil War.
- He established Yellowstone National Park as the nation's first national park.

19. Rutherford Birchard Hayes 1877-81
- Political party: Republican
- Vice president: William Wheeler
- First Lady: Lucy Hayes (Lemonade Lucy)
- State: Ohio
- Rutherford Hayes studied law at Harvard.
- He served as governor of Ohio.

20. James Abram Garfield 1881
- Political party: Republican
- Vice president: Chester A. Arthur
- State: Ohio
- James Garfield was shot on July 2, 1881 by Charles Guiteau and died on September 19th after serving 199 days.

42 *Presidents, Vice Presidents and First Ladies*

- His term was the second shortest of any president.
- He was the first left handed president.

21. *Chester Alan Arthur 1881-1885*
- Political party: Republican
- Vice President: none
- State: New York
- Chester Arthur became president upon the assassination of James Garfield.
- He renovated the White House.

22. *Grover Cleveland 1885-89*
- Political party: Democrat
- Vice President: Thomas Hendricks
- First Lady: Francis Folsom Cleveland
- State: New York
- Grover Cleveland served as governor of New York.
- He dedicated the Statue of Liberty, October 28, 1886.
- He was the first president married in the White House.
- He was the only president reelected after losing the presidency.
- His picture is on the $1,000 bill.

23. *Benjamin Harrison 1889-1893*
- Political party: Republican
- Vice president: Levi P. Morton
- First Lady: Caroline (Scott) Harrison
- State: Indiana
- Benjamin Harrison commanded Indiana's 70th Infantry during Civil War.
- He defeated incumbent Grover Cleveland in 1888.
- He was grandson of William Henry Harrison.

24. *Grover Cleveland 1893-97*
- Vice president: Adlai E. Stevenson
- He became the first and only president to serve non-consecutive terms.

25. *William McKinley 1897-1901*
- Political party: Republican
- Vice presidents: Garrett A. Hobart, Theodore Roosevelt
- First Lady: Ida (Saxton) McKinley
- State: Ohio (Canton)
- William McKinley was governor of Ohio.
- He promised a full dinner pail.
- He was assassinated in Buffalo, New York by Leon Czolgosz on Sept 6, 1901.
- His picture is on the $500 bill.

26. Theodore Roosevelt 1901-1909 (The Squire of Sagamore Hill)
- Political party: Republican
- Vice president first term: none
- Vice president second term: Charles W. Fairbanks (Fairbanks, Alaska namesake)
- First Lady: Edith Roosevelt
- State: New York
- Teddy Roosevelt's first wife died in 1884.
- He led the charge up San Juan Hill in the Spanish-American War.
- He became president when McKinley was assassinated.
- He was the youngest president to assume office. (JFK youngest elected)
- He sponsored antitrust legislation.
- He enacted Pure Food and Drug Act in 1906, which established the FDA.
- He was the first president to travel outside the USA during his presidency to dedicate the Panama Canal.
- He mediated an end to the Russo-Japanese War for which he won a Nobel Peace Prize.
- Was shot and wounded in 1912 while running for president as a candidate of the Bull Moose Party.
- His motto was "speak softly and carry a big stick".
- Had a daughter named Alice Blue.
- Teddy Bear was named after him.

27. William Howard Taft 1909-1913
- Political party: Republican
- Vice president: James S. Sherman
- First Lady: Helen (Herron) Taft
- State: Ohio
- William Taft served as civilian governor of the Philippines after the islands were ceded to United States at the end of the Spanish-American War.
- He was the only president to serve as Chief Justice of the Supreme Court.
- He was the heaviest president.
- He was president when the last of the contiguous U.S. states joined the union.
- He is buried in Arlington National Cemetery.

28. Woodrow Wilson 1913-21
- Political party: Democrat
- Vice president: Thomas R. Marshall
- First Lady: Edith (Galt) Wilson
- State: New Jersey
- Woodrow Wilson Graduated from Princeton University.
- He is the only president with a PH.D.
- He served as president of Princeton Univ. and governor of New Jersey.
- He brought the U.S. into WWI.
- He established peace program of 14 points at end of the war.
- He helped establish the League of Nations.
- He is the only president buried in Washington, DC.
- His picture is on the $100,000 bill.

29. Warren Gamaliel Harding 1921-23
- Political party: Republican
- Vice president: Calvin Coolidge
- First Lady: Florence (DeWolfe) Harding
- Warren Harding was president during the Teapot Dome Scandal in which his interior secretary Albert Fall was sent to jail for taking bribes to secure oil leases on federal lands.
- Herbert Hoover was his Secretary of Commerce.
- He died in office of an embolism.

30. John Calvin Coolidge 1923-29 (Silent Cal)
- Political party: Republican
- Vice president first term: none
- Vice president second term: Charles G. Dawes
- First Lady: Grace (Goodhue) Coolidge
- State: Massachusetts
- Calvin Coolidge became president upon the death of Warren Harding.
- Quoted, "The business of America is business".

31. Herbert Hoover 1929-33
- Political party: Republican
- Vice president: Charles Curtis
- First Lady: Lou Hoover
- State: Iowa
- Herbert Hoover had an engineering degree from Stanford University.
- He made his fortune with mining rights in Asia.
- He was in China with wife Lou during the Boxer Rebellion.
- He was Commerce Secretary under Harding and Coolidge.
- He was president during the start of the Great Depression, which ended his political career.

32. Franklin Delano Roosevelt 1933-1945
- Political party: Democrat
- Vice presidents: John Nance Garner, Henry A. Wallace, Harry S Truman
- First Lady: Eleanor (Roosevelt) Roosevelt, a distant cousin to FDR
- State: New York
- Franklin Roosevelt served as governor of New York.
- Was the only president elected four times.
- He had an advisory group called "The Brain Trust."
- He sponsored New Deal program in response to the Great Depression.
- He created the Tennessee Valley Authority.
- He contracted polio in 1921.
- He died in office April 12, 1945 of a cerebral hemorrhage.
- His father was a distant cousin of Theodore Roosevelt.
- He had dog named Fala.

33. Harry S Truman 1945-53
- Political party: Democrat
- Vice president first term: none
- Vice president second term: Alben W. Barkley
- First Lady: Elizabeth (Bess) Truman
- State: Missouri (Independence)
- Harry Truman served as an artillery commander during WWI.
- He became president upon the death of FDR.
- He made the decision to use the atom bomb to end WWII.
- He implemented the Marshall Plan to aid reconstruction of Europe after WWII.
- He sponsored legislative program "Fair Deal".
- He was the last president without a college degree.

34. Dwight David Eisenhower 1953-61
- Political party: Republican
- Vice president: Richard M. Nixon
- First Lady: Mamie (Doud) Eisenhower
- State: Texas
- "Ike" Eisenhower graduated from West Point Military Academy.
- He commanded a tank corp training center during WWI.
- He served as Allied Supreme Commander during WWII.
- He had an affair with his WWII chauffeur Kay Somersby.
- He was president of Columbia University.
- He did not hold public office before becoming president.
- He warned against the "military-industrial complex".
- His Secretary of State was John Foster Dulles.
- He had a home in Gettysburg, PA.
- He was the first president to have a pilot's license.

35. John Fitzgerald (Jack) Kennedy 1961-63
- Political party: Democrat
- Vice president: Lyndon Johnson
- First Lady: Jacqueline (Bouvier) Kennedy
- State: Massachusetts
- John F. Kennedy was the son of Joseph and Rose Kennedy.
- He graduated from Harvard University.
- He won Pulitzer Prize for his book *Profiles in Courage*.
- He served on the "PT-109", which was sunk during WWII.
- His father served as ambassador to Great Britain.
- He was the youngest president ever elected.
- He made "Ich bin ein Berliner" speech in West Berlin.
- He established the Peace Corps.
- He considered the failed Bay of Pigs invasion his worst personal embarrassment.
- He was president during the Cuban Missile Crisis.
- He laid the ground work for the manned moon missions.
- His brother Robert Kennedy was his Attorney General.

42 *Presidents, Vice Presidents and First Ladies*

- He was assassinated November 22, 1963 in Dallas, Texas by Lee Harvey Oswald.
- He is buried in Arlington National Cemetery .
- He had a home in Hyannisport, MA.

36. *Lyndon Baines Johnson 1963-69*
- Political party: Democrat
- Vice president first term: none
- Vice president second term: Hubert H. Humphrey
- First Lady: Lady Bird (Claudia Taylor) Johnson
- State: Texas (The Elms)
- Lyndon Johnson became president upon the death of JFK.
- He launched the "Great Society" program to raise living standards.
- He expanded the war in Vietnam.

37. *Richard Milhous Nixon 1969-74*
- Political party: Republican
- Vice presidents: Spiro Agnew (resigned), Gerald R. Ford (first VP named under the 25th amendment)
- First Lady: Pat Nixon
- State: California
- Richard Nixon served as a supply officer during WWII.
- He served as two term VP under Dwight Eisenhower.
- He had "Kitchen Debate" with Nikita Khrushchev.
- He was defeated by JFK in 1960 presidential election.
- He ordered gradual removal of U.S. troops during Vietnam War.
- He opened relations with communist China.
- He resigned presidency in 1974 due to Watergate Scandal.
- He was pardoned for "all offenses against the U.S." by Gerald Ford.
- He had a dog named Checkers.
- He had a home in Casa Pacifica, CA.

38. *Gerald R. Ford 1974-77*
- Political party: Republican
- Vice president: Nelson Rockefeller
- First Lady: Betty Ford
- State: Michigan
- Gerald Ford was born Leslie Lynch King, Jr.
- He played football at University of Michigan.
- He served on the commission investigating the assassination of JFK.
- He survived two assassination attempts by Lynette "Squeaky" Fromme and Sara Jane Moore.
- He was the only VP and president not to be elected by vote.

39. *Jimmy (James Earl) Carter 1977-81*
- Political party: Democrat
- Vice president: Walter F. Mondale

- First Lady: Rosalyn (Smith) Carter
- State: Georgia (Plains)
- Jimmy Carter graduated from the U.S. Naval Academy.
- He worked as a peanut farmer before his public life.
- He served as governor of Georgia.
- He signed Panama Canal Treaty and Salt II Treaty.
- He boycotted 1980 Summer Olympics due to USSR invasion of Afghanistan.
- He provided framework for Egyptian-Israeli peace treaty.
- He served during Iran hostage crisis.

40. *Ronald Wilson Reagan 1981-89 (The Great Communicator, Dutch)*
- Political party: Republican
- Vice president: George Bush
- First Lady: Nancy (Davis) Reagan
- State: California
- Ronald Reagan graduated from Eureka College in Illinois.
- He appeared in approximately 50 motion pictures.
- He served as president of the Screen Actors Guild.
- He served two terms as governor of California.
- He survived an assassination attempt by John Hinkley Jr.
- He initiated the Strategic Defense Initiative (SDI or Star Wars).
- He was the oldest president elected and the oldest to serve.
- He was the only divorced president.

41. *George Herbert Walker Bush 1989-93*
- Political party: Republican
- Vice president: Dan Quayle
- First Lady Barbara Bush (The Silver Fox)
- State: Texas
- George Bush was shot down as a fighter pilot in WWII.
- He served as director of CIA.
- He served as U.S. ambassador to the United Nations.
- He served two terms as VP under Ronald Reagan.
- He coordinated United Nations effort to win the Persian Gulf War.
- He has vacation home in Kennebunkport, Maine.
- His sons, George W. Bush and Jeb Bush, served as Governors of Texas and Florida respecitively.

42. *William Jefferson Clinton 1993-2001*
- Political party: Democrat
- Vice president: Al Gore
- First Lady: Hillary Rodham Clinton
- State: Arkansas
- Bill Clinton had an affair with White House intern Monica Lewinsky.
- He was impeached and acquitted during his second term.

43. George Walker Bush 2001-
Political party: Republican
Vice president: Richard Cheney
First Lady: Laura Bush
State: Texas
George W. Bush became the fourth president in U.S. history to lose the popular vote and still win the election.*
He is the second son of a president to become president.

Important Presidential facts:

President to serve the longest .... Franklin Roosevelt

President with shortest term .... William Harrison (32 days)

The shortest president .... James Madison

The tallest president .... Abraham Lincoln

The heaviest president .... William Howard Taft

First president born in a log cabin .... Andrew Jackson

First president born in the United States .... Martin van Buren

Last president born a British subject .... William H. Harrison

First president born in the 20th century .... John F. Kennedy

First president born west of the Mississippi River .... Herbert Hoover

First president born in a hospital .... Jimmy Carter

First left handed president .... James Garfield

Only president to hold a patent .... Abraham Lincoln

Only adopted president .... Gerald Ford

Only divorced president .... Ronald Reagan

Only president never married .... James Buchanan

Only president to return to the House after presidency .... John Quincy Adams

Only president to return to the Senate after presidency .... Andrew Johnson

First president sworn in office in the White House .... Thomas Jefferson

First president married in the White House .... Grover Cleveland

Last Whig president .... Millard Fillmore

"Trustbuster" president .... Theodore Roosevelt

President who served in Thomas Jefferson's cabinet .... James Monroe

President assassinated in Buffalo, NY .... William McKinley

He promised "a chicken in every pot" .... Herbert Hoover

* Others: J.Q. Adams v. Jackson, 1824, Hayes v. Tildon, 1876, Cleveland v. B. Harrison, 1888

He promised "a full dinner pail" .... William McKinley

The centennial president .... Ulysses S. Grant

The bicentennial president .... Gerald Ford

He was sworn into office at Love Field, Texas .... Lyndon Johnson

The only split term president .... Grover Cleveland

Iowa president .... Herbert Hoover

Illinois president .... Abraham Lincoln (born in Kentucky)

Missouri president .... Harry Truman

New Hampshire president .... Franklin Pierce

New Jersey president .... Woodrow Wilson

Georgia president .... Jimmy Carter

His middle initial S stood for nothing .... Harry Truman

President who won popular vote in 1888, but lost election

.... Grover Cleveland

President known for his 14 points .... Woodrow Wilson

The only president to be Secretary of Commerce .... Herbert Hoover

"Baby Ruth" was his daughter .... Grover Cleveland

"Alice Blue" was his daughter .... Theodore Roosevelt

The First Dark Horse .... James Polk

The Beast of Buffalo .... Grover Cleveland

The Duke of Braintree .... John Adams

The Schoolmaster in Politics .... Woodrow Wilson

The Sage of Montpelier .... James Madison

The Squire of Sagamore Hill .... Theodore Roosevelt

"Silent" president.. Calvin Coolidge

He wrote the Bill of Rights .... James Madison

President with an engineering degree from Stanford .... Herbert Hoover

President who survived two assassination attempts in one month

.... Gerald Ford

Presidents who never held public office before their presidency

.... George Washington, U.S. Grant, Dwight Eisenhower

President who lived in Blair House during White House renovation

.... Harry Truman

President who withdrew all funds from the Bank of the U.S.

.... Andrew Jackson

First Three Star General of the Army .... U. S. Grant

Jimmy Carter made him the only Six Star General .... George Washington

His initials F. P. can also stand for fourteenth president .... Franklin Pierce

Harriet Lane was his niece and hostess .... James Buchanan

President elected by the largest electoral margin .... Ronald Reagan (1984)

Only president to graduate from the U.S. Naval Academy

.... Jimmy Carter

Two presidents to graduate from West Point .... Grant, Eisenhower

Two presidents to sign The Declaration of Independence

.... J. Adams, Jefferson

Two presidents to sign the Constitution .... Washington, Madison

Two Whigs who died in office .... Taylor, W. H. Harrison

Two presidents who were in service during WWI .... Truman, Eisenhower

Two presidents who were not married when elected .... Buchanan, Cleveland

Two presidents buried at Arlington National Cemetery ... Taft, Kennedy

Two presidents from Braintree, MA .... J. Adams. J.Q. Adams

Two presidents to serve less than one year .... W. H. Harrison, Garfield

Four presidents for which state capitals were named .... Jackson, Lincoln, Jefferson, Madison

Five presidents not elected to office .... Tyler, Fillmore, A. Johnson, Arthur, Ford

State with the most presidents .... Virginia (8)

State with second most presidents .... Ohio (7)

Date presidents were inaugurated before the 20th amendment

.... March 4

Event that precipitated installation of the "hot line" to Moscow

.... The Cuban Missile Crisis

Vice Presidents:

First vice president not to be president .... Aaron Burr

First vice president to resign .... John C. Calhoun

Greek vice president who also resigned .... Spiro Agnew

Youngest vice president, South Civil War general .... John C. Breckenridge

Oldest vice president .... Alben Barkley

First two term vice president .... John Adams

Lincoln's first vice president .... Hannibal Hamlin

First vice president under the 25th amendment .... Gerald Ford

First vice president to serve under two presidents .... George Clinton

First vice president to rise to presidency upon the death of a president
.... John Tyler

Vice president involved in Credit Mobilier scandal .... Schuyler Colfax

Texas city named for a vice president .... Dallas

Alaska city named for a vice president .... Fairbanks

Vice president who won Nobel Peace Prize .... Charles Dawes

Vice presidents from Minnesota .... H. Humphrey, W. Mondale

State with most vice presidents .... New York (8)

Number of vice presidents to become president .... Fourteen

Vice presidents home .... Blair House

Vice president's official song .... Hail Columbia

First Ladies:

She had a degree in geology .... Lou Hoover

"Lemonade Lucy" banned alcohol in the White House .... Lucy Hayes

She also banned alcohol in the White House .... Sara Polk

She danced for Martha Graham .... Betty Ford

Val-kill was her retreat .... Eleanor Roosevelt

She graduated from University of Texas .... Lady Bird Johnson

Noted hostess of the early 19th century .... Dolley Madison

Bouvier was her maiden name .... Jackie Kennedy

Her maiden name was Thelma Patricia Ryan .... Pat Nixon

19th century first lady who spoke French fluently .... Mary Todd Lincoln

The Steel Magnolia .... Rosalyn Carter

The Silver Fox .... Barbara Bush

She has a law degree from Yale University .... Hillary Rodham Clinton

(only First Lady to hold public office)

43 *Religion*

Buddhism: Religion of four noble truths; 256 million believers

The Enlightened One	Buddha (Prince Siddhartha Gautama)
Head of Tibetan Buddhists	(14th) Dalai Lama
State of peaceful blessedness	Nirvana
Buddha's teachings, universal truth	Dharma
Branches of Buddhism	Tharavada, Mahayana and Gautama
Tantric form of Buddhism	Mantra
Ancient Cambodian temple	Angkor Wat

Christianity: 1.2 billion believers

Main divisions:

Roman Catholic:	806 million believers
Protestant:	343 million believers
Eastern Orthodox:	79 million believers

Bible versions:

Standard Latin Bible	Vulgate
First mass-produced Bible	Gutenberg Bible

Bible translation authorized by English monarch
.... King James Bible

"Isa Ibn Mary am"	Jesus
Holiday forty days before Easter	Ash Wednesday
Christmas story	Passion Play
Founder of the Quakers	George Fox
Founder of Methodism	John Wesley
Founder of the Shakers	Mother Ann Lee
Founder of Christian Science	Mary Baker Eddy
Founder of the Amish	Jacob Amman
Founder of the Jehovah's Witnesses	Charles Taze Russell
Founder of the Mormon Church	Joseph Smith

Mormon leader who led followers to Salt Lake City
.... Brigham Young (had 22 wives, 57 children)

Mormon prophet	Moroni
Mormon city in Illinois	Nauvoo
Protestant Reformation founder	Martin Luther
Number of Luther's theses	95
Swiss-French reformist	John Calvin
John Calvin's followers	Presbyterians
Scottish reformist	John Knox
Largest protestant sect	Lutheran (60 million)
French Protestants	Huguenots
Betsy Ross' religion	Quaker

Conservative Mennonite group from Pennsylvania
.... Amish

Preachers who traveled the old west .... Circuit riders (mostly Methodist)
Molokai priest .... Father Damian (died of leprosy)
Archbishop of Cyprus .... Archbishop Makarios
Apostle of California .... Junipero Serra
Archbishop of New York, 1939 .... Archbishop Spellman
Last anti-pope .... Felix V
Papal residence .... Castel Gandolfo
Vatican guard .... Swiss Guard
Home for nuns .... Convent
Site where the Virgin Mary was seen in 1917
.... Fatima, Portugal
Site where the Virgin Mary was seen in 1531
.... Guadeloupe, Mexico
1378 split of the Catholic church .... The Great Schism
Catholic order of friars with pointed hoods
.... Capuchin
First pope .... Peter
Recent Popes:
1922-39 .... Pius XI
1939-58 .... Pius XII
1958-63 .... John XXIII
1963-78 .... Paul VI
1978 .... John-Paul I ("The Smiling Pope")
1978- .... John-Paul II (264th successor to Peter)
Confucianism: 175 millions believers
Founder .... Confucius
Principal country .... China
Hare Krishna:
Spiritual leader .... Swami
Principal country .... India
Hinduism: The Eternal Law; 500 million believers
Trimurti of Gods: .... Brahma (The Preserver)
.... Shiva (The Destroyer)
.... Vishnu (The Creator)
Avatar of Vishnu .... Krishna
Hindu text .... Vedas ("knowledge")
Hindu universal spirit .... Brahman
Sacred rivers .... Ganges and five others
Two letter chant .... "Om"
Great epic .... Rada
Ancient scriptures: .... Badas
Islam: One billion believers
Founder .... Mohammed (570-632 A.D.)
Major sects .... Sunni (largest), Shiite
Holy book .... Koran
Highest office .... Caliphate

43 *Religion*

House of worship .... Mosque
Prayer tower .... Minaret
Holy cities .... Mecca, Medina, Jerusalem
Holy pilgrimage to Mecca .... Hajj
Number of pillars of Islam .... Five
Holy house in Mecca .... Kabaa
Kabaa center piece .... Black Stone
Month of fasting .... Ramadan
Holy war .... Jihad
Movement founded by Wali Fard, 1934
.... Nation of Islam

Jainism: 4.3 million believers
Principal country .... India

Judaism: 17 million believers
Founder .... Abraham
Holy city .... Jerusalem
Feast of lights or feast of dedication .... Hannukah
New year; day of judgement .... Rosh Hashana
Day of atonement .... Yom Kippur
Passover feast .... Seder
Jewish mourners prayer .... Caddish
Coming of age rite .... Bar Mitzvah (male); Bat Mitzvah (female)
Wedding rite .... Breaking of the glass
Mountain fortress .... Masada
Jewish population outside Israel .... Diaspora
Candelabra .... Menorah
Door post .... Mazuzah
Scull cap .... Yarmulke

Rastafarianism:
Principal country .... Jamaica

Shintoism: Contains principles of Confucianism and Buddhism
Principal country .... Japan

Sikhism: Monotheist religion of the Punjab region of India
Founders .... Kabir and Nanak

Taoism: Chinese philosophical and religious system
Founder .... Lao-Tse (c. 400 B.C.)
Chief God .... Jade Emperor

Unification Church:
Founder .... Sun Myung Moon
Principal countries .... South Korea and USA

Voodoo:
Principal country .... Haiti

Zoroastrianism: 250,000 believers
Founder .... Zoroaster (c. 600 B.C.)
Principal countries .... India and Iran

Revolutionary War 44

Patriotic group established in 1765 .... Sons of Liberty
Street clash on March 5, 1770 .... Boston Massacre
Lawyer who defended British soldiers of Boston Massacre
.... John Adams
December 17, 1773 raid .... Boston Tea Party
Patriot who captured Fort Ticonderoga .... Ethan Allen
Organization of patriots founded by Ethan Allen .... The Green Mountain Boys
Battle of Monmouth heroine .... Molly Pitcher
Revolution pamphleteer and *Common Sense* author .... Thomas Paine
"The scribe of the revolution" .... Thomas Jefferson
Prussian advisor to George Washington .... Baron von Steuben
Polish general who helped Colonists .... Count Pulaski
Pole who aided in the Battle of Saratoga .... Thaddeus Kosciusko
French aide to George Washington .... Marquis de Lafayette
Colonial officer, father of Robert E. Lee .... Henry (Light Horse Harry) Lee
Federalist Papers (85 essays) author .... Alexander Hamilton
Patriot spy caught and hanged .... Nathan Hale
Colonial ambassador to France .... Benjamin Franklin
Colonists who favored the British .... Tories
General who defected to the British .... Benedict Arnold
Major who defected to the British .... Major John Andre
Virginia lawyer and war advocate .... Patrick Henry
Sea captain who took the war to Britain .... John Paul Jones
South Carolina "Swamp Fox" .... Francis Marion
British-German mercenaries .... Hessians
George Washington's command .... Continental Army
First battle of the war .... Battle of Lexington
Second battle of the war .... Battle of Concord
Battle near Boston, 1775 .... Battle of Bunker Hill
                                                (actually fought on Breed's Hill)
Battle leading to the fall of Philadelphia .... Brandywine
General who captured Montreal in 1777 .... Richard Montgomery
"Mad" Colonial general .... Anthony Wayne
Colonial victory that brought French into the war .... Saratoga
British general who surrendered at Saratoga, 1777 .... John Burgoyne
General who defeated Burgoyne .... Horatio Gates
Battle that decided the war .... Battle of Yorktown, VA
General who surrendered to Washington at Yorktown ..... Charles Cornwallis
Treaty ending the war .... Treaty of Paris

45 *The Roman Empire*

31-476 A.D.

Emperors:

First triumvirate of Rome: Julius Caesar, Crassus and Pompey

Julius Caesar: Assassinated in 44 B.C. only one month after being declared dictator for life.

Anthony and Cleopatra: Defeated by Augustus in 31 B.C. in the Battle of Actium

Augustus Caesar: (Octavian) 27 B.C.-14 A.D.

Tiberius: 14-37 A.D. (Augustus' stepson)

Caligula: 37-41 (rumor says he made his horse a member of government)

Claudius: 41-54 (stammering emperor)

Nero: 54-68 (Claudius' adopted son)

Trajan: 98-117 (column designer)

Hadrian: 117-138 (built namesake wall in Scotland and the Pantheon)

Constantine: 306-337 (built new capital at Constantinople)

Ancient Roman Points of Interest:

Pantheon: Temple built by Hadrian

Temple of Jupiter

Circus Maximus: Used for chariot races

Colosseum, a.k.a. Flavian Amphitheater

Other Facts:

River that Caesar crossed .... Rubicon

Caesar's message to Rome .... "Veni, Vidi, Vici"

(I came, I saw, I conquered)

64 AD event .... Fire in Rome (Nero did not fiddle)

79 AD event .... Mt.Vesuvius eruption

Roman priestesses .... Vestal Virgins

Roman imperial guards .... Praetorian Guards

Praetorian Guard leader .... Prefect

Roman tax collector .... Publican

Noble class of Rome .... Patrician

Roman commoner .... Plebeian

Nero's mother .... Aggrapina

Author of *Aeneid* .... Virgil

Orator, statesman and philosopher .... Cicero

Roman comic playwright .... Plautus

Rebel slave leader .... Spartacus

Judean Military governor, 37-4 B.C. .... Herod (the Great)

Judean Military governor, 26-36 A.D. .... Pontius Pilot

Roman governor of Egypt .... Mohammed Ali

Roman naturalist, wrote of Mt. Vesuvius eruption

.... Pliny the Elder

Roman astronomer .... Ptolemy (published geocentric

observations that would be used for over 1400 years)

Roman inner courtyard .... Atrium

Roman public gathering .... Forum

Roman ruling body .... Senate

Roman road .... Appian Way

Roman-Carthage wars .... Punic Wars

Roman peace .... Pax Romana

Cities Vesuvius buried .... Pompeii and Herculaneum

Wall in Scotland .... Hadrian's Wall

Color of trim on Roman togas .... Purple

Legendary founders of Rome, 753 B.C. .... Romulus and Remus

Roman name for:

France .... Gaul

Ireland .... Hibernia

Wales .... Cambria

Scotland .... Caledonia

The first two Caesars formulated our twelve-month, 365-day calendar (Julian calendar). They added the months of July (Julius) and August (Augustus). That is why September, which means seventh month, is actually the ninth month, October the tenth month and so on.

46 *Royalty*

Current Royalty:

Belgium	Albert II
Denmark	Margarethe II
Japan	Akihito
Jordan	King Abdullah Hussein
Liechtenstein	Prince Hans Adam II
Luxembourg	Grand Duke Henri
Monaco	Prince Rainier
Netherlands	Beatrix
Norway	Harold V
Saudi Arabia	King Faud
Spain	King Juan Carlos
Sweden	Carl XVI Gustaf
Thailand	King Bhumibol
United Kingdom	Elizabeth II

English Royalty:

ROYAL	YEAR	DYNASTY
Egbert	829-39	Saxon
Alfred the Great	871-99	Saxon
Ethelred the Unready	978-1016	Saxon
Harold I	1035-40	Danish
Edward the Confessor	1042-66	Saxon
Harold II	1066	Saxon
William I, the Conqueror	1066-87	Norman
William II	1087-1100	Norman
Henry I	1100-35	Norman
Stephen	1135-54	Norman
Henry II	1154-1189	Plantagenet
Richard I, the Lionhearted	1189-99	Plantagenet
John	1199-1216	Plantagenet
Henry III	1216-72	Plantagenet
Edward I	1272-1307	Plantagenet
Edward II	1307-27	Plantagenet
Edward III	1327-77	Plantagenet
Richard II	1377-99	Plantagenet
Henry IV	1399-1413	Lancaster
Henry V	1413-22	Lancaster
Henry VI	1422-71	Lancaster
Edward IV	1471-83	York
Edward V	1483	York

Richard III	1483-1485	York
Henry VII	1485-1509	Tudor
Henry VIII	1509-1547	Tudor
Edward VI	1547-53	Tudor
Lady Jane Grey	Uncrowned	Tudor
Mary	1553-58	Tudor
Elizabeth I	1558-1603	Tudor
James I	1603-25	Stuart
Charles I	1625-49	Stuart
Charles II	1660-85	Stuart
James II	1685-88	Stuart
William III	1689-1702	Orange
Mary II	1689-1694	Orange
Anne	1702-14	Stuart
George I	1714-27	Hanover
George II	1727-60	Hanover
George III	1760-1820	Hanover
George IV	1820-30	Hanover
William IV	1830-37	Hanover
Victoria	1837	Saxe-Coburg-Gotha
Edward VII	1901-10	Saxe-Coburg-Gotha
George V	1910-36	Windsor
Edward VIII	1936	Windsor
George VI	1936-52	Windsor
Elizabeth II	1952-	Windsor

Spouses of English Royals:
Henry II
.... Eleanor of Aquitaine (mother of Richard the Lionhearted and King John)
Henry VIII
.... Catherine of Aragon (mother of Mary I)
.... Anne Boleyn (mother of Elizabeth I)
.... Jane Seymour (mother of Edward VI)
.... Anne of Cleves
.... Catherine Howard
.... Catherine Parr
Victoria .... Prince Albert (father of Edward VII)
George VI .... Mary, a.k.a. "Queen Mum"
Elizabeth II ...... Prince Philip (Mountbatten)

Heirs to the British Throne:
Charles, Prince of Wales (would be Charles III)
William, Prince of Wales (would be William V)
Henry, Prince of Wales
Prince Andrew, Duke of York

Royalty

Beatrice, Princess of York
Eugeni, Princess of York
Prince Edward, The Earl of Wessex
Princess Anne, The Princess Royal

Scottish Royalty:

ROYAL	YEAR
Malcolm II	1005-34
Duncan	1513
James V	1513-42
Mary, Queen of Scots	1542-67
James VI (James I of England)	1567-1625
Charles I (also of England)	1625-49
Charles II (also of England)	1660-85
James VII (James II of England)	1685-88
William II (William III of England)	1688-1702
Anne (also of England)	1702-14

French Royalty:

ROYAL	YEAR	DYNASTY
Charles Martel	714-741	Carolingian
Pepin III (the Short)	751-768	Carolingian
Charlemagne	768-814	Carolingian
Hugh Capet	987-996	Capetian
Louis IX (St. Louis)	1226-70	Capetian
Charles V (the Wise)	1364-80	Valois
Louis XIII	1610-43	Bourbon
Louis XIV	1643-1715	Bourbon
Louis XV	1715-74	Bourbon
Louis XVI	1774-93	Bourbon
Napoleon I	1804-14	Bonaparte
Louis XVIII	1814-24	Bourbon
Charles X	1824-30	Bourbon
Louis-Philippe	1830-48	Bonaparte
Louis Napoleon	1848-51	Bonaparte
Napoleon III	1852-70	Bonaparte

Facts about royalty:

British monarch who died in 1910	Edward VII
Mother to Elizabeth I	Anne Boleyn
Chakkri family rules here	Thailand
He abdicated the British throne in 1936	Edward VIII
The name of five Hawaiian kings	Kamehameha
Last Hawaiian queen	Liliuokalani
Country with ten kings named Christian	Denmark

He preceded King David of Israel .... King Saul
He was the first Stuart king of England .... James I
Louisiana was named after him .... Louis XIV
The Merry Monarch .... Charles II
He was king of Thebes .... Oedipus
She was the last of the Ptolomy dynasty .... Cleopatra (VII)
King of Egypt when the Suez Canal opened .... King Farouk
"Good" king of Bohemia .... King Wencenslaus
Youngest daughter Nicholas II and Alexandra .... Anastasia
King that "lost" the American colonies .... George III
Prince Andrew's younger brother .... Prince Edward
Constantine VIII's empire, c. 1042 .... Byzantine
Country of Yi dynasty, 1392-1910 .... Korea
Magyar prince of Hungary, c. 997 .... St. Stephen
The House of Orange rules here .... Netherlands
Olav I ruled here .... Norway
State of Georgia is named for him .... George II
Richard the Lionhearted and King John's mother ..... Eleanor of Aquitaine
Captain Mark Phillips was married to her .... Princess Anne
Longest ruling Danish monarch .... Christian IV
Catherine of Aragon's mother .... Isabella (of Aragon)
Marie Antoinette's mother .... Maria Teresa
To quote her, "We are not amused" .... Queen Victoria
Guy Fawkes tried to blow up this king in the gunpowder plot
.... James I
A Grand Duke rules here .... Luxembourg
Malcolm Candor killed this king in 1057 .... Macbeth
Carl XVI Gustav rules here .... Sweden
She is divorced from Lord Snowden .... Princess Margaret
Wilhelmina was her mother and Beatrix is her daughter
.... Juliana
Carol II was king here .... Romania
The last British emperor of India .... George VI
Caroline and Stephanie's younger brother .... Prince Albert
King of the Franks, 500 A.D. .... Clovis I
This prince consort died of typhoid in 1861 .... Prince Albert
The Black Prince .... Prince Edward
Longest ruling French king .... Louis XIV
Longest ruling English monarch .... Victoria
Irish king who defeated the Danish, 1014 .... Brian Baramha
Uncrowned Queen of England .... Lady Jane Grey
Mary, Queen of Scot's son .... James I of England
Byzantine emperor, 527-564 .... Justinian I
Prussian king, 1740-82 .... Frederick II (the Great)
Germany's last kaiser .... Wilhelm II
Henry Brolingbrook a.k.a. .... Henry IV

Mad king who built Neuschwanstein Castle .... Ludwig II
He is married to Princess Sophia of Greece .... King Juan Carlos
Scottish king killed by his own people .... Charles I
Age begun in England, 1901, ending Victorian Age. Edwardian Age
Holy Roman Empire founder .... Otto I
Regina, Saskatchewan is named for her .... Queen Victoria
French king who was canonized .... Louis IX (St. Louis)
Virginia was named for her .... Elizabeth I (Virgin Queen)
King Manual I was from this country .... Portugal
King Alfonzo XIII was from this country .... Spain
Umberto I was from this country .... Italy
Country of Pedro I and Pedro II .... Brazil
He was Europe's longest-reigning monarch when he died in 1993
.... Baudouin I (of Belgium)
England's longest-reigning dynasty .... Plantagenet
The last Stuart queen (granted a patent for the typewriter, 1714)
.... Queen Anne
"The Young Chevalier" .... Charles Edward Stewart
"Country Girl" who became princess of Monaco ..... Princess Grace
English king who won the Battle of Crecy, 1346 ...... Edward III
King Zod's country .... Albania
"The Crusader Queen" .... Eleanor of Aquitaine
"The Citizen King" .... Louis Phillip
She built the Hermitage .... Catherine the Great
King beheaded by is own people, 1793 .... Louis XVI
First king of a united Italy, 1861 .... Victor Emanuel
Last French king, 1870 .... Nopoleon III
The Dutchess of Windsor... Wallace Simpson
Nickname of French King Louis VI .... Louis the Fat
English king made a saint in 1161 .... Edward the Confessor
The Jacobites supported him .... Bonnie Prince Charlie
Florence ruling family .... Medici
Milan ruling family .... Sforza
Robert I ruling house .... Bruce
Austro-Hungarian ruling family .... Habsburg
Prussian ruling family.. Hohenzollern
Queen Beatrix ruling family .... Orange
Queen Elizabeth II ruling family .... Windsor
Portuguese ruling family.. Braganza
King Juan Carlos ruling family .... Bourbon
Monaco ruling family .... Grimaldi

Saints 47

Patron saint of Finland	St. Henry
Patron saint of France	St. Denis
Patron saint of Germany	St. Boniface
Patron saint of Hungary	St. Stephen
Patron saint of Ireland	St. Patrick
Patron saint of Italy	St. Francis of Assisi
Patron saint of Mexico	Our Lady of Guadalupe
Patron saint of Norway	St. Olaf
Patron saint of Poland	St. Stanislaus
Patron saint of England	St. George
Patron saint of Scotland	St. Andrew
Patron saint of Spain	St. James
Patron saint of Sweden	St. Catherine
Patron saint of Wales	St. David
Patron saint of Rome	St. Peter
Patron saint of Lima	St. Rose
Patron saint of Venice	St. Mark
Patron saint of travelers	St. Christopher
Patron saint of children	St. Nicholas
Patron saint of animals	St. Francis
Patron saint of lovers	St Valentine
Patron saint of mountain climbers	St. Bernard
Patron saint of lost causes	St. Jude
Patron saint of fishermen	St. Andrew
Patron saint of the poor	St. Anthony of Padua
Patron saint of carpenters	St. Joseph
Patron saint of students	St. Thomas Aquinas
Patron saint of accountants	St. Matthew
The Lady of Lourdes	St. Bernadette
The Bishop of Hippo	St. Augustine
6th century Irish nun	St. Bridgette
Founder of the Jesuits	St Ignatius of Loyola
Founder of the Friars, he received Jesus' wounds	St. Francis of Assisi
Cyrillic alphabet founder	St. Cyril
Saint beheaded in London, 1535	St. Thomas More
Female saint who followed St. Francis	St. Clair (The Poor Clairs)
First U.S. citizen made a saint	Mother Cabrini
First American-born saint	Mother Seton

48 *Science*

The science of heredity .... Genetics
The science of sound .... Acoustics
The science of light .... Optics
The science of heat and energy transfer .... Thermodynamics
The science of agriculture .... Agronomy
The science of projectiles .... Ballistics
The science of crime prevention and punishment .... Penology
Ancient science of changing metal into other metals .... Alchemy
The study of rocks .... Petrology
The study of man .... Anthropology
The study of fossils .... Paleontology
The study of the past .... Archaeology
Ionic or covalent bonds join these .... Atoms
Atoms of an element with the same number of protons and different number of neutrons
.... Isotope
Negatively charged atomic particle .... Electron
Center of an atom .... Nucleus
Positively charged particle in the nucleus .... Proton
Neutral particle in an atom's nucleus .... Neutron
General term for subatomic particles .... Quarks
Particle or packet of light .... Photon
Electron is this type of particle .... Lepton
Quark that holds nucleus of an atom together .... Gluon
The act of splitting atoms .... Fission
The act of joining atoms together .... Fusion
The three states of matter .... Solid, liquid, gas
The fourth state of matter .... Plasma
Term for the time it takes radioactivity of an element to decrease by 50%
.... Half life
Least amount of material needed for a nuclear reaction .... Critical mass
Scientific name for laughing gas .... Nitrous oxide
LOX .... Liquid oxygen
Bitter almond smelling gas .... (Hydrogen) cyanide
NH_3 .... Ammonia
CO .... Carbon monoxide
CO_2 .... Carbon dioxide
H_2SO_4 .... Sulfuric acid
HCl, found in the human stomach .... Hydrochloric acid
NACL .... Salt
Tri-atomic oxygen.. Ozone (O_3)
Solid carbon dioxide .... Dry ice
Force applied to a body to maintain a circular orbit .... Centripetal force

Equal and opposite force of centripetal force .... Centrifugal force
The four forces of nature .... Electromagnetic force
.... Weak nuclear force
.... Strong nuclear force
.... Gravity
Theory that seeks to unite the four forces of nature .... Unified field theory
Acid made from oak bark .... Tannic acid
Acidic level "factor" .... ph factor
It turns red in acid and blue in alkaline .... Litmus paper
Citric acid "cycle" .... Krebs cycle
-273.16° Centigrade, -459.69° Fahrenheit or 0° Kelvin ... Absolute zero
Fahrenheit heat unit .... BTU
Celsius heat unit .... Calorie
Broadest measure of living things .... Kingdom
Poikilothermic animal .... Cold blooded
Mutually beneficial relationship between two animals ...... Symbiosis
What oviparous animals do .... Lay eggs
Organisms that combine algae and fungi .... Lichens
Amoeba-like single celled organisms .... Protozoans
Fossilized resin from prehistoric pines .... Amber
The period between ice ages .... Interglacial
Hygrometer measures this .... (Relative) humidity
Wind velocity scale .... Beaufort Scale
Term for wind speed above 72 miles per hour .... Hurricane
Atmospheric layer 7 to 30 miles up .... Stratosphere
Clouds formed by convection .... Cumulus
Rainy thunder head cloud type .... Cumulo-nimbus
Clouds composed of ice crystals .... Cirrus
Low-lying clouds .... Stratus
Fast tropospheric winds .... Jet stream
Lakes at high altitude .... Seamount
Term for water circling around a drain .... Corolis effect
The first plastic developed .... Celluloid
3-D imaging process .... Holography
Term for a mineral that glows under an ultra-violet light
.... Fluorescence
Wavelength just longer than visible light .... Infrared
Wavelength just shorter than visible light .... Ultraviolet
Term for the "skin" that develops on surface of water .... Surface tension
Geologic epoch when man developed .... Pleistocene
The solar wind colliding with Earth's magnetic field creates this effect
.... Northern and southern lights
Scientific name for northern lights .... Aurora Borealis
Scientific name for southern lights .... Aurora Australis
Lowest ignition point of a vapor .... Flash point
Hydrogen isotope with atomic weight of two .... Deuterium

Hydrogen isotope with atomic weight of three .... Tritium
Materials made from two or more metals .... Alloys
Copper and zinc alloy .... Brass
Copper and tin alloy .... Bronze
Copper and silver alloy .... Sterling silver
Silver and tin alloy .... Pewter

Scientists:

Father of atom bomb (Manhattan Project) .... Robert Oppenheimer
Father of hydrogen bomb .... Edward Teller
Father of nuclear navy or nuclear submarine .... Hyram Rickover
English father of modern chemistry .... Robert Boyle
French father of modern chemistry .... Antoin Lavoissier
Father of Soviet hydrogen bomb .... Andrei Sakharov
Father of rocketry .... Robert Goddard
Saturn Five rocket developer .... Werner von Braun
Astronomer with metal nose .... Tycho Brahe
Second English Astronomer Royal .... Sir Edmund Halley
Astronomer who proposed heliocentric solar system .... Copernicus
Scientist who proved yellow fever was caused by mosquitos
.... Walter Reed
Monk who discovered the principals of genetics .... Gregor Mendel
Russian who developed theory of conditioned reflex .... Ivan Pavlov
Scientist who discovered electromagnetic waves .... Heinrich Hertz
Scientist who discovered the structure of the atom .... Neils Bohr
Scientist who established the Periodic Table of Elements
.... Dimitri Mendeleyev
English scientist who discovered the properties of hydrogen
.... Henry Cavendish
English scientist who discovered sodium and potassium .. Sir Humphry Davy
Italian physicist who discovered radioactive elements .... Enrico Fermi
French scientist of optics and geometry .... René Descartes
German scientist who established quantum theory of radiation
.... Max Plank
Scientist who first learned of fermentation .... Louis Pasteur
Scientist who proposed theory of expanding universe ...... Edwin Hubble

Elements:

Lightest element .... Hydrogen (H)
Second-lightest element .... Helium (He)
Heaviest non-man made element.................................... Uranium (U)
Earth's most abundant element .... Oxygen (O)
Earth's second-most abundant element .... Silicon (Si)
Atmosphere's most abundant element........................... Nitrogen (N)
Lightest metal .... Lithium (Li)
Second-lightest metal... Potassium (K)
Lightest common metal .... Magnesium (Mg)
Earth's most abundant metal... Aluminum (Al)

Blue metal .... Cobalt (Co)
Light metal used in fighter aircraft .... Titanium (Ti)
Metal which is liquid at room temperature .... Mercury (Hg)
Grey filament metal with highest melting temperature . Tungsten (W)
Element found in seaweed .... Iodine (I)
Nevada state metal, best electrical conductor .... Silver (Ag)
Most malleable and ductile metal .... Gold (Au)
Graphite element .... Carbon (Co)
Element banned from aerosol .... Freon (Fr)
Element found in bones .... Calcium (Ca)
Element used in flourescent lights .... Neon (Ne)
Element used to galvanize steel .... Zinc (Zn)
Element used in car batteries .... Lead (Pb)
Elements used in rechargeable batteries .... Nickel (Ni), Cadmium (Cd)
"Color" element .... Chromium (Cr)
Last element in alphabetical order .... Zirconium (Zr)
Superman's home planet .... Krypton (Kr)

Other common elements and symbols:

Am .... Americium (named for America)
Ar .... Argon
As .... Arsenic
B .... Boron
Bi .... Bismuth
Cl .... Chlorine
Cm .... Curium (named for Marie and Pierre Curie)
Es .... Einsteinium (named for Albert Einstein)
F .... Fluorine
Fe .... Iron
Fm .... Fermium (named after Enrico Fermi)
Fr .... Francium
Ga .... Gallium
Ge .... Germanium (used in transistors)
Ho .... Holmium (named for Stockholm)
Mn .... Manganese
Na .... Sodium (part of the NaCl in salt)
No .... Nobelium (named for Alfred Nobel)
P .... Phosphorus
Po .... Polonium (named for Poland)
Pt .... Platinum
Pu .... Plutonium
Ra .... Radium
Rn .... Radon
S .... Sulfur (found in gunpowder)
Sb .... Antimony
Se .... Selenium
Xe .... Xenon

49 *The Seven Wonders of the World*

(Listed Chronologically)

1. The Great Pyramid of Giza:
The tomb of Egyptian Pharaoh Khufu. It's the oldest of the seven wonders and the only one still standing

2. The Hanging Gardens of Babylon:
A palace along the banks of the Euphrates River built by King Nebuchadnezzar II

3. The Statue of Zeus at Olympia:
An enormous statue carved by Pheidias

4. The Temple of Artemis at Ephesus:
A beautiful temple in Asia Minor

5. The Mausoleum at Halicarnassus:
A tomb constructed for Persian King Maussollos

6. The Colossus of Rhodes:
A huge statue of the sun god Helios that overlooked a harbor on the island of Rhodes

7. The Lighthouse (Pharaohs) at Alexandria:
Built by the Ptolomies

Shakespeare 50

All's Well That Ends Well
    Characters:
        Bertram, Count of Rousillon
        Helena
        The King of France
    Setting: Florence

Antony and Cleopatra
    Characters:
        Mark Antony (commits suicide)
        Cleopatra (commits suicide with the bite of an asp)
        Octavius
    Setting: Egypt
    Quote: *"I am dying Egypt, dying."* (Mark Antony)

As You Like It
    Characters:
        Oliver
        Orlando
        Rosalind
        Duke Federick
        Jaques the jester
    Setting: The Forest of Arden
    Quote: *"All the world's a stage, all the men and women merely players."* (Jaques)

Comedy of Errors
    Characters:
        Aegeon
        Anipholus (twins with the same name)
        Dromio (two servants with the same name)

Hamlet (Shakespeare's longest play)
    Characters:
        Hamlet, Prince of Denmark
        Gertrude (Hamlet's mother, poisoned with drink meant for Hamlet)
        King Claudius (Hamlet's uncle, kills Hamlet's father, killed by Hamlet)
        Horatio (Hamlet's friend)
        Polonius (killed by Hamlet)
        Laertes (Polonius' son, stabbed by Hamlet)
        Ophelia (Polonius' daughter, goes mad and drowns in a river)
        Rosencrantz and Guildenstern
    Setting: Denmark
    Castle: Elsinore
    Hamlet's dead friend, dug up by the gravedigger: Yorick

50   *Shakespeare*

Quotes:
  "Something is rotten in the state of Denmark" (Marcellus)
  "To be, or not to be: that is the question" (Hamlet)
  "To sleep, perchance to dream" (Hamlet)
  "Alas poor Yorick, I knew him well" (Hamlet)
  "Neither a borrower nor a lender be" (Polonius)
  "Brevity is the soul of wit" (Polonius)

Henry V
  Characters:
    King Henry V (wins the Battle of Agincourt)
    The Dauphin of France
    Princess Katherine of France (courted by Henry)

Henry VIII (the last play performed in the Globe Theater)
  Characters:
    Henry VIII
    Katherine of Aragon (divorced by Henry)
    Anne Boleyn
    Cardinal Wolsey
    Archbishop Thomas Cranmer

Julius Caesar
  Characters:
    Julius Caesar
    Brutus and Cassius (they kill Julius Caesar and commit suicide in the end)
    Mark Antony
    Octavius (Caesar's nephew)
  Quotes:
    "Beware the Ides of March" (Soothsayer)
    "A coward dies many deaths, a brave man but once" (Caesar)
    "I have come to bury Caesar, not to praise him" (Mark Antony)
    "Cry havoc and let slip the dogs of war!" (Mark Antony)
    "This was the most unkindest cut of all." (Mark Antony)

King Lear
  Characters:
    King Lear, king of ancient Britain
    Goneril, Regan and Cordelia (King Lear's daughters)
    Quote: *"Sharper than a serpent's tooth it is to have a thankless child"* (King Lear)

Love's Lobours Lost
  Characters:
    Ferdinand, the king of Navarre
    The princess of France

Macbeth ("The Scottish Play")
  Characters:
    Macbeth, The Thane of Glamis

Lady Macbeth
King Duncan (killed by Macbeth)
Macduff (kills Macbeth in battle)
Malcolm (becomes king upon the death of Macbeth)
The three witches
Setting: Scotland
Castle: Dunsinane
Quotes:
"Double, double toil and trouble, fire burn and cauldron bubble" (Witches)
"Out, damned spot! Out, I say!" (Lady Macbeth)

The Merchant of Venice
Characters:
Antonio (the merchant of Venice, borrows money from Shylock)
Shylock (the moneylender)
Portia
Quotes:
"If you prick us, do we not bleed" (Shylock)
"The quality of mercy is not strained" (Portia)

The Merry Wives of Windsor
Character: Falstaff (he appears in three of Shakespeare's plays)

A Midsummer Night's Dream
Characters:
Theseus, the Duke of Athens
Hippolyta (Queen of the Amazons)
Oberon (King of the faireis)
Titania (Oberon's wife)
Puck (the fairy)
Setting: Athens
Quote: *"Lord, what fools these mortals be"* (Puck)

Othello
Characters:
Othello the Moor
Desdemona (Othello's wife)
Iago and Cassio (Othello's lieutenants)
Setting: Cyprus and Venice
Quotes:
"Beware of jealousy, it is a green-eyed monster" (Othello)
"Then you must speak of one that loved not wisely, but too well" (Othello)

Richard III
Characters:
Richard III (of the House of York)
King Edward IV (of the House of Lancaster)
Edward and Richard (King Edward's sons)
Setting: 15th century England

50 *Shakespeare*

Battle: The Battle of Bosworth Field
Quotes:
  "Now is the winter of our discontent" (Richard III)
  "A horse, a horse, my kingdom for a horse! (Richard III)

Romeo and Juliet
Characters:
  Romeo, of the House of Montague
  Juliet, of the House of Capulet
  Tybalt (Juliet's nephew, killed by Romeo)
Setting: Verona
Quotes:
  "That which we call a rose by any other name would smell as sweet" (Juliet)
  "But soft, what light through yonder window breaks. It is the East and Juliet is the sun"
  (Romeo)

The Taming of the Shrew (basis for the musical *Kiss Me Kate*)
Characters:
  Katherina and Bianca (sisters)
  Petruchio

The Tempest (Shakespeare's last play)
Characters:
  Prospero, former Duke of Milan
  Miranda (Prospero's daughter)
  Antonio
  Ariel the sprite
  Caliban (a deformed slave)
Quotes:
  "We are such stuff as dreams are make of." (Prospero)
  "O brave new world that has such people in it!" (Aldous Huxley used this quote for the
title of his book *Brave New World*)

Titus Andronicus
Setting: Ancient Rome

Troilus and Cressida
Characters:
  Troilus and Cressida
  Aeneas and Hector (Troilus' brothers)
Setting: Ancient Troy

Twelfth Night (As You Will)
Characters:
  Duke Orsino
  Countess Olivia
Quote: *"If music be the food of love, play on"* (Duke Orsino)

Two Gentlemen of Verona
    Characters:
        Valentine and Proteus (the two gentlemen)
        Silvia and Julia (their girlfriends)

The Winter's Tale
    Setting: Sicaly

Other Facts:

William Shakespeare's wife .... Ann Hathaway

Shakespeare's nickname .... The Bard of Avon

Kind Lears daughter's .... Regan, Cordelia, Goneril

The Scottish play .... Macbeth

Fictional Black Moor .... Othello

Twelfth Night's other name .... *As You Will*

Play set on a ship wrecked island .... *The Tempest*

The Tempest sprite .... Ariel

A Midsummer Night's Dream sprite .... Puck

Mistress in *Henry IV, V,* and *The Merry Wives of Windsor*

.... Quickly

Shakespeare's longest play .... Hamlet

Hamlet kills this king .... Claudius

Macbeth kills this king .... Duncan

He kills Macbeth .... Macduff

He kills Tybalt .... Romeo

Early actor in many Shakespeare films .... Laurence Olivier

Recent actor in many Shakespeare films .... Kenneth Branagh

Italian director of many Shakespeare films .... Franco Zeffirelli

Early London Shakespearean theater .... The Globe

Shakespearean actor who built The Globe .... Richard Burbage

51 *Ships*

Ship of:

Charles Darwin	*Beagle*
Sir Francis Drake	*The Golden Hind*
Pilgrims	*Mayflower*
Henry Hudson (crew mutinied)	*Half Moon*
Captain Bligh	*The Bounty*
Admiral Horatio Nelson	*Victory*
John Paul Jones	*Bonhomme Richard*
Christopher Columbus (flagship)	*Santa Maria*
Captain Cook	*Discovery*
Captain Ahab (fictional)	*Pequod*
Captain Nemo's submarine (fictional)	*Nautilus*
Roald Amundsen	*Fram*
Thor Heyerdahl's raft	*Kon-Tiki*
Oliver Hazard Peary	*Lawrence*
Robert Fulton	*Clermont*
Jacques Yves Cousteau	*Calypso*
	(sung about by John Denver)

Other facts:

Monitor's ironclad adversary	*Merrimack*
Merrimack's southern name	*Virginia*
USS Constitution	"Old Ironsides"
"Small vessel" sailing ship	Caravel
Fastest sailing ship	Clipper ship
Clipper ship that set New York to San Francisco record, 1851	*Flying Cloud*
Clipper ship of fame	*Cutty Sark*
One-masted ship	Sloop
Ship with one mast and a single jib	Schooner

Four-masted ship .... Barquentine (Barque)

Ships that sailed to Jamestown, 1607 .... *Susan Constant, Discovery,*
Godspeed

Ghost ship destined to sail the seas forever .... *Flying Dutchman*

Ship of the 1839 slave mutiny .... *Amistad*

First steam powered ship to cross the Atlantic .... *Savannah*

Ship that sank on April 14, 1912 .... *Titanic*

Ship that came to the Titanic's rescue .... *Carpathia*

Ship that sank on May 7, 1915 .... *Lusitania*

Ship that sank in 1956 collision with *Stockholm* .. *Andrea Doria*

"Ghost ship" found abandoned in 1872 .... *Marie Celeste*

Ship sunk in Havana harbor, 1898 .... *Maine*

Titanic's sister ships .... *Brittanic, Olympic*

Lusitania's sister ship .... *Mauritania*

Russian ship where crew mutinied .... *Potempkin*

German pocket battleship scuttled in Montevideo in 1939
.... *Graf Spee*

Ill-fated German battleship .... *Bismarck*

Ship hijacked by North Korea .... *Pueblo*

Ship hijacked by Cambodia .... *Mayaguez*

First nuclear-powered submarine .... *Nautilus*

Freighter that sank in Lake Superior, 1975 .... *Edmond Fitzgerald*

Liner hijacked by Palestinians, 1985 .... *Achille Lauro*

Greenpeace research vessel, sank in 1985 .... *Rainbow Warrior*

Dennis Conner's America's Cup yacht, 1987 .... *Stars and Stripes*

Alaskan oil spill ship, 1989 .... *Exxon Valdez*

Only liner currently making Atlantic crossing .... *Queen Elizabeth II (QE2)*

John F. Kennedy's PT-boat *PT-109*

Lieutenant Commander McHale's PT-boat *PT-73*

52 Sickness and Health

Twenty-four hour human biological rhythm .... Circadian rhythm

Common name for pertussis .... Whooping cough

Common name for neoplasm .... Tumor

Common name for consumption .... Tuberculosis

Common name for rubella .... German Measles

Common baby disease .... Colic

Common name for myopia .... Near sightedness

Common name for conjunctivitis .... Pink eye

Common name for Daltonism .... Color blindness

Common name for alopecia .... Baldness

Common name for amyotrophic lateral sclerosis .... Lou Gehrig's Disease

Hyperactive child disorder .... Attention deficit hyperactive disorder

Damaged brain stem disease .... Polio

Disease of hardening of the artery walls .... Arteriosclerosis

Inflamation, pain, and swelling of the joints .... Arthritis

Memory loss associated with the elderly .... Alzheimer's disease

Disease that destroys myelin sheaths in nerve fibers .... Multiple sclerosis

Bacterial disease causing abdominal pain and dehydration
.... Cholera

Diver's condition of nitrogen bubbles in the blood .... Bends

Chronic respiratory disease that includes spasms .... Asthma

Scar tissue of the liver caused by alcoholime .... Cirrhosis

Reduced bone mass disease .... Osteoporosis

Iron or hemoglobin deficiency .... Anemia

Hereditary bleeding disease .... Hemophilia

Low blood pressure .... Hypotension

High blood pressure .... Hypertension

Low blood sugar .... Hypoglycemia

When body temperature drops below 95 degrees .... Hypothermia

Sudden sleep attacks .... Narcolepsy

Anxiety about health .... Hypochondria

"Splitting of the mind" phenomenon .... Schizophrenia

Hansen's or Father Damian's Disease .... Leprosy

Insulin deficiency disorder... Diabetes

Enlargement of the thyroid gland by iodine deficiency .... Goiter

Disorder resulting in weakness of the facial muscles .... Bell's palsy

Septal defect .... Hole in the heart

Plague that spread across 14th century Europe .... Bubonic plague or Black Death

Mary Mallon's disease (1904-15) .... Typhoid

"Kissing disease" .... Mononucleosis

Mononucleosis germ .... Epstein-Barr

Scarlet fever germ .... Streptococci

Virus that appeared in Zaire in 1995 .... Ebola

Mutation bacteria that causes paralyzing cramps .... E. coli

Common virus that causes colds .... Rhino virus

Paralyzing food poisoning caused by a toxin .... Botulism

Food poisoning that effects gastrointestinal tract.............. Salmonella

Blockage of an artery by a bubble or blood clot .... Embolism

Bulge in an artery wall... Aneurysm

When the spinal cord blocks pain .... Analgesia

Inflamation of the tongue... Glossalgia

Steroid that relieves arthritis pain .... Cortisone

Malaria medicine from chinchona tree bark .... Quinine

Disease of the gum .... Gingivitis

Gum doctor.. Periodontist

Thyroid disease... Grave's Disease

Food aversion disorder... Anorexia nervosa

Binge eating and purging disease .... Bulimia

Syndrome involving barking and cursing .... Tourette's Syndrome

Disorder of the wrist.. Carpal tunnel Syndrome

Retardation caused by an extra chromosome .... Down syndrome

Yellowing of the skin caused by excessive bile .... Jaundice

Brief stopping of breathing during sleep .... Sleep apnea

52 *Sickness and Health*

Disease with raised fluid pressure on the eye .... Glaucoma

Clouding of the eye's lens .... Cataracts

Eye lens defect .... Astigmatism

Affliction in which children are socially withdrawn .... Autism

Rhinitis affects this .... Nose

Encephalitis is a disease of this organ .... Brain

Pyelonephritis is a disease of this organ .... Kidney

Tuberculocus is a disease of this organ .... Lungs

Hepatitis is a disease of this organ .... Liver

Hormone prescribed to promote fertility .... Estrogen

Swelling of salivary glands is symptom of this .... Mumps

Compound carried by high and low density lipoproteins . Cholesterol

Most common cause of death in America .... Heart disease

Second-most common cause of death in America .... Cancer

First organ to be transplanted, 1954 .... Kidney

How fetal defects are detected .... Amniocentesis

"Picture" of an unborn child .... Sonogram

Equipment used to electrically restart the heart .... Defibrillator

Surgery to correct myopia... Radio caritodimy

Common name of diazapam .... Valium

The study of cancer .... Oncology

RICE .... Rest, ice, compression, elevation

PTSD .... Post traumatic stress disorder

Vitamin deficiency causing night blindness .... A (retinol)

Vitamin deficiency causing beriberi .... B-1 (thiamine)

Vitamin deficiency causing lesions .... B-2 (riboflavin)

Vitamin deficiency causing anemia .... B-6 (niacin)

Vitamin deficiency causing pernicious anemia .... B-12 (folic acid)

Vitamin deficiency causing scurvy .... C (ascorbic acid)

Vitamin deficiency causing rickets..................................... D

Blood clotting vitamin... K

Sports **53**

The National Hockey League:
NHL championship trophy .... Lord Stanley's Cup
NHL MVP trophy.. Hart Trophy
Team with most Stanley Cup wins .... Montreal Canadiens (24)
American team with most Stanley Cup wins .... Detroit Red Wings
Most goals in a season .... Wayne Gretzky (92)
Most career goals .... Wayne Gretzky (894)
Second most career goals .... Gordie Howe (801)
Most career goals by a defenseman .... Bobby Orr
Coach with most career wins .... Scotty Bowman

The National Football League:
NFL championship trophy .... Lombardi Trophy
Teams with most Super Bowl victories (5) .... San Francisco 49ers and
                                                     Dallas Cowboys
Most career points .... Gary Anderson (2003+)
Most rushing yards, career .... Walter Payton (16,726)
Most rushing yards in a season .... Eric Dickerson (2,105)
Most rushing yards in a game .... Corey Dillon (278)
Most passing yards, career.................................... Dan Marino (55,416)
Most passing yards in a season .... Dan Marino (5,084)
Most touchdown passes in a career .... Dan Marino (420)
Most touchdown passes in a season .... Dan Marino (48)
Most pass receptions in a career .... Jerry Rice (1262)
Most pass receptions in a season .... Herman Moore (123)
Most touchdowns in a career .... Jerry Rice (167)
Most touchdowns in a season .... Marchall Faulk (26)
Longest field goal (tied) .... Tom Dempsey,
                                                     Jason Elam (63 yds.)

The National Basketball Association:
Team with most NBA championships .... Boston Celtics (16)
Team with most wins in a season .... Chicago Bulls (72, 1995-96)
Team with longest winning streak .... LA Lakers (33, 1971-72)
Most career points .... Kareem Abdul-Jabbar (38,387)
Most points in a game .... Wilt Chamberlain (100)
Most career assists .... John Stockton (active)
Most career games .... Robert Parish (1,611)
Coach with most career wins .... Lenny Wilkens
Coach with most playoff wins .... Pat Riley
Coach with most NBA titles................................. Red Auerbach (9)

Major League Baseball:

Award for best pitcher in each league .... Cy Young Award
Team with most World Series wins, either league . New York Yankees
Team with most World Series wins, National League
    .... St. Louis Cardinals (9)
Player with highest season batting average .... Rogers Hornsby (.424)
Player with highest career batting average .... Ty Cobb (.367)
Player with most career home runs .... Hank Aaron (755)
Player with second most career home runs .... Babe Ruth (714)
Player with most home runs in a season .... Mark McGwire (70)
Player with second most home runs in a season .... Sammy Sosa (66)
Player with most RBI's in a season .... Hack Wilson (190)
Player with most career RBI's .... Hank Aaron (2297)
Player with most career hits .... Pete Rose (4256)
Player with longest consecutive game hitting streak .. Joe DiMaggio (56)
Player with most stolen bases for a season .... Rickey Henderson (130)
Player with most career stolen bases .... Rickey Henderson (1265+)
Pitcher with most career wins .... Cy Young (511)
Pitcher with most career strikeouts .... Nolan Ryan (5714)
Pitcher with most strike outs in a season .... Nolan Ryan (383)
Pitcher with most strike outs in a game .... Roger Clemens and
                                                                         Kerry Wood (20)
Pitcher with most career no hitters .... Nolan Ryan (7)
Pitcher with most Cy Young Awards .... Roger Clemens (5)
Pitcher with lowest ERA for a season .... Bob Gibson (1.12)
Pitcher with most consecutive scoreless innings .... Orel Hershiser (59)
Only pitcher to throw back to back no-hitters ...... Johnny Vander Meer
Only pitcher to throw perfect game in a World Series
    .... Don Larsen (1956)
Last player to win the triple crown .... Carl Yastrzemski (1967)
Last Major Leaguer to hit .400 .... Ted Williams
Player playing in most consecutive games .... Cal Ripken, Jr. (2632)
Baseball's first pro team, 1869 .... Cincinnati Red Stockings
Year of first world series 1903
Last Cub's World Series championship 1908
First baseball commissioner, 1921 .... Kenesaw Mountain Landis
Baseball Hall of Fame's five charter members .... Babe Ruth, Ty Cobb, Walter
                              Johnson, Honus Wagner, Christy Mathewson

Boxing: ("The Sweet Science")

Last bare-knuckle heavyweight champion .... John L. Sullivan
Longest reign as heavyweight champion .... Joe Louis (11 years)
Only undefeated heavyweight champion .... Rocky Marciano (49-0)
Most professional knockouts .... Archie Moore (129)
Cassius Clay defeated him to win heavyweight title . Sonny Liston

Fighters in the "Thrilla' in Manila" .... Ali and Foreman
Fighters in the "Rumble in the Jungle" (Kinshasa, Zaire)
.... Ali and Frazier
Rules governing pro boxing .... Marquis of Queensberry

College Basketball:
Team with most NCAA titles .... UCLA (11)
Team with second most NCAA titles .... Kentucky
Team with longest winning streak .... UCLA (88 games)
UCLA coach for 10 championship seasons .... John Wooden
All-time leading scorer .... "Pistol" Pete Maravich

College Football:
Award for best college player .... Heisman Trophy
Award for best college defenceman .... Bronko Nagurski Award
Team with longest winning streak .... Oklahoma (47 games)
Only player to win two Heisman Trophies .... Archie Griffin
Home to the Cotton Bowl .... Dallas, TX
Home to the Fiesta Bowl .... Tempe, AZ
Home to the Liberty Bowl .... Memphis, TN
Home to the Orange Bowl .... Miami, FL
Home to the Peach Bowl .... Atlanta, GA
Home to the Rose Bowl .... Pasadena, CA
Home to the Sugar Bowl .... New Orleans, LA
Home to the Sun Bowl .... El Paso, TX
Colleges of first intercollegiate football game .... Princeton and Rutgers (1869)

Golf:
Golfer with most tournament wins .... Sam Snead (81)
Golfer with most major tournament wins .... Jack Nicklaus (18)
First golfer to win $1,000,000 .... Arnold Palmer (1963)
Youngest Masters winner .... Tiger Woods
All time leading money winner .... Hale Irwin

Tennis:
First female to win the grand slam .... Maureen Connolly
Female with most grand slam wins .... Margaret Court (24)
Male with most grand slam wins (tied) .... Roy Emerson, Pete Sampras (12)
Youngest female Wimbledon champion .... Martina Hingis (15 yrs.)
Youngest male Wimbledon champion .... Boris Becker (17 yrs.)
Player with most Wimbledon singles titles .... Martina Navratilova (9)
Only player to win Grand Slam twice .... Rod Laver
#1 woman tennis player, 1991-97 .... Steffie Graf
First female to make over $100,000 .... Billie Jean King (1971)

53 *Sports*

Sports Halls of Fame:

Pro Football	Canton, OH
Pro Basketball	Springfield, MA
Pro Hockey	Toronto, Ontario
Major League Baseball	Cooperstown, NY
Tennis	Newport, RI
Bowling	St. Louis, MO
Figure Skating	Colorado Springs, CO
Skiing	Vail, CO
College Football	South Bend, IN

Other Facts:

Basketball inventor	Dr. James A. Naismith
Daytona 500 winner seven times	Richard Petty
Indianapolis 500 winners four times	A. J. Foyt, Jr, Al Unser, Sr. and Rick Mears
Notre Dame football coach, 1918-31	Knute Rockne
Brazilian-American soccer player	Pele
First non-European to win the Tour de France	Greg LeMond
Tour de France winner 1999 and 2000	Lance Armstrong
First man to run the mile in under four minutes, 1954	Roger Bannister
First high schooler to run the mile in under four minutes	Jim Ryan
The Galloping Ghost	Harold (Red) Grange
Crazy Legs	Elroy Hirsch
The Brown Bomber	Joe Louis
The Manassa Mauler	Jack Dempsey
The Louisville Lip	Muhammed Ali
Dr. J	Julius Erving
Ice Man	George Gervin
The Big O	Oscar Robertson
The Iron Horse	Lou Gehrig
The Georgia Peach	Ty Cobb
The Yankee Clipper	Joe DiMaggio
The Splendid Splinter	Ted Williams
The Big Train	Walter Johnson
The Duke of Flatbush	Duke Snider
The Say Hey Kid	Willie Mays
The Sultan of Swat	Babe Ruth
The house that Ruth built	Yankee Stadium
1927 Yankees lineup	Murderer's Row
Mr. October	Reggie Jackson
The Wizard of Westwood	John Wooden
The Shark	Greg Norman

Rocket .... Rod Laver, Maurice Richard
The Golden Jet .... Bobby Hull
Italian skier nicknamed La Bomba .... Alberto Tomba
Mike Tyson's promoter .... Don King
"Highland" game .... Caber tossing
Amateur boxing association for all ages .... Golden Gloves
English racket sport .... Squash
Game played with a stone and brooms .... Curling
Player banned for Chicago "Black Sox" scandal, 1919
.... "Shoeless" Joe Jackson (and seven others)
World's longest dog sled race .... Iditirod
Female Iditirod winner four times .... Susan Butcher
Federation International de Football's championship
.... World Cup
Country with most World Cup wins .... Brazil (4)
Player on three Brazil World Cup teams .... Pele

The Olympic Games
(all athletes are American unless otherwise noted)
Gold Medal winners in:
Basketball
Men
    1904-1968, 1976-1984 .... USA
    1992-2000 .... USA ("Dream Teams")
    1972, 1988 .... Soviet Union
Women
    2000, 1996, 1984 .... USA

Boxing
Heavyweight
    1964 .... Joe Frazier
    1968 .... George Foreman
Light Heavyweight
    1960 .... Cassius Clay
Middleweight
    1952 .... Floyd Patterson
    1976 .... Michael Spinks

Decathlon
    1912 .... Jim Thorpe
    1948, 1952 .... Bob Mathias
    1960 .... Rafer Johnson
    1968 .... Bill Toomey
    1976 .... Bruce Jenner
    1996 .... Dan O'Brien

53 *Sports*

Discus
> 1956,1960,1964,1968 .... Al Oerter

Greco-Roman wrestling
> 2000 .... Rulon Gardner

Gymnastics
> 1972 ..... Two Gold for Olga Korbut of the Soviet Union
> 1976 ..... Three gold for Nadia Comaneci of Romania (coached by Bela Karolyi)
> 1984 ..... Mary Lou Retton wins first USA gymnastics gold in the vault
> 1984 ..... Bart Conner wins USA gold in parallel bars
> 1984 ..... USA men's team gold
> 1992 ..... Shannon Miller wins USA gold in the balance beam
> 1996 ..... USA women's team gold
>   (Shannon Miller, Dominique Dawes, Kerri Strug, Dominique Moceanu,
>   Amy Chow and Jaycee Phelps)

High Jump
> 1968 .... Dick Fosbury revolutionized high
>   jumping forever with his "Fosbury Flop."

Heptathlon, women
> 1988, 1992 .... Jackie Joyner-Kersee

Figure skating
> Men
> 1948, 1952 .... Dick Button
> 1984 .... Scott Hamilton
> Women
> 1928, 1932, 1936 .... Sonja Henie (Norway)
> 1956 .... Tenley Albright
> 1960 .... Carol Heiss
> 1968 .... Peggy Fleming
> 1976 .... Dorothy Hamill
> 1984, 1988 .... Katarina Witt (East Germany)
> 1992 .... Kristi Yamaguchi
> 1994 .... Oksana Baiul (Ukraine)
> 1994 (Silver) .... Nancy Kerrigan
> 1998 .... Tara Lipinski

Javelin
> Women
> 1932 .... Babe Didrikson

Long Jump
> Men
> 1968 .... Bob Beamon
> 1984, 1988, 1992, 1994 .... Carl Lewis

Marathon
  Women
    1984 .... Joan Benoit
  Men
    1972 .... Frank Shorter
    1960, 1964 .... Abebe Bikila (Ethiopia, ran barefoot)

Pole Vault
  Men
    1952, 1956 .... Bob Richards
    1968 .... Bob Seagren

Skiing
  Women
    1998 .... Picabo Street
  Men
    1968 (3 gold) .... Jean-Claude Killy (France)
    1984 .... Phil Mahre
    1992 .... Tommy Moe

Speed Skating
  Women
    1988, 1992, 1994 (5 gold) .... Bonnie Blair
  Men
    1980 (5 gold) .... Eric Heiden

Swimming
  Women
    1924 .... Gertrude Ederle
  Men
    1912 .... Duke Kahanamoku
    1924, 1928 .... Johnny Weissmuller
    1932 .... Buster Crabbe
    1968 (2 gold) .... Mark Spitz
    1972 (7 gold) .... Mark Spitz
    1988 (5 gold) .... Matt Biondi

Track
  Women
    1960 (3 gold) .... Wilma Rudolph
    1988 (2 gold) .... Florence Griffith-Joyner
  Men
    1936 (2 gold) .... Jesse Owens
    1996 (2 gold) .... Michael Johnson
    1984, 1988, 1992 (5 gold) .... Carl Lewis

53 *Sports*

Olympic cities:
Summer

1896	Athens, Greece
1900	Paris, France
1904	St. Louis, Missouri
1908	London, England
1912	Stockholm, Sweden
1920	Antwerp, Belgium
1924	Paris, France
1928	Amsterdam, Netherlands
1932	Los Angeles, California
1936	Berlin, Germany
1948	London, England
1952	Helsinki, Finland
1956	Melbourne, Australia
1960	Rome, Italy
1964	Tokyo, Japan
1968	Mexico City, Mexico
1972	Munich, Germany
1976	Montreal, Canada
1980	Moscow, USSR
1984	Los Angeles, California
1988	Seoul, South Korea
1992	Barcelona, Spain
1996	Atlanta, Georgia
2000	Sydney, Australia
2004	Athens, Greece

Winter

1924	Chamonix, France
1928	St. Moritz, Switzerland
1932	Lake Placid, New York
1936	Garmish-Partenkirchen, Germany
1948	St. Moritz, Switzerland
1952	Oslo, Norway
1956	Contina d'Ampezzo, Italy
1960	Squaw Valley, California
1964	Innsbruck, Austria
1968	Grenoble, France
1972	Sapporo, Japan
1976	Innsbruck, Austria
1980	Lake Placid, New York
1984	Sarajevo, Yugoslavia
1988	Calgary, Canada
1992	Albertville, France
1994	Lillehammer, Norway

1998 .... Nagano, Japan
2002 .... Salt Lake City, Utah

Other Olympic facts:

Modern Olympics founder .... Baron Pierre de Coubertin

Native American sprinting star, 1912 .... Jim Thorpe

American sprinter who embarrassed Hitler, 1936

.... Jesse Owens

American woman who won 3 track golds, 1960 ... Wilma Rudolph

American skiing twin brothers who won gold and silver in same event, 1984

.... Phil and Steve Mahre

Ameican who won back to back decathalon titles

.... Bob Mathias

She won first Olympic women's marathon .... Joan Benoit

American female speed skater with five gold medals

.... Bonnie Blair

American male speed skater with five gold medals

.... Eric Heiden

Man who won five swimming golds, 1988 .... Matt Biondi

Man who won seven swimming golds, 1972 .... Mark Spitz

Male swimming star, 1924 .... Johnny Weissmuller

"Flying Finn" who won gold in three Olympics ... Paavo Nurmi

Man who broke long jump record by two feet, 1968

.... Bob Beamon

Four-time discus champion .... Al Oerter

Four-time long jump champion .... Carl Lewis

Man who won the marathon twice barefoot .... Abebe Bikila (Ethopia)

Only man to win the 200 and 400 meter races ..... Michael Johnson

Years Olympics were canceled due to war 1916, 1940, 1944

54 *Television*

Television Shows:

Clayton Moore and Jay Silverheels western .... *The Lone Ranger*
Gale Storm and Charles Ferrell sitcom .... *My Little Margie*
Gene Barry western .... *Bat Masterson*
Ann Sothern sitcom... *My Mother, the Car*
George Reeves action series....................................... *Superman*
Fred Gwynne police comedy .... *Car 54, Where are You?*
Efrem Zimbalist, Jr. private detective series .... *77 Sunset Strip*
Broderick Crawford police drama .... *Highway Patrol*
Walter Brennan and Richard Crenna comedy .... *The Real McCoys*
Dwayne Hickman Bob Denver comedy .... *Dobie Gillis*
Duncan Renaldo and Leo Carrillo western .... *The Cisco Kid*
June Lockhart and Jon Provost family series .... *Lassie*
Robert Young and Jane Wyatt family series .... *Father Knows Best*
Robert Stack G-Man series .... *The Untouchables*
Barbara Stanwyck and Lee Majors western .... *The Big Valley*
Lorne Greene and Michael Landon western .... *Bonanza*
Bret Reed and Bruce Lee action series .... *The Green Hornet*
Adam West and Burt Ward action series .... *Batman*
Robert Vaughn and David McCallum spy series .... *The Man From U.N.C.L.E.*
Robert Culp and Bill Cosby spy series .... *I Spy*
Diana Rigg and Patrick Macnee spy drama............ *The Avengers*
Bea Benaderet and Edgar Buchanan comedy .... *Petticoat Junction*
Stacy Keach detective series....................................... *Mike Hammer*
Danny Thomas and Marjorie Lord comedy .... *The Danny Thomas Show*
James Arness and Amanda Blake western .... *Gunsmoke*
Jack Webb and Harry Morgan police series .... *Dragnet*
June Lockhart and Guy Williams sci-fi series .... *Lost in Space*
Brian Keith and Sebastian Cabot family series.................. *Family Affair*
Clint Eastwood and Eric Fleming western .... *Rawhide*
Eddie Albert and Eva Gabor comedy...................... *Green Acres*
Lynda Carter action series... *Wonder Woman*
Suzanne Somers and John Ritter sitcom .... *Three's Company*
Don Johnson and Philip Michael Thomas police drama .. *Miami Vice*
Raymond Burr and Barbara Hale murder series.... *Perry Mason*
Alan Hale and Bob Denver comedy .... *Gilligan's Island*
Ken Berry and Forrest Tucker comedy............................. *F Troop*
Rod Serling sci-fi show, 1959-65 .... *The Twilight Zone*
Rod Serling sci-fi show, 1970-73.............................. *Night Gallery*
Robert Young medical drama .... *Marcus Welby, M.D.*
Buddy Ebsen and Irene Ryan comedy .... *The Beverley Hillbillies*

Chuck Connors western .... *The Rifleman*
Robert Wagner drama .... *It Takes a Thief*
Vince Edwards and Sam Jaffe medical drama .... *Ben Casey*
Elizabeth Montgomery and Agnes Moorehead comedy .... *Bewitched*
Richard Thomas and Michael Learned drama .... *The Waltons*
Richard Boone western .... *Have Gun, Will Travel*
Hugh Beaumont and Barbara Billingsley comedy .... *Leave It To Beaver*
Ernest Borgnine and Tim Conway comedy .... *McHale's Navy*
Shirley Booth and Don DeFore comedy .... *Hazel*
Chad Everett medical drama .... *Medical Center*
Gabe Kaplan and John Travolta comedy .... *Welcome Back, Kotter*
Jack Lord and James MacArthur police series .... *Hawaii Five-O*
John Amos and Jimmie Walker comedy .... *Good Times*
Peter Falk detective series .... *Columbo*
Michael J. Fox and Meredith Baxter-Birney sitcom .... *Family Ties*
James Garner and Jack Kelly western .... *Maverick*
Richard Chamberlain medical series .... *Dr. Kildare*
Robert Wagner and Stefanie Powers mystery series .... *Hart to Hart*
William Shatner and Leonard Nimoy sci-fi series .... *Star Trek*
William Conrad detective series .... *Cannon*
Dick Van Patten family drama .... *Eight is Enough*
Erik Estrada and Larry Wilcox police series .... *CHIPS*
Linda Lavin and Polly Holliday sitcom .... *Alice*
Tom Selleck and John Hillerman detective series .. *Magnum P.I.*
Telly Savalas police drama .... *Kojak*
Robert Blake and Fred the cockatoo police drama *Baretta*
Raymond Burr disabled detective legal drama ...... *Ironside*
Andy Griffith legal drama .... *Matlock*
Fred Gwynne and Yvonne DeCarlo comedy .... *The Munsters*
John Astin and Carolyn Jones comedy .... *The Addams Family*
Bob Crane and Werner Klemperer comedy .... *Hogan's Heroes*
Marlin Perkins and Jim Fowler wildlife program .... *Wild Kingdom*
Louise Lasser comedy/soap opera .... *Mary Hartman, Mary Hartman*
Ed Asner newspaper drama .... *Lou Grant*
David Carradine action series .... *Kung Fu*
Sharon Gless and Tyne Daly police drama .... *Cagney and Lacey*
Larry Hagman and Barbara Eden comedy .... *I Dream of Jeannie*
Rock Hudson and Susan St. James police drama ... *McMillan and Wife*
Ron Howard and Tom Bosley comedy .... *Happy Days*
Bea Arthur and Adrienne Barbeau comedy .... *Maude*
Sherman Hemsley and Isabel Sanford sitcom .... *The Jeffersons*
Buddy Ebsen detective drama .... *Barnaby Jones*
George Peppard detective drama .... *Banacek*
Dennis Franz and Rick Schroder police drama ...... *N.Y.P.D. Blue*
Candice Bergen sitcom .... *Murphy Brown*

Florence Henderson and Robert Reed sitcom	*The Brady Bunch*
Mackenzie Phillips and Valerie Bertinelli sitcom	*One Day at a Time*
Jane Wyman and Lorenzo Lamas drama	*Falcon Crest*
Carroll O'Connor and Howard Rollins police drama	*In the Heat of the Night*
Dennis Weaver police show	*McCloud*
Robert Guillaume and Inga Swenson comedy	*Benson*
Bea Arthur and Estelle Getty comedy	*The Golden Girls*
Karl Malden and Michael Douglas police drama	*The Streets of San Francisco*
Jack Klugman medical drama	*Quincy, M.E.*
Mike Connors detective drama	*Mannix*
Tony Danza and Judith Light sitcom	*Who's the Boss?*
Robin Williams and Pam Dawber comedy	*Mork & Mindy*
Angie Dickinson police series	*Police Woman*
Alan Alda and Loretta Swit comedy	*M*A*S*H**
Daniel Travanti and Ed Marinaro police show	*Hill Street Blues*
Delta Burke and Dixie Carter sitcom	*Designing Women*
Ted Danson and Rhea Pearlman comedy	*Cheers*
Angela Lansbury mystery series	*Murder, She Wrote*
Jane Seymour western drama	*Dr. Quinn, Medicine Woman*
Pernell Roberts medical drama	*Trapper John, M.D.*
Ed O'Neill and Katey Sagal sitcom	*Married ..... With Children*
Robert Stack mystery series	*Unsolved Mysteries*
James Burke history series	*Connections*
Tom Skerrit and Kathy Baker comedy	*Picket Fences*
Brook Shields sitcom	*Suddenly Susan*
Chuck Norris action series	*Walker, Texas Ranger*
Michael J. Fox and Barry Bostwick sitcom	*Spin City*
David Duchovny and Gillian Anderson sci-fi drama	*The X-Files*
Dick Van Dyke murder-mystery series	*Diagnosis Murder*
Anthony Edwards and George Clooney medical drama	*ER*
Sam Waterston and Christopher North police/legal drama	*Law & Order*
Richard Dysart and Alan Rachins legal drama	*L.A. Law*
Andrew Shue and Grant Show drama	*Melrose Place*
Tim Allen and Patricia Richardson sitcom	*Home Improvement*
Tim Daly and Steven Weber sitcom	*Wings*
Paul Reiser and Helen Hunt sitcom	*Mad About You*
Kelsey Grammar sitcom	*Frasier*
John Lithgow and Jane Curtin comedy	*Third Rock From the Sun*
Jason Alexander and Julia Louis-Dreyfus sitcom	*Seinfeld*
Teri Hatcher and Dean Cain sci-fi show	*Superman*
ABC news magazine, 1978-	*20/20*
Linda Lawless action show	*Xena*
Kevin Sorbo action show	*Hercules*

Spin Offs:

All in the Family	The Jeffersons
	Maude
	Good Times
	Gloria
Happy Days	Mork and Mindy
	Laverne and Shirley
	Joanie Loves Chachi
The Mary Tyler Moore Show	Rhoda
	Phyllis
	Lou Grant
Cheers	Frasier
	The Tortellis
The Cosby Show	A Different World
Soap	Benson
Dynasty	The Colbys
Alice	Flo
Dallas	Knots Landing
Sanford and Son	Grady

Game Show and Other Hosts:

See It Now host	Edward R. Murrow
Firing Line host	William F. Buckley
60 Minutes original hosts	Mike Wallace and Harry Reasoner
20-20 female co-host	Barbara Walters
Inside Edition host	Deborah Norville
Late, Late Show host	Tom Snyder
Politically Incorrect host	Bill Maher
The Joker's Wild host	Jack Barry
Concentration original host	Hugh Downs
Password host	Allen Ludden
House Party host	Art Linkletter
The Original Amateur Hour host	Ted Mack
ABC's Wide World of Sports host	Jim McKay
Hollywood Squares original host	Peter Marshall
College Bowl original host	Allen Ludden
To Tell the Truth host	Bud Collyer
This is Your Life host	Ralph Edwards
Truth of Consequences host	Bob Barker
What's My Line host	John Daly
I've Got a Secret host	Garry Moore
Let's Make a Deal host	Monty Hall
American Bandstand host	Dick Clark
The Newlywed Game host	Bob Eubanks
Family Feud original host	Richard Dawson

The Price is Right current host	Bob Barker
The $10,000 ($25,000) Pyramid host	Dick Clark
Original *Jeopardy!* host	Art Fleming
Current *Jeopardy!* host	Alex Trebek
America's Funniest Home Videos host	Bob Saget
Who Wants To Be A Millionaire? host	Regis Philbin
Twenty-One host	Maury Povich
Greed host	Chuck Wollery
Original *Soul Train* host	Don Cornileous
The 700 Club host	Pat Robertson
Original *Monday Night Football* hosts	Don Meredith, Keith Jackson, Howard Cosell

Other Facts:

Longest-running program	*Meet the Press*
Longest-running prime time program	*60 Minutes*
Most-watched single episode	Last episode of *M*A*S*H**
Most-watched mini-series	*Roots*
Most-watched movie on television	*Gone With the Wind*
Most-watched syndicated program	*Wheel of Fortune*
Program syndicated in the most countries	*Baywatch*
Program rated #1 for longest consecutive time	*All in the Family* (5 years)
Show rated #1 for five nonconsecutive years in the 1950s	*I Love Lucy*
Program nominated for the most Emmys	*Cheers (117)*
Program to win the most Emmys	*The Mary Tyler Moore Show (29)*
Pay channel with the most subscribers	HBO
Cable channel in the most homes	ESPN
PBS top rated show	*Antiques Road Show*
Largest Christian network	Trinity (TBN)
Largest Spanish speaking network	Univision
The "Channel for Women"	Lifetime
First TV mini-series	*Rich Man, Poor Man*
First televised political debate, 1960	Nixon vs. Kennedy
Longest-running animated prime time program	*The Simpsons*
Second longest-running animated prime-time program	*The Flintstones*
The Untouchables narrator	Walter Winchell
Phil Silver's sitcom character	Sgt. Ernie Bilko
The Skipper's name on *Gilligan's Island*	Jonas Grumby
"The Galloping Gourmet"	Graham Kerr
Game show host with 14 Emmys	Bob Barker
Jeopardy! And *Wheel of Fortune* creator	Merv Griffin
Star Trek creator	Gene Roddenberry
Saturday Night Live producer	Lorne Michaels

U.S. Government 55

The Constitution of the United States: (established 1787)

Bill of Rights:

1. Freedom of the press, speech and religion
2. The right to keep and bear arms
3. The government cannot keep troops in homes
4. Regulation of search and seizure
5. Freedom from double jeopardy; the right to due process
6. Right to a speedy trial and to call witnesses
7. Right to trial by jury
8. Excessive bail is prohibited; a ban on cruel and unusual punishment
9. Enumeration of rights in the Constitution does not take away rights retained by the people (rule of construction)
10. Rights not delegated by the Constitution are retained by the people

Additional Amendments:

11. Limits federal judicial powers
12. Separate electoral ballots for president and vice president
13. Abolishes slavery
14. Rights of citizenship unabridged
15. Race will be no exemption to voting rights
16. Allows for federal income tax
17. Allows for direct election of U.S. senators
18. Prohibition
19. Women's suffrage (right to vote)
20. Lame duck amendment (sets presidential inauguration day to January 20)
21. Repeal of Prohibition
22. Presidential two-term limit
23. Citizens of the District of Columbia can vote in presidential election
24. Bans poll tax
25. Presidential succession and disability
26. Voting age set to 18 years

Cabinet of the President:

President George W. Bush's Cabinet:

Secretary of Agriculture	Ann Veneman
Secretary of Commerce	Don Evans
Secretary of Defense	Donald Rumsfeld
Secretary of Education	Rod Paige
Secretary of Energy	Spencer Abraham
Secretary of Health and Human Services	Tommy Thompson
Secretary of Housing and Urban Development	Mel Martinez

Attorney General .... John Ashcroft
Secretary of the Interior .... Gale Norton
Secretary of Labor .... Linda Chavez
Secretary of State .... Colin Powell
Secretary of Transportation .... Norman Mineta
Secretary of the Treasury .... Paul O'Neill
Secretary of Veterans Affairs .... Anthony Principi

* These positions change frequently. This list could be outdated anytime after the publication of this book

George Washington's Cabinet:

Secretary of the Treasury .... Alexander Hamilton
Secretary of War .... Henry Knox (Fort Knox)
Secretary of State .... Thomas Jefferson
Attorney General .... Edmund Randolph

Other Prominent Presidential Cabinet Members:

Abraham Lincoln's Secretary of State .... William Seward
Chester Arthur's Secretary of War .... Robert Lincoln (Abe's son)
Secretary of State from Maine, 1889-92 .... James Blaine
Wilson's Secretary of State .... William Jennings Bryan
First Secretary of Defence, 1947 .... James Forrestall
Eisenhower's Secretary of State .... John Foster Dulles
Kennedy & Johnson's Secretary of Defense, 1961-68 ... Robert McNamara
Kennedy and Johnson's Secretary of State .... Dean Rusk
Ford and Nixon's Secretary of State .... Henry Kissinger
Reagan's first Secretary of State ("I'm in charge here") .. Alexander Haig
Reagan's second Secretary of State .... George Shultz
Reagan's Secretary of Defense .... Caspar Weinberger
Bush's Secretary of State .... James Baker III
Clinton's Secretary of Commerce, killed in plane crash
.... Ron Brown

Cabinet Department Divisions:
Treasury:
Customs
Secret Service
Internal Revenue Service
Bureau of Alcohol, Tobacco and Firearms
Transportation:
Coast Guard
St. Lawrence Seaway

Commerce Department:
National Bureau of Standards
Census Bureau

Agriculture:
Food Stamps
Forestry

Justice Department:
Immigration and Naturalization Service
Federal Bureau of Investigation

Interior Department:
Bureau of Mines
Bureau of Indian Affairs
National Park Service
Geological Service

Order of Presidential Succession:
President
Vice President
Speaker of the House of Representatives
President Pro Tem of the Senate
Secretary of State
Secretary of the Treasury
Secretary of Defense

The United States Supreme Court:
Current Judges in order of appointment:
William Rehnquist-Chief Justice (appointed by Nixon)
John Paul Stephens (appointed by Ford)
Sandra Day O'Conner (first female justice, appointed by Reagan)
Antonin Scalia (Judge for Watergate hearings, appointed by Reagan)
Anthony Kennedy (appointed by Reagan after Bork failed)
David Souter (replaced Brennan, appointed by Bush)
Clarence Thomas (appointed by Bush)
Ruth Bader Ginsburg (appointed in 1993 by Clinton)
Stephen Breyer (appointed in 1994 by Clinton)
Previous Chief Justices:
John Jay; 1789-95 (first chief justice)
John Marshall; 1801-35 (4th chief justice, longest-serving chief justice)
Roger Taney; 1836-64 (presided over Dred Scott Decision)
Salmon P. Chase; 1864-73 (presided over Andrew Johnson's impeachment trial)
William Howard Taft; 1921-30
Charles Evans Hughes; 1930-41
Earl Warren; 1953-69 (presided over *Brown vs. Board of Education*)
Warren Burger; 1969-94

Other Justices:
Oliver Wendell Holmes (The Great Dissenter)
Whizzer White (pro football player)
Harry Blackmun (wrote the opinion on *Roe vs. Wade*)
Thurgood Marshall (first Black justice)
Louis Brandeis (first Jewish justice)
William O. Douglas (Justice with the longest term on the court)

Other Facts:

Republican presidential ticket, 1996 .... Robert Dole and Jack Kemp
Republican presidential ticket, 1992 .... George Bush and Dan Quayle
Democratic presidential ticket, 1988 .... Michael Dukakis and Lloyd Bentson
Democratic presidential ticket, 1984 .... Walter Mondale and Geraldine Ferraro
Democratic presidential ticket, 1980 .... Jimmy Carter and Walter Mondale
Republican presidential ticket, 1976 .... Gerald Ford and Robert Dole
Democratic presidential ticket, 1972 .... George McGovern and Sargent Shriver
Democratic presidential ticket, 1968 .... Hubert Humphrey and Ed Muskie
Republican presidential ticket, 1964 .... Barry Goldwater and William Miller
Republican presidential ticket, 1960 .... Richard Nixon and Henry Cabot Lodge
Democratic presidential candidate 1952, 1956 .... Adlai Stevenson
Republican presidential candidate 1944, 1948 .... Thomas E. Dewey
Democratic presidential candidate 1896, 1900, 1908
.... William Jennings Bryan
Presidential candidate 1824, 1832, 1844 (different parties)
.... Henry Clay
Last 3rd party presidential candidate to receive electoral votes
.... George Wallace (1968)
Independent presidential candidate, 1992, 1996 ...... Ross Perot
Five-time Social Democrat Presidential candidate .... Eugene Debs
First Republican candidate, 1856 .... John C. Fremont
First Republican president, 1860 .... Abraham Lincoln
Independent presidential candidate, 1980 .... John Anderson
"Flamboyant" New York city mayor .... Jimmy Walker
Speaker of the House of Representatives, 1977-87 ... Thomas "Tip" O'Neill, Jr.
Speaker of the House of Representatives, 1995-98 ... Newt Gingrich
Speaker of the House of Representatives, 1998- .... Dennis Hastert
Arizona congressman, 1912-69 (longest term in Congress)
.... Carl Hayden
Texas congressman, 1912-61 (also had longest term as Speaker of House)
.... Sam Rayburn
"The Happy Warrior" .... Al Smith
Ditch-digging New York governor (Erie Canal) .... De Witt Clinton
The "Eggheads'" candidate .... Adlai Stevenson

"Dixiecrats" candidate (elected by write-in vote, 1954)
.... Strom Thurmond
Golden Fleece award giver .... William Proxmire
"Tail gunner Joe" .... Joseph McCarthy
Governor of Kansas, 1933-37 .... Alf Landon
Alf Landon's daughter .... Nancy Landon Kassebaum
Thomas Eagleton's replacement for V.P. candidate, 1972
.... Sargent Shriver
Number of Congress, January 2000 .... 106th
Number of Senators 100
Number of Representatives 435
Site of *U.S. Constitution* and *Declaration of Independence*
.... National Archives
Where tax bills originate .... House of Representatives
Congressional viewing area .... The Gallery
Assistant to a party leader .... Whip
Opinion passed by the House or Senate .... Resolution
Person representing U.S. Government in Supreme Court
.... Solicitor General
President of the Senate .... Vice President
Body that decides on impeachment .... House of Representatives
Listing of who's who in congress .... Congressional Directory
Body that elects the V.P. in case of a tie .... Senate
Federal National Mortgage Association .... "Fannie Mae"
Student loan association .... "Sallie Mae"
Body that names the U.S. Poet Laureate .... Library of Congress
Intermediary between the government and citizens .. Ombudsman
FBI director, 1924-77 .... J. Edgar Hoover
Location of FBI headquarters .... Quantico, Va
Location of CIA headquarters .... Langley, Va
Term for congressional seniority .... Ranking
Power of the government to take private property for public use
.... Eminent Domain
Central U.S. banking authority .... The Federal Reserve
Chairman of the Federal Reserve, 1979-87 .... Paul Volcker
Chairman of the Federal Reserve, 1987- .... Alan Greenspan
Person with picture on the:
    Fifty cent coin .... John F. Kennedy
    Old one dollar coin .... Susan B. Anthony
    New one dollar coin .... Sacajawea
    Two dollar bill .... Thomas Jefferson
    $500 bill .... William McKinley
    $1,000 bill .... Grover Cleveland
    $5,000 bill .... James Madison
    $10,000 bill .... Salmon P. Chase
    $100,000 bill .... Woodrow Wilson

56 U. S. History

Colonial History

First permanent settlement, 1565 .... St. Augustine
First English colony, 1588 .... Roanoke Island
Virginia colony, 1607 .... Jamestown
Massachusetts colony, 1620 .... Plymouth
First Pilgrim at Plymouth Rock and colonial barrel maker
.... John Alden
First governor of Plymouth, died during first winter .... John Carver
Plymouth father, elected Plymouth governor 30 times ..... William Bradford
Pilgrim known as "Little Shrimp".................................... Miles Standish
First legislature in Virginia, 1619 .... House of Burgesses
Dutch settlement, 1624... New Netherlands
New York City's original name .... New Amsterdam
Boston to New York road established in 1672 .... Boston Post Road
Virginia rebellion, 1676 .... Bacon's Rebellion
Colonial capital of Virginia .... Williamsburg
Virginia namesake .... Queen Elizabeth I (The Virgin Queen)
Man who claimed Virginia for England .... Sir Walter Raleigh
He purchased Manhattan from the Indians .... Peter Minuit
Providence and Rhode Island founder .... Roger Williams
Dutch governor of New Netherlands .... Peter Stuyvesant
Maryland founder .... Cecil Calvert (second Lord Baltimore)
Georgia founder .... James Oglethorpe
Fort Orange location .... Albany
Philadelphia founder .... William Penn
Colonial silversmith, engraver and gunpowder maker ...... Paul Revere
Puritan husband of Maria Cotton .... Increase Mather
Increase Mather's son.. Cotton Mather
He married Pocahontas .... John Rolfe
Pocahontas' father... Powhattan
Man Pocahontas saved .... John Smith
Pocahontas' burial place.. Gravesend Church, England
Detroit founder .... Antoine Cadillac
John Adams' cousin and Boston Tea Party organizer .... Samuel Adams
Colonial seamstress... Betsy Ross
Boston hall, "The Cradle of Liberty" .... Faneuil Hall
Pre-Revolutionary War patriotic societies .... Sons of Liberty
New England religious revival, 1730-50 .... Great Awakening
Father of the Great Awakening, fire and brimstone preacher
.... Jonathan Edwards
Act passed by British Parliament in 1763 .... Stamp Act
Street clash that killed five colonists in 1770 .... Boston Massacre

Dumping of British tea into Boston Harbor in 1773 .... Boston Tea Party
British acts legislated because of Boston Tea Party .... Intolerable Acts
Colonial legislature established in 1774 .... First Continental Congress
Kentucky frontiersman, 1775 .... Daniel Boone

American History:

First constitution, Nov. 15, 1777 .... Articles of Confederation
First president under the Articles of Confederation .... John Hanson
Body representing the colonies, 1774-89 .... Continental Congress
Continental Congress president, 1775-77 .... John Hancock
Continental Congress last president .... Cyrus Griffin
Party of the first two presidents .... Federalist Party
Roadway across Appalachians .... Cumberland Road
Designer of the American flag .... Francis Hopkins
U.S. capital from 1775-83 .... Philadelphia
U.S. capital, 1783 .... Annapolis
U.S. capital from 1789-90 .... New York City
Massachusetts farmers rebellion of 1786 .... Shays' Rebellion
Document established in 1787 .... U.S. Constitution
Hamilton's 1790 report .... Report on public credit
He founded the Bank of America, 1791 .... Alexander Hamilton
First Secretary of War .... John Knox (Fort Knox)
First Secretary of Treasury.. Alexander Hamilton
Hamilton's 85 essays .... Federalist papers
Duelist who shot Alexander Hamilton .... Aaron Burr
Eli Whitney's invention, 1791 .... Cotton gin
Liquor tax rebellion of 1794... Whiskey Rebellion
Diplomatic incident with France in 1797 .... XYZ affair
American frigate launched in Boston, 1797 .... *USS Constitution* (Old Ironsides)
U.S. land purchase of 1803 .... Louisiana Purchase ($15 Million)
Case declared unconstitutinal by Supreme Court, 1803 .. Marberry vs. Madison
Man who burned the *Philadelphia* in Tripoli harbor, 1804
.... Stephen Decatur (Decatur, IL)
"The Pathfinder" who was governor of the Arizona Territory
.... John C. Fremont
Louisiana Purchase explorers of northern territory .... Meriwether Lewis and
　　　　　　　　　　　　　　　　　　　　　　　　　　　William Clark
William Clark's frontiersman brother .... George Rogers Clark
Louisiana Purchase explorer of southern territory............. Zebulon Pike (Pike's Peak)
Winner of the Battle of Lake Erie in 1813 .... Oliver Hazard Perry
Fort bombed by British in 1814 .... Fort McHenry
Man who wrote *Star Spangled Banner* in 1814 .... Francis Scott Key
Man who captured New Orleans in 1815 .... Andrew Jackson
Pirate who aided in Battle of New Orleans .... Jean Lafitte
1815 treaty that officially ended the War of 1812 .... Treaty of Ghent (Belgium)

"The Great Compromiser;" he negotiated the Treaty of Ghent
.... Henry Clay
Territory of states in the Ohio Valley and northward .... Northwest Territory
States fighting in the Toledo War .... Ohio and Michigan
Political party established by Henry Clay & Daniel Webster
.... Whigs
1820 compromise that temporarily ended slavery dispute
.... Missouri Compromise
Doctrine warning Europe not to interfere in Western Hemisphere, 1823
.... Monroe Doctrine
Man-made waterway that opened in 1825 .... Erie Canal
He led unsuccessful slave rebellion, 1831 .... Nat Turner
I t rang for the last time in 1835 .... Liberty Bell
San Antonio shrine of Texas War of Independence .... Alamo
Commander at the Alamo, 1836 .... William Travis
Tennessee frontiersman killed at Alamo .... Davy Crockett
Knife inventor killed at the Alamo .... Jim Bowie
Northwest land dispute motto, 1844 .... "54-40 or fight"
"Old Fuss and Feathers;" he captured Mexico City in 1847
.... Winfield Scott
Treaty that ended Mexican-American War .... Treaty of Guadeloupe Hidalgo
Langtree, Texas judge, "The law west of the Pecos" .... Judge Roy Bean
Short-lived U.S. state in western Tennessee .... Franklin
Birthplace of the Conestoga wagon .... Lancaster, PA
Settlers trapped in Sierra Madres, 1846-47 .... Donner party
Site where gold was discovered in 1848 .... Sutter's Mill
First U.S. steamship commander, he negotiated a trading treaty with Japan in 1853
.... Commodore Matthew Perry
Territory bought from Mexico, 1853 .... Gadsden Purchas
1854 act that nullified Missouri Compromise .... Kansas-Nebraska Act
Women's Christian Temperance Union (WCTU) party ... Prohibition Party
"Paper note party" .... Greenbacks
"Ignorant party" .... Know Nothings
Harriet Beecher Stowe's preacher brother .... Henry Ward Beecher
Supreme Court decision,1857 (a slave is not a citizen) ..... Dred Scott Decision
He debated with Abe Lincoln, 1858 .... Stephen Douglas
He raided Harper's Ferry, 1859 .... John Brown
"The boss of Tammany Hall" in the 1860s...................... (William Marcy) "Boss" Tweed
Mail delivery service, 1860-61 .... Pony Express
Pony Express terminals .... St. Joseph, MO & Sacramento, CA
Congressional act giving land to settlers, 1862 .... Homestead Act
Land purchase, 1867, a.k.a. Seward's Folley .... Alaska Territory ($7.2 million)
He instituted the national banking system .... Salmon P. Chase
Transportation route, completed 1869 .... Transcontinental Railroad
Utah point where the transcontinental railroad met .... Promontory Point
Railroads that met at Promontory Point .... Union Pacific and Central Pacific

City of the great fire, 1871 .... Chicago
Laws enacted for segregation in the 1880s .... Jim Crow laws
Tombstone, AZ marshall, 1881 .... Wyatt Earp
Famous Tombstone, AZ gunfight, 1881 .... Gunfight at the OK Corral
Feuding families of West Virginia and Kentucky, 1882 .... Hatfields and McCoys
"The Son of Morning Star" who died at Little Big Horn
.... George Armstrong Custer
Statue that was dedicated in 1886 .... Statue of Liberty
Chicago riots, 1886 .... Haymarket riots
Pennsylvania flood of 1889 .... Johnstown flood
1890 trust busting act .... Sherman Anti-trust Act
American Railway Union founder, 1893 .... Eugene Debs
1894 rail workers strike .... Pullman Strike
"Separate, but equal" Supreme Court decision, 1896 .... Plessy vs. Ferguson
1896 William Jennings Bryan speech .... "Cross of Gold"
Ship that exploded in Havana Harbor in 1898 ....: *Maine*
War that commenced in 1898 .... Spanish-American War
He won the Battle of Manila Bay, 1898 .... Commodore George Dewey
Disaster that killed 6,000, 1900 .... Galveston hurricane
Five-time Socialist presidential candidate, starting 1900 .. Eugene Debs
Disaster that killed 500, 1906 .... San Francisco earthquake
Railroad "robber baron" who organized U.S. Steel, 1901
.... J. P. Morgan
Oil baron who was first billionaire in the U.S. .... J. D. Rockefeller
"Saloon Smasher," 1910 .... Carry Nation
William Howard Taft's policy toward Latin America .... Dollar Diplomacy
1912 health claims act .... Pure Food and Drug Act
Central U.S. banking authority created in 1913 .... Federal Reserve System
He established the first auto assembly line, 1913 .... Henry Ford
Agency created to prevent unfair business practices, 1914
.... Federal Trade Commission
Teddy Roosevelt's independent party .... Progressive or Bull Moose Party
He chased Pancho Villa into Mexico .... John (Black Jack) Pershing
Law that banned export of alcohol, 1919 .... Volsted Act
Major police strike, 1919 .... Boston police strike
He organized the U.S. Communist Party in 1919 .... John Reed
Baseball scandal, 1919-20 .... "Black Sox" scandal
U.S. declined to join this body, 1920 .... League of Nations
Harding pardoned this Socialist in 1921 .... Eugene Debs
Wyoming oil leasing scandal, 1923 .... Teapot Dome Scandal
Tennessee trial on teaching evolution in schools, 1925 .... Scopes (monkey) trial
He launched first liquid fueled rocket, 1926 .... Robert Goddard
First U.S. underwater tunnel, 1927 .... Holland Tunnel
Voting league established, 1928 .... League of Women Voters
Beaumont, Texas oil field .... Spindle Top Field
Secretary of Interior convicted of taking bribes, 1929 ...... Albert Fall

Date of the stock market crash .... October 29, 1929 ("Black Tuesday")
FDR established this holiday in 1933 .... Bank Holiday
FDR's 1933 program to end the depression .... New Deal
Group of dams built as part of the New Deal .... Tennessee Valley Authority (TVA)
Louisiana senator shot, 1935 .... Huey Long
U.S. gold repository, established in 1935 .... Fort Knox
Chicago to L.A. highway; "Main Street of America" .... Route 66
He set around-the-world flying record, 1938 .... Howard Hughes
He broadcast "The War of the Worlds" in 1938 .... Orson Welles
Boston night club fire in which 491 people were killed, 1942
.... Coconut Grove
Site of first atomic bomb test in 1945 .... Alamogordo, New Mexico
Statesman awarded Nobel Peace Prize, 1945 .... Cordell Hull
Site of first postwar atomic bomb test in 1946 .... Bikini Atoll
He broke the sound barrier, 1947 .... Chuck Yeager
Law that banned closed union shops, 1948 .... Taft-Hartley Act
Army Chief of Staff, 1948 .... Omar Bradley (last five star general)
Sex researcher at Indiana University, 1948 .... Alfred Kinsey
Statesman convicted of lying to HUAC, 1948 .... Alger Hiss
Time magazine editor involved with Alger Hiss .... Whitaker Chambers
Great robbery of 1950 .... Brinks robbery
First computer, 1950 .... ENIAC
Computer used by U.S. Census Bureau, 1951 .... UNIVAC
Tennessee senator who held organized crime hearings, 1951
.... Estes Kefauver
Pacific site of first H-bomb test, 1951 .... Eniwetok
"Hollywood Ten" were investigated by this committee ..... HUAC
"Hollywood Ten" spokesman .... Humphrey Bogart
First U.S. nuclear powered submarine, 1954 .... *Nautilus*
Post WW II generation .... "Baby Boomers"
Generation that followed baby boomers .... "Generation X"
Supreme Court anti-segregation decision, 1954 .... Brown vs. the Board of Education
Bus boycott city, 1955 .... Montgomery
Man who created first state board of education .... Horace Mann
High school integration city, 1957 .... Little Rock
He was a 14-year-old U.S. chess champion in 1957 .... Bobby Fischer
Man given the correct answers to quiz show questions ..... Charles Van Doren
J. F. Dulles' brother and head of the CIA .... Allen Dulles
They participated in the "Kitchen Debate", 1959 .... Richard Nixon and
                                                                            Nikita Khrushchev
Failed Cuban invasion site, 1961 .... Bay of Pigs
Nightclub comedian arrested for obscenity, 1961 .... Lenny Bruce
Doctor defended by F. Lee Bailey before the Supreme Court in 1962
.... Sam Shepard
Member of the Weavers and political activist .... Pete Seeger
American pilot exchanged for Soviet spy Rudolph Abel ... Francis Gary Powers

Nuclear weapons treaty of 1963 .... Test Ban Treaty
Commission set up to investigate JFK assassination .... Warren Commission
Cities of Martin Luther King's 1965 Freedom March ...... Selma to Montgomery
LBJ's social program .... Great Society
Law that opened up government files, 1966 .... Freedom of Information Act
Spring, 1968, North Vietnam offensive .... Tet Offensive
Event that occurred on July 20, 1969 .... Moon landing
Base on the Moon, 1969 .... Tranquility Base
Name of Apollo 11 space capsule .... Eagle
Rock concert at Bethyl, New York, 1969 .... Woodstock
Air quality standards act of 1970 .... Clean Air Act
Ads banned, 1971 .... Cigarette ads
Nixon's attorney-general who resigned in 1972 .... John Mitchell
Analyst who leaked the Pentagon Papers .... Daniel Ellsberg
Nixon's White House Chief of Staff .... H.R. Haldeman
He directed the Watergate Hotel burglary .... E. Howard Hunt
White House lawyer caught up in Watergate .... John Dean
Head of committee investigating Watergate .... Sam Irvin
Company given $1.5 billion government bailout in 1973
        .... Chrysler
Environmental act of 1973 .... Endangered Species Act
Disease first recognized in Philadelphia, 1976 .... Legionaire's Disease
Oil artery finished in 1977 .... Alaska pipeline
This became an American territory in 1978 .... American Samoa
News program established to cover Iran hostage crisis ...... *Nightline*
Number of days of the Iran hostage crisis 444
Site of nuclear power accident, 1979 .... Three Mile Island
Peace agreement worked out by President Carter, 1979 ... Camp David Accords
Volcano that erupted in 1980 .... Mt. St. Helens
He funneled arms sales profits to Nicaraguan Contras ..... Oliver North
Admiral indicted over Iran-Contra affair .... John Poindexter
Commission that presided over Iran-Contra hearings ...... Tower Commission
Bill intended to balance U.S. budget, 1985 .... Graham-Rudman (Hollings)
Gun bill named for White House press secretary .... Brady Bill
Idaho site of FBI standoff, 1992 .... Ruby Ridge
Banker whose conviction was overturned in 1993 .... Charles Keating
Trade agreement ratified in 1993 .... NAFTA
World trade agreement ratified in 1994 .... GATT
Malitia who had an 81 days standoff with the U.S. government, 1996
        .... Montana Freemen

57 *U.S. States and Territories*

U.S. STATES:

Alabama:

Capital	Montgomery (first Confederate capital)
Largest city	Birmingham (Pittsburgh of the South)
Port	Mobile
Bay	Mobile Bay
NASA city	Huntsville (home to Marshall Flight Center)
University	University of Alabama (Crimson Tide)
Governor three times	George Wallace
Senator	Trent Lott
Female governor, 1967-71	Lurleen Wallace
Indians	Creek
Forest	Talladega National Forest

Alaska:

The Last Frontier, Russian America (Largest state, least in population density)

Capital	Juneau (largest state capital in area)
Largest city	Anchorage (on Cook Inlet)
Second largest city	Fairbanks (named after V.P. Charles Fairbanks)
Oil shipping port	Valdez
Northern-most U.S. point	Point Barrow
Nicknames	Seward's Folly, Seward's Icebox
Largest Island	Kodiak Island
Island chain	Aleutians
River	Yukon
Northern mountain range	Brooks Range
Peninsulas	Alaska Peninsula, Seward Peninsula
Strait	Bering Strait
Inlet	Cook Inlet
Sea	Bering Sea
Bering Sea islands	Pribilof Islands, Little Diamede
Sound	Prince William Sound
Northern bay	Prudhoe Bay (oil drilling center)
National parks	Denali, Glacier Bay, Gates of the Arctic
Holiday	Seward's Day
Eskimos	Inuits
University	University of Alaska at Anchorage
Pop singer	Jewel

Arizona:
The Grand Canyon State
Capital and largest city	Phoenix (largest state capital, city that rose from the ashes of a Spanish mission)
Second largest city	Tucson
Phoenix valley	Valley of the Sun
Largest Indian tribe	Navajo
Lake	Lake Havasu (home to the London Bridge)
River	Colorado
Forest	Tonto National Forest
National park	Grand Canyon
Ancient forest ruins	Petrified Forest
Desert	Sonora
Valley filmed in many westerns	Monument Valley
"Colorful" desert	Painted Desert
Dam	Hoover Dam (formerly Boulder Dam)
Hoover Dam lake	Lake Mead
Mine	Lost Dutchman Mine
Governor	Bruce Babbitt
Senator, 1953-65, 1979-87	Barry Goldwater
Longtime congressman	Carl Hayden
Supreme Court justices	William Rehnquist, Sandra Day O'Connor
Universities	University of Arizona at Tucson (Wildcats)
	Arizona State University at Tempe (Sun Devils)

Pro sports teams:
NBA	Phoenix Suns
NFL	Arizona Cardinals
NHL	Phoenix Coyotes
MLB	Arizona Diamondbacks

Arkansas:
The Land of Opportunity
Capital and largest city	Little Rock
Mountains	Ozarks
Rivers	Arkansas, Red
National park	Hot Springs
State park	Crater of Diamonds
President	Bill Clinton
Clinton's home town	Hope
Senators	Dale Bumpers, William Fulbright
Governors	Bill Clinton, Dale Bumpers, Winthrop Rockefeller, Jim Guy Tucker (resigned due to Whitewater)
Bentonville business	Wal-Mart

57 | *U.S. States and Territories*

California:
The Golden State (most populous state)

Capital	Sacramento
Largest city	Los Angeles
Second largest city	San Francisco
Mountains	Sierra Nevada (where Donner Party met its fate)
National parks	Yosemite, King's Canyon, Redwood, Sequoia
Fault line	San Andreas Fault
USA's lowest elevation	Death Valley
Lake	Lake Tahoe
Wine country	Napa Valley
Desert	Mojave
Forest	Shasta National Forest
Winter Olympics site, 1960	Squaw Valley
San Diego founder	Junipero Serra
Los Angeles asphalt bog	La Brea Tar Pits
Landmark glass church	Crystal Cathedral
Presidents	Richard Nixon, Ronald Reagan
Senators	Diane Feinstein, Barbara Boxer
Governors	Pete Wilson, Ronald Reagan, Jerry Brown, Earl Warren
Universities	Berkeley
	UCLA (Bruins)
	University of California (Golden Bears)
	USC (Trojans)
	Stanford (Cardinals)
	Cal Tech at Pasadena
	Pepperdine at Malibu
	Scripps Institution of Oceanography at San Diego
	University of San Francisco
Pro Sports teams:	
NFL	Oakland Raiders
	San Diego Chargers
	San Francisco 49ers
NBA	Los Angles Lakers (formerly Minnesota Lakers)
	Los Angeles Clippers
	Golden State Warriors
	Sacramento Kings
NHL	Los Angeles Kings
	Anaheim Mighty Ducks
	San Jose Sharks
MLB	San Diego Padres
	Los Angeles Dodgers (formerly Brooklyn Dodgers)
	Los Angeles Angels
	San Francisco Giants (formerly New York Giants)
	Oakland Athletics (formerly Kansas City Athletics)

Colorado:
Centennial State (joined the union in 1876)
Capital and largest city .... Denver (Mile High City)
Second largest city .... Colorado Springs
Mountains .... Mt. Elbert (Colorado's tallest), Pike's Peak
National parks .... Rocky Mountain, Mesa Verde
Gorge.. Royal Gorge
Silver mine city .... Leadville (highest incorporated U.S. city)
Denver natural amphitheater .... Red Rocks
Congresswoman .... Patricia Schroeder
University .... University of Colorado at Boulder (Buffaloes)
Pro sports teams:
NBA .... Denver Nuggets
NFL.. Denver Broncos
NHL... Colorado Avalanche (former Quebec Nordiques)
MLB .... Colorado Rockies

Connecticut:
The Nutmeg State, The Constitution State
Capital .... Hartford (The Insurance Capital of the World)
Largest city .... Bridgeport
Female Governor .... Ella Grasso
Congresswoman .... Clair Booth Luce
Senators .... Christopher Dodd, Joseph Lieberman
Universities .... Yale at New Haven (Bulldogs)
.... University of Connecticut at Storrs (Huskies)

Delaware:
The First State, The Blue Hen State
Capital .... Dover
Largest city .... Wilmington
Number of counties .... Three
Namesake .... Lord de la War

Florida:
The Sunshine State
Capital .... Miami
Largest city .... Jacksonville
Governor .... Jeb Bush
Space center .... John F. Kennedy Space Center
Space port at Cape Kennedy .... Cape Canaveral
First settlement .... St. Augustine
Lake .... Okeechobee
Swamp .... Okefenokee (with Georgia)
Island chain .... Florida Keys
Major keys .... Key Largo, Key West (farthest south)

57 U.S. States and Territories

National parks .... Everglades, Dry Tortugas
Universities .... Florida State University (Seminoles) at Tallahassee
.... University of Florida (Gators) at Gainesville
.... University of Miami (Hurricanes)
Pro sports teams:
NBA .... Orlando Magic
.... Miami Heat
NFL .... Miami Dolphins
.... Jacksonville Jaguars
.... Tampa Bay Buccaneers
NHL .... Florida Panthers
.... Tampa Bay Lightning
MLB .... Florida Marlins
.... Tampa Bay Devil Rays

Georgia:
The Peach State, The Empire State of the South (largest state east of the Mississippi)
Capital and largest city .... Atlanta
Second largest city .... Columbus
Port .... Savannah
Founder .... James Oglethorpe
Mountain near Atlanta .... Stone Mountain
Mountains .... Blue Ridge Mountains
Swamp .... Okefenokee
Universities .... Georgia Tech at Atlanta,
.... Spelman at Atlanta
.... University of Georgia at Athens (Bulldogs)
Pro sports teams:
NFL .... Atlanta Falcons
NBA .... Atlanta Hawks (former St. Louis Hawks)
NHL .... Atlanta Thrashers
MLB .... Atlanta Braves (owned by Ted Turner)

Hawaii:
The Aloha State (was independent country from 1849-89)
Capital and largest city .... Honolulu
King .... Kamehameha
Queen .... Liliuokalani
Major islands: .... Hawaii (The Big Island)
.... Kauai (oldest island)
.... Lanai (The Pineapple Island)
.... Molokai (Leper Island, home to Father Damian)
.... Oahu (second largest island)
.... Maui (The Garden Island)
National parks .... Volcanos on Hawaii, Haleakala on Maui
Oahu mountain .... Diamond Head

North Oahu surfing area .... Bonsai Pipeline
Harbor .... Pearl Harbor
Beach party .... Luau
Dance .... Hula
Cooked taro dish .... Poi
Polynesian god .... Maui

Idaho:
The Gem State
Capital and largest city .... Boise
River .... Snake
Canyon .... Hell's Canyon (deepest gorge in U.S.)
Monument .... Craters of the Moon
Ski area .... Sun Valley
FBI standoff site, 1992 .... Ruby Ridge

Illinois:
The Land of Lincoln, The Prairie State
Capital .... Springfield
Largest city .... Chicago
President .... Abraham Lincoln
Longtime senator .... Evertt Dirkson
Female senator .... Carol Moseley-Braun
Governors .... Adlai Stevenson, Jim Thompson
Poet .... Carl Sandburg
Poet Laureate .... Gwendolyn Brooks
Universities .... University of Illinois at Champaign (Fighting Illini)
.... Northwestern University at Chicago & Evanston (Huskies)
.... Bradley at Peoria,
.... Loyola at Chicago,
.... Illinois State University at Normal
Pro Sports teams:
NBA .... Chicago Bulls
NFL .... Chicago Bears
NHL .... Chicago Blackhawks
MLB .... Chicago Cubs, Chicago White Sox

Indiana:
The Hoosier State
Capital and largest city .... Indianapolis
Lake Michigan port .... Gary
River .... Wabash
Vice President .... Dan Quayle
Governor .... Evan Bayh
Universities .... Purdue at West Lafayette (Boilermakers)
.... Notre Dame at South Bend (Fighting Irish)

U.S. States and Territories

Pro Sports teams:
NBA .... Indiana Pacers (came from ABA)
NFL .... Indianapolis Colts (former Baltimore Colts)

Iowa:
The Hawkeye State
    Capital and largest city .... Des Moines
    River .... Des Moines
    President .... Herbert Hoover
    Author .... James Waller
    Artist... Grant Wood
    Universities .... University of Iowa at Iowa City (Hawkeyes)
    .... Iowa State at Ames (Cyclones)
    .... Drake at Des Moines

Kansas:
The Sunflower State
    Capital .... Topeka
    Largest city .... Wichita
    Historic western city .... Dodge City
    Topeka clinic .... Menninger Clinic
    Senators .... Bob Dole, Alf Landon, Nancy Landon Kassebaum
    Bob Dole's home town .... Russell
    Universities .... University of Kansas at Overland Park (Jayhawks)
    .... Kansas State at Overland Park

Kentucky:
The Bluegrass State (Commonwealth, Abe Lincoln's birthplace)
    Capital .... Frankfort
    Largest city .... Louisville
    First capital .... Bowling Green
    City named after Massachusetts city
    .... Lexington
    U.S. gold reserve .... Fort Knox
    Museum... Kentucky Derby Museum
    National park .... Mammoth Cave
    Universities .... University of Kentucky (Wildcats)
    .... University of Louisville (Cardinals)

Louisiana:
The Pelican State (Commonwealth)
    Capital .... Baton Rouge
    Largest city .... New Orleans (The Big Easy, The Crescent City)
    Lake .... Lake Pontchartrain
    Assassinated governor .... Huey Long ("Kingfish")

French Canadian descendants .... Cajuns
County-like divisions .... Parishes
New Orleans historic area .... French quarter
New Orleans historic hall .... Preservation Hall
Universities .... Southern University at Shreveport
.... Tulane at New Orleans (Green Wave)
.... Loyola at New Orleans
.... Louisiana State University at Baton Rouge (Tigers)
Pro sport team:
NFL .... New Orleans Saints

Maine:
The Pine Tree State (the only one-syllable state, the only state bordered by only one other state)
Capital .... Augusta
Largest city .... Portland
Overseas refueling stop .... Bangor
National Park.................................. Acadia
River .... Kennebunk
Author .... Stephen King
Senator .... Margaret Chase Smith
19th century Secretary of State .... James Blaine
20th century Secretary of State .... Edwin Muskie

Maryland:
The Old Line State, The Star Spangled Banner State
Capital .... Annapolis (named after Queen Anne)
Largest city .... Baltimore
Flower... Black-Eyed Susan
Founder .... Cecil Calvert
Bay .... Chesapeake Bay
Island .... Kent Island
Fort... Fort McHenry
Baltimore critic .... H. L. Mencken
Vice president .... Spiro Agnew
Representative and senator .... Barbra Mikulski
Universities .... Johns Hopkins at Baltimore,
................................United States Naval Academy at Annapolis (Midshipmen)
Pro sports teams:
NFL .... Baltimore Ravens (named after Poe's "The Raven")
NBA .... Baltimore Wizards (formerly Washington Bullets)
MLB .... Baltimore Orioles (formerly St. Louis Browns)

Massachusetts:
The Bay State (Commonwealth)
Capital and largest city .... Boston
Boston church/landmark .... Old North Church

57 *U.S. States and Territories*

Boston park .... Boston Common
Boston hall .... Faneuil Hall
Witch trial city, 1697 .... Salem
Lizzy Borden's home town .... Fall River
Music festival city .... Tanglewood
Resort islands .... Martha's Vineyard, Nantucket Island
Capes .... Cape Ann, Cape Cod
Bays .... Buzzard's Bay, Cape Cod Bay
Sound .... Nantucket Sound
Lowell artist .... James Whistler
Hills .... Berkshires
Amherst poet .... Emily Dickinson
Salem author .... Nathaniel Hawthorne
Presidents....................................... John Adams, John Quincy Adams, John F. Kennedy
Senators .... Ted Kennedy, Henry Cabot Lodge, John Kerry
Governors .... Hugh Carey, Calvin Coolidge
Universities .... Harvard (Bulldogs)
.... Massachusetts Institute of Technology
Pro sports teams:
NFL .... New England Patriots
NBA .... Boston Celtics
NHL .... Boston Bruins
MLB .... Boston Red Sox

Michigan:
The Wolverine State
Capital .... Lansing
Largest city .... Detroit
National park................................... Isle Royal
Strait .... Strait of Mackinac
President .... Gerald Ford
Governor .... George Romney
Universities .... University of Michigan at Ann Arbor (Wolverines)
.... Michigan State University at Lansing (Spartans)
Pro sports teams:
NFL .... Detroit Lions
NBA .... Detroit Pistons
NHL .... Detroit Red Wings
MLB .... Detroit Tigers

Minnesota:
The Gopher State, Land of 10,000 Lakes (farthest north of the lower 48 states)
Capital .... St. Paul
Largest city .... Minneapolis
Port .... Duluth
Rochester clinic .... Mayo (Brothers) Clinic

Mountain range .... Masabi (known for its iron ore deposits)
Source of Mississippi River .... Lake Itaska
National park .... Voyagers
Sauk Center author .... Sinclair Lewis
Walnut Grove author .... Laura Ingalls Wilder
Vice presidents .... Hubert Humphrey, Walter (Fritz) Mondale
Governor, 1998- .... Jesse ("the Body") Ventura
University .... University of Minnesota at St. Paul (Golden
                                                        Gophers)
Pro sports teams:
NFL .... Minnesota Vikings
NBA .... Minnesota Timberwolves
NHL .... Minnesota Wild
MLB .... Minnesota Twins (formerly Washinton Senators)

Mississippi:
The Magnolia State
    Capital and largest city .... Jackson (named for Andrew Jackson)
    Ports .... Biloxi, Gulfport
    Senator .... Trent Lott
    Oxford author .... William Faulkner
    Elvis Presley's birthplace................. Tupelo
    Short story writer .... Eudora Welty
    Indian trail .... Natchez Trace
    University .... University of Mississippi at Oxford (Ole Miss)

Missouri:
The Show Me State
    Capital .... Jefferson City
    Largest city .... St. Louis
    Second largest city .... Kansas City
    Start of the Pony Express .... St. Joseph
    Harry Truman's home .... Independence
    Mountains .... Ozarks
    Muralist .... Thomas Hart Benton
    Astronomer .... Edwin Hubble
    Outlaws .... The James Gang
    President .... Harry Truman
    Senators .... Thomas Eagleton, John Danforth
    Universities .... University of Missouri at Columbia (Tigers)
    .... Washington University in St. Louis
Pro sports teams:
NFL.. St. Louis Rams, Kansas City Chiefs
NHL... St. Louis Blues
MLB .... St. Louis Cardinals, Kansas City Royals

Montana:
The Treasure State
    Capital .... Helena (home of Last Chance Gulch)
    Largest city .... Billings
    River .... Missouri
    Battlefield .... Little Big Horn
    National parks .... Glacier, Waterton-Glacier International Peace Park
        (shared with Canada)
    University .... University of Montana at Missoula

Nebraska:
The Cornhusker State, The Beef State
    Capital .... Lincoln
    Legislature type .... Unicameral (only one house)
    Largest city .... Omaha
    River .... (North) Platte
    Home for boys near Omaha .... Boys Town
    Author .... Willa Cather
    Comedian .... Johnny Carson
    Politician .... William Jennings Bryan (3-time presidential candidate)
    University .... University of Nebraska at Lincoln (Cornhuskers)

Nevada:
The Silver State, The Battle Born State, The Sagebrush State
    Capital .... Carson City (named after Kit Carson)
    Largest city .... Las Vegas
    Second largest city .... Reno
    Largest river .... Humboldt
    Reno River .... Truckee
    Silver mine .... Comstock lode
    Comstock lode city .... Virginia City
    Lakes .... Lake Tahoe (shared with California)

New Hampshire:
The Granite State
    Capital .... Concord
    Largest city .... Manchester
    Port .... Portsmouth
    Mountain .... Mt. Washington
    Mountain range .... Presidential Range
    Prep school .... Exeter
    President .... Franklin Pierce

New Jersey:
The Garden State (most densely populated state)
    Capital .... Trenton

Largest city .... Newark
Gambling city .... Atlantic City
Cape .... Cape May
Governor .... Christine Todd Whitman
Senator .... Bill Bradley
Universities .... Princeton
.... Rutgers at Newark
Pro sports teams:
NFL .... New York Giants, New York Jets
NBA .... New Jersey Nets
NHL .... New Jersey Devils

New Mexico:
The Land of Enchantment
Capital .... Santa Fe
Largest city .... Albuquerque
Ski city .... Taos
UFO crash site .... Roswell
Atomic research center .... Los Alamos
First atomic bomb site .... Trinity
City near Trinity .... Alamogordo
River .... Rio Grande ("Big River")
State bird .... Roadrunner
National park .... Carlsbad Caverns
National monument .... White Sands National Monument
University .... University of New Mexico at Albuquerque

New York:
The Empire State
Capital .... Albany (site of Fort Orange)
Largest city .... New York City
Second largest city .... Buffalo
Long Island nuclear research center .. Brookhaven National Laboratory
Northern mountains .... Adirondacks
Southern mountains .... Catskills
River .... Hudson
Hudson tributary .... Mohawk
Lakes .... Finger Lakes, Lake Champlain (shared with
                                            Vermont)
Winter Olympics site, 1932, 1980 . Lake Placid
Presidents .... Martin van Buren, Chester Arthur, Grover
                                            Cleveland, Theodore Roosevelt, Franklin Roosevelt
Vice Presidents .... Aaron Burr, Nelson Rockefeller
Governors .... Dewitt Clinton, Al Smith, Thomas Dewey, Nelson
                                            Rockefeller, Mario Cuomo, Hugh Carey
Senators .... Daniel Moynihan, Alfonse D'Amato, Hillary Clinton

57 U.S. States and Territories

New York City mayors .... Fiorello La Guardia, Mario Cuomo, Ed Koch,
                                         David Dinkins, Rudolph Giuliani
Universities .... City University of New York (CUNY)
.... Colgate at Hamilton
.... Columbia at New York City
.... Cornell at Ithaca
.... Syracuse
.... Vassar at Poughkeepsie
Pro sports teams:
NFL .... Buffalo Bills
NBA .... New York Knicks
NHL .... Buffalo Sabres, New York Islanders, New York Rangers
MLB .... New York Mets, New York Yankees

North Carolina:
The Tarheel State
Capital .... Raleigh
Largest city .... Charlotte
Mountains .... Blue Ridge Mountains (shared with Georgia)
National park .... Great Smoky Mountains (shared with Tennessee)
Capes .... Cape Hatteras, Cape Fear
Sounds .... Pamilco, Albemarle
Island .... Roanoke
Cradle of aviation .... Kitty Hawk
Author .... Thomas Wolfe
Senator .... Sam Irvin, Jesse Helms
Universities .... Duke at Durham (Blue Devils)
.... University of North Carolina at Chapel Hil (Tarheels)
.... Wake Forest at Winston-Salem (Deamon Decons)
.... North Carolina State at Raleigh
Pro sports teams:
NFL .... Carolina Panthers
NBA .... Charlotte Hornets
NHL .... Carolina Hurricanes

North Dakota:
The Peace Garden State, The Sioux State (geographic center of North America)
Capital .... Bismarck
Largest city .... Fargo
Rivers .... Red River (of the North), Missouri
National park .... Theodore Roosevelt

Ohio:
The Buckeye State
Capital .... Columbus
Largest city .... Cleveland (on Lake Erie)

First capital .... Zanesville
Pro Football Hall of Fame .... Canton
Rubber capital .... Akron
Wright Brothers city .... Dayton
Presidents .... U. S. Grant, Rutherford B. Hayes, James Garfield,
.... William McKinley, William Taft
Senator .... John Glenn
Author .... Toni Morrison
Universities .... Ohio State University (Buckeyes)
.... Miami of Ohio
.... University of Cincinnati (Bearcats)
Pro sports teams:
NFL .... Cincinnati Bengals
NBA .... Cleveland Cavaliers
NHL .... Columbus Blue Jackets
MLB .... Cleveland Indians, Cincinnati Reds

Oklahoma:
The Sooner State
Capital and largest city .... Oklahoma City
Second largest city .... Tulsa ("The Oil Capital of the World")
Universities .... University of Oklahoma at Norman (Sooners)
.... Oklahoma State University at Stillwater (Cowboys)
.... Oral Roberts at Tulsa

Oregon:
The Beaver State
Capital .... Salem
Largest city .... Portland
End of Oregon Trail .... Astoria (named for John Jacob Astor)
Rivers .... Columbia, Willamette
Senator .... Bob Packwood (forced to resign, 1995)
National park .... Crater Lake
Crater Lake island .... Wizard's Island
Waterfall .... Klammath Falls
Universities .... University of Oregon at Eugene (Beavers)
.... Willamette University at Salem
Pro sports team:
NBA .... Portland Trailblazers

Pennsylvania:
The Keystone State
Capital .... Harrisburg
Largest city .... Philadelphia
Philadelphia statehouse .... Independence Hall

57   *U.S. States and Territories*

Philadelphia seat of Continental Congress, 1774
.... Carpenter's Hall
Second largest city .... Pittsburgh
Port .... Erie
Flood city .... Johnstown
Chocolate-making city .... Hershey
Founder .... William Penn
Nationality of first settlers .... Swedish
Religious sects .... Pennsylvania Dutch, Quakers
Pittsburgh rivers .... Allegheny, Monongahela, Ohio
Universities .... Penn State at State College (Nittany Lions),
.... Pittsburgh University
.... Lehigh at Bethlehem
Pro Sports teams:
NFL .... Philadelphia Eagles, Pittsburgh Steelers
NBA .... Philadelphia Seventy-Sixers
NHL .... Philadelphia Flyers, Pittsburgh Penguins
MLB .... Philadelphia Phillies, Pittsburgh Pirates

Rhode Island:
The Ocean State (the smallest state)
    Capital and largest city .... Providence (founded by Roger Williams)
    Port and jazz festival city .... Newport
    Bay .... Narragansett Bay
    Painter .... Gilbert Stewart

South Carolina:
The Palmetto State
    Capital and largest city .... Columbia
    Port .... Charleston
    Beach .... Myrtle Beach
    Island .... Hilton Head Island
    River .... Savannah
    Fort .... Fort Sumter
    "Swamp Fox" .... Francis Marion
    Spanish Explorer .... Gardillo
    Senator .... Strom Thurmond
    Strom Thurmond supporters .... "Dixiecrats"
    Military academy .... The Citadel

South Dakota:
The Sunshine State, The Coyote State
    Capital .... Pierre
    Largest city .... Sioux Falls
    Hills .... Black Hills
    National monument .... Mt. Rushmore

River .... Missouri
National parks .... Badlands, Windcave

Tennessee:
The Volunteer State
Capital .... Nashville
Largest city .... Memphis
Civil War capital .... Bowling Green
World's Fair city .... Knoxville
Nuclear research center .... Oak Ridge
Highest point .... Clingman's Dome
National park .... Great Smoky Mountains
Bird .... Tennessee Warbler
Horse .... Tennessee Walker
Presidents .... Andrew Jackson, Andrew Johnson, James Polk
Vice president .... Al Gore
Senators .... Howard Baker, Fred Thompson
Congressman .... Davy Crockett
Governor .... Lamar Alexander
Universities .... University of Tennessee at Knoxville (Volunteers)
.... Vanderbilt at Nashville
Pro sports team:
NFL .... Tennessee Titans (former Houston Oilers)

Texas:
The Lone Star State (second largest state; independent country from 1836-45)
Capital .... Austin
Largest city .... Houston
Second largest city .... Dallas (named after V.P. George M. Dallas)
Southernmost city .... Brownsville
State flower .... Bluebonnet
River .... Rio Grande
National parks .... Big Bend, Guadaloupe Mountains
Island .... Padre Island
Large ranch .... King Ranch
NASA center in Houston .... Johnson Space Center
Oil field .... Spindle Top Gusher
Lawmen .... Texas Rangers
Texas Rangers founder .... Stephen Austin
Presidents .... Dwight Eisenhower, Lyndon Johnson
Senators .... Lloyd Bentson, Phil Grahm
Governors .... Sam Houston, John Connally, Ann Richards,
                                                        George W. Bush
Representatives .... Sam Rayburn, Barbara Jordan
Universities: .... University of Texas at Austin (Longhorns)
.... Texas Tech at Lubbock

57 *U.S. States and Territories*

.... Baylor at Waco
.... Rice at Houston
.... TCU at Fort Worth
.... SMU at Dallas
Pro sports teams:
NFL .... Dallas Cowboys
NBA .... Dallas Mavericks, Houston Rockets,
　　　　　　　　　　　　　　　　San Antonio Spurs
NHL .... Dallas Stars
MLB .... Texas Rangers, Houston Astros

Utah:
The Beehive State
Capital and largest city .... Salt Lake City (the only three-word state capital)
Highest point .... King's Peak
Senator .... Orrin Hatch
National parks .... Canyonlands, Arches, Bryce Canyon, Zion
Ancient lake .... Lake Bonneville
University .... Brigham Young University at Provo
Pro sports team:
NBA .... Utah Jazz (formerly New Orleans Jazz)

Vermont:
The Green Mountain State (independent country from 1777-91)
Capital .... Montpelier
Largest city .... Burlington
Lake .... Lake Champlain
President .... Calvin Coolidge
Senator .... Patrick Leahy

Virginia:
Old Dominion State
Capital .... Richmond
Largest city and port .... Norfolk
Colonial capital .... Williamsburg
Motto .... Sic Semper Tyrannis
Rivers .... James, Potomac
Mountains .... Blue Ridge
Swamp .... Dismal Swamp
Cemetery .... Arlington National Cemetery
Senator .... Charles Robb
Author .... William Styron
Orator .... Patrick Henry
National park .... Shenandoah
Presidents .... George Washington, Thomas Jefferson, James
　　　　　　　　　　　　　　　　Madison, James Monroe

Chief Justice .... John Marshall
Universities ...... William & Mary at Williamsburg (Second oldest university in the U.S.)
.... University of Virginia at Charlottesville (founded by Thomas
Jefferson)

Washington:
The Evergreen State
Capital .... Olympia
Largest city .... Seattle (named after Chief Seattle)
Highest mountain .... Mt. Rainier
Volcano .... Mt. St. Helens
River .... Columbia
Dam .... Grand Coulee
Sound .... Puget Sound
Female Governor .... Dixie Lee Ray
Airframe manufacturer .... Boeing at Everett
National parks .... Mt. Rainier, Olympic, North Cascades
University .... University of Washington at Seattle (Huskies)
Pro sports teams:
NFL .... Seattle Seahawks
NBA .... Seattle Supersonics
MLB .... Seattle Mariners

West Virginia:
The Mountain State (the only state to secede from another state, the newest state east of the
Mississippi)
Capital and largest city .... Charleston
Ferry .... Harper's Ferry
Senator .... Robert Byrd

Wisconsin:
The Badger State
Capital .... Madison
Largest city .... Milwaukee
Senators .... Joseph McCarthy, William Proxmire (noted for his
"Golden Fleece Award")
Universities .... University of Wisconsin (Badgers)
.... Marquette University at Milwaukee
Pro sports teams:
NFL .... Green Bay Packers
NBA .... Milwaukee Bucks
MLB .... Milwaukee Brewers

Wyoming:
The Equality State, The Equal Rights Banner State (least populous state, home to USA's first female governor)

Capital .... Cheyenne
Largest city .... Casper
National monument .... Devil's Tower
National parks .... Yellowstone (the first national park), Grand Teton
Oil scandal site .... Teapot Dome

UNITED STATES TERRITORIES:

Puerto Rico:
(acquired in the Spanish-American War)
Capital: San Juan
Island group: Greater Antilles

Guam: ("Where Americia's day begins")
(acquired in the Spanish-American War)
Capital: Agana
Island group: Marianas

U.S. Virgin Islands:
(acquired from Denmark, 1917)
Capital: Charlotte Amalie
Island group: Virgin Islands
Main islands: St. Thomas, St. Croix, St. John

American Samoa:
(southernmost U.S. possession)
Capital and port: Pango Pango (pronounced Pago Pago)
Island group: Samoan Island Group

Wake Island

Midway Islands

Northern Mariana Islands

Johnson Atoll

Baker, Howland, and Jarvis Islands

Kingman Reef

Navassa Island

Palmyra Atoll

United Nations 58

Secretary Generals:

Trygve Lie of Norway, 1946-53

Dag Hammarskjold of Sweden, 1953-61 (won posthumous Nobel Peace Prize)

U-Thant of Burma, 1961-71

Kurt Waldheim of Austria, 1972-81

Javier Perez de Cuellar of Peru, 1982-91

Boutros Boutros-Ghali of Egypt, 1991-96

Kofi Annon of Ghana, 1997-

U.S. Ambassadors to the United Nations:

Henry Cabot Lodge, Jr. (1953-60)

Adlai Stevenson (1961-65)

George Bush (1971-73)

Daniel Moynihan (1975-76)

Andrew Young (1977-79)

Jeanne Kirkpatrick (1981-85)

Madeleine Albright (1993-96)

Richard Holbrooke (1999-)

Security Council Permanent Members:

China

France

Russia

United Kingdom

United States

Agencies of the United Nations:

International Monetary Fund (IMF)

U.N. Educational, Scientific and Cultural Organization (UNESCO)

U.N. International Children's Emergency Fund (UNICEF)

World Bank (in Washington, D.C.)

World Health Organization (HQ in Vienna)

International Court of Justice (at The Hague)

There are currently 158 countries that are members of the United Nations

59 *Women*

First Woman:

Born in an American colony	Virginia Dare
Winner of two Nobel Prizes	Marie Curie
To receive the Congressional Medal of Honor	Mary Walker
In Congress	Jeannette Rankin (1916)
Senator	Hattie Caraway (1932)
Elected in both houses of Congress	Margaret Chase Smith
Presidential cabinet member	Frances Perkins (FDR administration)
Secretary of State	Madeleine Albright
Supreme Court Justice	Sandra Day O'Connor
Secretary of Transportation	Elizabeth Dole
Surgeon General	Jocelyn Elders
Attorney General	Janet Reno
To break sound barrier	Janet Cochrin
To fly nonstop around the world	Jeanna Yeager
To swim the English Channel	Gertrude Ederle
American doctor	Elizabeth Blackwell
American astronomer	Maria Mitchell
Presidential candidate	Victoria Woodhull (1872)
Major party V.P. candidate	Geraldine Ferraro
To co-anchor major network news	Barbara Walters
Time Woman of the Year	Wallis Simpson
In Gymnastics Hall of Fame	Mary Lou Retton
U.S. balance beam gold medalist	Shannon Miller
Miss America	Margaret Gorman (1921)
Citadel cadet	Shannon Faulkner
Stewardess	Ellen Church
To win $100,000 on *Star Search*	Jenny Jones
In the Indianapolis 500	Janet Guthrie

Other facts:

Prime Minister of India, 1966-77, 1980-84	Indira Gandhi
Prime Minister of Israel, 1969-74	Golda Meir (raised in Milwaukee)
President of Argentina, 1975-76	Isabel Peron
Prime Minister of Great Britain, 1979-90	Margaret Thatcher
President of the Philippines, 1986-92	Corazon Aquino
Prime Minister of Pakistan, 1988-90	Benazir Bhutto
President of Nicaragua, 1990-	Violetta Chamorro
Prime Minister of Canada, 1993	Kim Campbell
Andre Sacarov's disident wife	Elana Bonner

Poetess from the island of Lesbos	Sappho
Lady from Coventry, England	Lady Godiva
Titanic survivor from Leadville, CO	(Unsinkable) Molly Brown
Pilot lost over the Pacific, 1937	Amelia Earhart
She went around world in 72 days, 1890	Nelly Bly
Franco-Prussian war nurse, Red Cross founder	Clara Barton
Frontier woman from Deadwood, SD	Calamity Jane
Wild West Show sharp-shooter	Annie Oakley
Friend of the James Gang	Belle Starr
Deaf Radcliffe graduate, 1904	Helen Keller
Helen Keller's teacher	Anne Sullivan
Hull House founder	Jane Addams
Lord Nelson's lover	Emma (Lady) Hamilton
Founder of Bryn Mawr school for girls	Edith Hamilton
Austrian born pioneer of child psychoanalysis	Anna Freud
First president, National Women's Suffrage Assn.	Susan B. Anthony
Women's rights leader from Seneca Falls, NY	Elizabeth Cady Stanton
Burlesque queen who lived in France	Josephine Baker
Minsky's and Ziegfeld Follies burlesque dancer	Gypsy Rose Lee
American impressionist painter	Mary Cassatt
Southwestern painter of flowers and skyscapes	Georgia O'Keefe
Amsterdam diarist	Anne Frank
1920s etiquette advisor	Emily Post
1990s etiquette advisor	Martha Stewart
Original platinum blond	Jean Harlow
"The Lady With the Lamp"	Florence Nightingale
"The Bird Woman"	Sacajawea
"The Poor Little Rich Girl"	Barbara Hutton
"The Blonde Bombshell"	Jayne Mansfield
"America's Sweetheart"	Mary Pickford
"First Lady of the Silent Screen"	Lillian Gish
"Girl in the Red Velvet Swing"	Evelyn Nesbit Thaw
"Peekaboo Girl"	Veronica Lake
"Sweater Girl"	Lana Turner
"Sarong Girl"	Dorothy Lamour
"It Girl"	Clara Bow
"The Pinup Girl"	Betty Grable
"First Lady of Song"	Ella Fitzgerald
"First Lady of the American Stage"	Helen Hayes
"Queen of the Swash Bucklers"	Maureen O'Hara
"Queen of the West"	Dale Evans
"Queen of the Surf"	Esther Williams
"Queen of Soul"	Aretha Franklin
"Queen of Disco"	Donna Summer
Algonquin Hotel "round table wit"	Dorothy Parker
Four Square Gospel founder	Aimee Semple McPherson

59 *Women*

She studied mountain gorillas	Dian Fossey
She studied chimpanzees	Jane Goodall
The Nun of Amherst or the Belle of Amherst	Emily Dickinson
Emily Dickinson's advisor	Helen Hunt Jackson
Italian teaching method innovator	Maria Montessori
Abe Lincoln's young love	Ann Rutledge
Dante's love	Beatrice
Frederic Chopin's lover	George Sand
Dashiell Hammet's lover	Lillian Hellman
Time-Life Korean War photographer	Margaret Bourke-White
"The last of the red hot mamas"	Sophie Tucker
Bob Fosse's "Red Headed" wife	Gwen Verdon
She said "Call me madam"	Ethel Merman
CNN's British-Iranian reporter	Christiane Amanpour
Heiress kidnapped on February 5, 1974	Patty Hearst
Nobel Peace Prize winner in 1979	Mother Teresa
Slain Tejano singer	Selena
Red-headed country music star	Reba McIntyre
New Jersey governor	Christie Todd Whitman
Texas governor, 1991-95	Ann Richards
Washington governor, 1995-	Dixie Lee Ray
Connecticut governor, 1975-80	Ella Grasso
Connecticut representative, 1943-47	Clare Booth Luce
Maryland senator and congressperson	Barbara Mikulski
Chicago mayor, 1979	Jane Burn
U.S. ambassador to Ghana	Shirley Temple Black
U.S. ambassador to Italy, 1953	Clare Booth Luce
Paleoanthropologist who died in 1996	Mary Leaky
Supreme Court Justice appointed in 1993	Ruth Bader Ginsburg
Teacher who perished in the *Challenger* disaster	Christa McAuliffe
Most down-loaded model on the internet	Cindy Margolis
She testified against Clarence Thomas	Anita Hill
White House corrispondant who retired after 40 years	Helen Thomas
First test tube baby	Louise Brown
Child was pulled from a Texas well, 1984	Baby Jessica (McClure)
Miss America winners:	
1945	Bess Myerson
1955	Lee Meriwether
1971	Phyllis George
1984	Vanessa Williams
She replaced Vanessa Williams	Suzette Charles

World Geography 60

Bodies of Water:

World's Oceans (in order of size):
1. Pacific Ocean
2. Atlantic Ocean
3. Indian Ocean
4. Arctic Ocean

The Great Lakes (in order of size):
1. Superior
2. Huron
3. Michigan
4. Erie
5. Ontario

World's Largest Lakes:
1. Caspian Sea
2. Lake Superior
3. Lake Victoria
4. Aral Sea
5. Lake Huron
6. Lake Michigan
7. Lake Tanganyika
8. Lake Baikal
9. Great Bear Lake
10. Malawi Lake

Seas of the World:
Sea between Russian and Alaska .... Bering Sea
Sea between Italy and Balkan Peninsula .... Adriatic Sea
Sea between China and Korea .... Yellow Sea
Sea west of Vietnam, east of the Philippines .... South China Sea
Sea east of Australia, home to Great Barrier Reef .... Coral Sea
Sea between India and Arabian peninsula .... Arabian Sea
Belgium, Norway and Denmark sea .... North Sea
Latvia, Lithuania and Estonia sea .... Baltic Sea
Sea between Ireland and Great Britain .... Irish Sea
World's saltiest body of water .... Dead Sea
Sea between Egypt and Saudi Arabia .... Red Sea
Georgia, Bulgaria and Ukraine sea .... Black Sea
Sea north of Black Sea and Crimean Peninsula .... Sea of Azov
Sea between Greece and Turkey .... Aegean Sea
Sea separating Asian and European Turkey .... Sea of Marmara
Sea in Israel, a.k.a. Lake Tiberias .... Sea of Galilee
Kazakhstan-Uzbekistan sea .... Aral Sea

Other bodies of water facts:

World's largest sea .... South China Sea
World's largest swamp .... Gran Pantanal (Brazil)
World's largest marsh .... Everglades
World's largest bay .... Hudson Bay
World's largest gulf .... Gulf of Mexico
World's highest tide .... Bay of Fundy (Canada)
World's deepest lake .... Lake Baikal (Siberia, Russia)
World's longest freshwater lake .... Lake Tanganyika
Largest lake in South America .... Lake Titicaca
Deepest lake in the U.S. .... Crater Lake
Largest lake lying within U.S. boundaries .... Lake Michigan
Source of Mississippi River .... Lake Itaska, Minnesota
World's longest strait .... Strait of Malacca (Indonesia)
Persian Gulf strait .... Strait of Hormuz
Strait between English Channel and North Sea .... Strait of Dover
Strait at southern end of South America .... Strait of Magellan
Strait dividing Asia and North America .... Bering Strait
Strait dividing Spain and Morocco .... Strait of Gibralter
Strait separating Italy and Sicily .... Strait of Messina
Strait separating North and South Islands of New Zealand
.... Cook Strait
Swedish-Finnish Gulf .... Gulf of Bothnia
Prince Edward Island gulf .... Gulf of St. Lawrence
Gulf between Iran and Arabian peninsula .... Persian Gulf
Gulf of western Africa .... Gulf of Guinea
Bay on Beaufort Sea .... Prudhoe Bay
Bangladesh bay .... Bay of Bengal
Spanish-French bay .... Bay of Biscay
Liffey River bay .... Dublin Bay
Sound south of Cape Cod .... Nantucket Sound
Washington state sound .... Puget Sound
Canals in Venice and China .... Grand Canals
Canal connecting Hudson River and Great Lakes .... Erie Canal
Lake between Switzerland and France .... Lake Geneva
Lake behind Grand Coulee Dam .... Franklin D. Roosevelt Lake
Lake behind Hoover Dam .... Lake Mead
Lake behind Aswan High Dam .... Lake Nasser
New York-Vermont lake .... Lake Champlain

Deserts:

North African desert .... Sahara Desert (world's largest)
Southern African desert .... Kalahari Desert
Southwest African desert .... Namib
Indian/Pakistani desert .... Thar Desert

Australian deserts .... Victoria & Great Sandy Deserts
Chinese/Mongolian desert .... Gobi Desert
Southwest American desert .... Mojave Desert
South American desert .... Atacama (world's driest place)
Israeli desert .... Negev
Southwest USA/Northern Mexico desert .... Sonora
Highest temperature ever recorded .... 136 degrees in Libyan Sahara

Islands:

World's largest islands:
1. Greenland (administered by Denmark)
2. New Guinea (Indonesia and Papua New Guinea)
3. Borneo (Indonesia, Malaysia and Brunei)
4. Madagascar (formerly Malagasy Republic, a French colony)
5. Baffin Island (Canada)
6. Sumatra (Indonesia)
7. Honshu (Japan)
8. Great Britain
9. Victoria Island (Canada)
10. Ellesmere Island (Canada)

Caribbean Sea's largest islands (all part of Greater Antilles):
1. Cuba
2. Hispaniola
3. Jamaica
4. Puerto Rico

Napoleon's islands:
Corsica (birthplace)
Elba (exiled there for 100 days)
St. Helena (in the south Atlantic, where he died)

French Caribbean islands:
Guadeloupe
Martinique
St. Maarten (owned with The Netherlands)

Oceania's Islands:
Small islands .... Micronesia
Black islands .... Melanesia
Many islands .... Polynesia

Other island facts:
Caribbean *ABC* islands .... Aruba, Bonaire, Curaçao
Australia's largest island .... Tasmania

New Zealand's main islands	North and South Island
Chile's Pacific island	Easter Island
Chile and Argentina's southern island	Tierra del Fuego
Equador's Pacific islands	Galapagos
Blue Grotto island	Capri
Irish Sea island	Isle of Man
"Pony" island in English Channel	Shetland Island
Danish islands between Iceland and Great Britain	Faroe Islands
Islands 500 miles northwest of Scotland	Hebrides
Europe's smallest island nation	Malta
Islands of the world's worst airline disaster, owned by Spain	Canary Islands
Portuguese islands in Atlantic	Azores
Bahama's most populous island	New Providence
Texas island that is one hundred miles long	Padre Island
The Statue of Liberty sits on this island	Bedloe's Island
Island that welcomed 19th century U.S. immigrants	Ellis Island
California immigrant island	Angel Island
Disney World island	Pleasure Island
Prison located on San Francisco bay island	Alcatraz
Bounty mutineer's island	Pitcairn
Major Dreyfus and Papillon were exiled here	Devil's Island
Island of Mt. Suribachi	Iwo Jima
Marshall Island's site of first atomic test in Pacific	Eniwetok
Marshall Island's site of first hydrogen bomb test	Bikini
Largest tropical island	New Guinea
Island of giant monitor lizards	Komodo
Brunei's island	Borneo
Jakarta's island	Java
Indonesia's western-most main island	Sumatra
Largest island in Mediterranean	Sicily
Second-largest island in the Mediterranean	Sardinia
Asia's smallest island country	Singapore
Island just south of India	Sri Lanka (formerly Ceylon)
Tanzania's island	Zanzibar
Formerly known as Cook Islands	New Zealand
Formerly known as Sandwich Islands	Hawaii
Formerly known as the Malagasy Republic	Madagascar
U.S. naval base in southern Indian Ocean	Diego Garcia
Main island of the Philippines	Luzon
Island in Manila Bay	Corregidor
Main island of Japan	Honshu
Large northern island of Japan	Hokkaido
Large southern island of Japan	Kyushu
Largest island in the United States	Hawaii (the Big Island)
Alaska's largest island	Kodiak Island

Canada's largest island	Baffin island
Canada's northern-most island	Ellesmere Island
Western Canada's largest island	Vancouver Island
Nova Scotia island	Cape Breton
Europe's largest island	Great Britain
Antigua's sister island	Barbuda
Largest island of Netherland Antilles	Curaçao
St. Vincent's sister island	Grenadines
Tahiti island group	Society Islands
Bikini island group	Marshall Islands
Guam island group	Mariana or Micronesia
Guadalcanal island group	Solomon Islands
Mallorca and Ibiza island group	Balearic Islands
Island group including Tenerife	Canary Islands
St. Croix and St. Thomas island group	Virgin Islands

Mountains

World's highest	Mt. Everest
World's second highest	K2 (Mt. Godwin-Austen)
World's highest mountain chain	Himalayas
World's second highest mountain chain	Andes

Highest mountain in:

Antarctica	Vinson Massif
Africa	Mt. Kilamanjaro
Asia	Mt. Everest
Australia	Mt. Kosciusko
Europe	Mt. Blanc
North America	Mt. McKinley (a.k.a. Danili)
South America	Mt. Aconcagua
Lower 48 states	Mt. Whitney, CA
East of the Mississippi	Mt. Mitchell, NC
Colorado	Mt. Elbert
Hawaii	Mauna Kea
Oregon	Mt. Hood
New Hampshire	Mt. Washington
Tennessee	Clingman's Dome
Washington	Mt. Rainier
Turkey	Mt. Ararat
Greece	Mt. Olympus
Israel	Mt. Marion
Japan	Mt. Fuji (Fujiyama)
Great Britain	Ben Nevis
Canada	Mt. Logan

World Geography

Mountain Chains:

Arkansas-Missouri	Ozarks
California	Sierra Nevada
Georgia-North Carolina	Blue Ridge Mountains
Minnesota	Masabi Range
Montana-Wyoming	Bighorn Mountains
New England	Presidential Range
Northeastern New York	Adirondacks (home to Algonquin Peak)
Eastern Pennsylvania	Poconos
Southern New York	Catskills
South Dakota	Black Hills
Tennessee-North Carolina	Great Smoky Mountains
Vermont	Green Mountains
Washington-Oregon	Cascades
Wyoming	(Grand) Tetons
Canada-USA-Mexico	Rockies
Eastern USA	Appalachians
South central Europe	Alps
Eastern Europe	Carpathian
French-Spanish border	Pyrenees
New Zealand	Southern Alps
Northwest Africa	Atlas
North central Italy	Domolites
Central Italy	Apennines
India-Asia divider	Himalayas
Europe-Asia divider	Urals
Southwest Russia	Caucasus
South America	Andes
Spain	Sierra Nevada
Eastern United States	Appalachians

Famous mountains:

Ten Commandments	Mt. Sinai
Rio de Janeiro	Sugarloaf
Italian-Swiss border	Matterhorn
Iwo Jima	Mt. Suribachi
Atlanta	Stone Mountain
New Hampshire profile	Great Stone Face

Rivers:

World's longest rivers:
1. Nile
2. Amazon
3. Yangtze (China)
4. Mississippi
5. Ob-Irtysh (Russia)

Major River of:

Atlanta	Chattahoochee
Boston	Charles
Harrisburg, PA	Susquehanna (Three Mile Island)
Little Rock	Arkansas
Louisville-Cincinnati	Ohio
Washington, D.C.	Potomac
Alaska	Yukon
Idaho	Snake
Iowa	Des Moines
Montana	Missouri
Nebraska	(North) Platte
New York state	Hudson
New England	Connecticut
Hudson tributary	Mohawk
North Dakota	Red River (of the North)
Texas-New Mexico	Rio Grande
Virginia	James
West of the Rockies	Colorado
Baghdad	Tigris
Budapest	Danube
Cairo	Nile
Dublin	Liffey
Florence	Arno
Hamburg	Elbe
Kiev	Dnieper
Lisbon	Tagus
Liverpool	Mersey
London	Thames
Montreal	St. Lawrence
Paris	Seine
Rome	Tiber
Stalingrad	Volga
St. Petersburg	Neva
Vienna	Danube
Argentina-Uruguay	Rio de la Plata
Northwest Canada	Mackenzie

West central France	Loire
Northeast India	Ganges
Ireland	Shannon
Israel	Jordan
Pakistan	Indus
Poland	Vistula
Scotland	Clyde
Spain	Ebro
South Africa	Orange
Turkey	Meander
Venezuela	Orinoco
Vietnam and Cambodia	Mekong
Northern Vietnam	Red River
East Africa	Zambezi
West Africa	Congo
North and east Africa	Nile
Northwest Europe	Rhine
River that feeds Lake Geneva	Rhone
"Big Muddy" river	Missouri
Robert Burns' "Sweet" river	Afton

Volcanos:

Alaska	Mt. Readout
Hawaii	Kilauea
Washington	Mt. St. Helens
Indonesia	Krakatoa
Italian mainland	Mt. Vesuvius
Martinique	Mt. Pelee
Mexico	Paracuten
Montserrat	Soufriere
Philippines	Mt. Pinitubo
Sicily	Mt. Etna (Europe's highest volcano)
Antarctica	Mt. Erebus
Iceland	Mt. Hekla

Waterfalls:

World's highest waterfall	Angel Falls, Venezuela
U.S. highest waterfall	Ribbon Falls, Yosemite
Falls on the Zambezi River	Victoria Falls, Zimbabwe
Falls on the Brazil-Argentina border	Iguazu Falls
Falls between Lakes Erie and Ontario	Niagra Falls
Major Falls in Natal, South Africa	Tugela Falls

World War I 61

World War I's original name before WW II .... The Great War

His assassination started the war .... Archduke Francis Ferdinand

City where Francis Ferdinand was assassinated .... Sarajevo

Germany, Austria-Hungary alliance .... Central Powers

Britain, France, and Russia alliance .... Triple Entente

General of U.S. Armies, 1918 .... Gen. John "Blackjack" Pershing

French leader .... Georges Clemenceau

German leader .... Kaiser Wilhelm II

German flying ace .... Baron Manfred von Richtofen
                                                                                (The Red Baron, 80 kills)

Maker of Richtofen's airplane type .... Fokker

American flying ace .... Eddie Rickenbacker

Battle that stopped German advance, 1914 .... First Battle of the Marne

British passinger liner sank, May, 1915 .... Lusitania

British-German naval battle for the North Sea, 1916 .... Battle of Jutland

Major French/German battle, 1916....................................... Battle of Verdun

Start of Allied offensive, 1918 .... Second Battle of the Marne

French Marshall at the Battle of the Marne .... Marshall Ferdinand Foch

Hero of the Battle of Argonne .... Alvin York

Female spy for Germany in France .... Mata Hari

Mata Hari's native country .... The Netherlands

Ill-fated Turkish landing site .... Gallipoli

Woodrow Wilson's post-war policy .... Fourteen points

Belgian cemetery .... Flanders Field

German 43-ton Howitzer .... "Big Bertha"

British nurse executed by the Germans................................. Dame Edith Cavell

Salvation Army worker .... Evangeline Booth

Treaty ending the war .... Treaty of Versailles

62 *World War II*

Allied Supreme Commander .... Dwight Eisenhower
American general of the 12th Army Group in Europe .... Omar Bradley
American general of the 3rd Army in Europe .... George S. Patton
British general in North Africa .... Bernard Montgomery
Top French general .... Charles De Gaulle
German tank commander known as "Desert Fox".................... Erwin Rommel
British leader who declared "Peace in our time" .... Neville Chamberlain
British leader following Chamberlain .... Winston Churchill
Nazi SS chief .... Heinrich Himmler
Nazi air force reichsmarschall .... Herman Goering
Nazi propaganda chief .... Joseph Goebbels
Nazi architect .... Albert Speer
Nazi foreign minister .... Joachim von Ribbentrop
"The Butcher of Lyon" .... Klaus Barbie
Hitler aide who parachuted into Scotland .... Rudolf Hess
Nazi doctor known as the "Angel of Death" .... Josef Mengele
Nazi captured in Argentina and hanged in 1962 .... Adolf Eichmann
Hitler's mistress .... EvaBraun
German secret state police .... Gestapo
Chief of the U.S. Army air forces .... Hap Arnold
U.S. ambassador to Great Britain at start of war .... Joseph Kennedy
Seat of the occupied French government .... Vichy
Head of the Vichy French government and WW I hero .... Henri Petain
French defense line facing Germany .... Maginot Line
Part of Czechoslovakia ceded to Germany by Munich Pact ...... Sudetenland
Country divided by Germany and Soviet Union, 1939 .... Poland
Russian who signed non-agression pact with Hitler .... Vyacheslav Molotov
Head of Germany's V2 rocket program .... Werner von Braun
Country invaded by Italy in 1939 .... Albania
French port where 337,000 soldiers were evacuated in 1940 .... Dunkirk
Cooperation agreement signed by FDR and Churchill .... Atlantic Charter
Agreement by the U.S. to aid Britain with war materials .... Lend/Lease
Hitler's mountain hideaway .... Berchtesgarten
German "lightning war" .... Blitzkrieg
German pocket battleship scuttled in Montevideo harbor .... *Graf Spee*
German battleship that sunk the *HMS Hood* .... *Bismarck*
Location of decisive allied victory in North Africa .... El-Alamein
Air battle between the RAF and the Luftwaffe .... The Battle of Britain
Code name for German invasion of Soviet Union .... Operation Barbarossa
Code name for D-Day invasion .... Operation Overlord
D-Day date .... June 6, 1944

D-Day beaches..Omaha, Sword, Juno, Gold, Utah
Beach with the most casualties .... Omaha
Germany's final western offensive .... Battle of the Bulge
Response given by General McAuliffe at Bastogne .... "Nuts!"
Largest land battle in history, central Russia .... Battle of Kursk
Most decorated U.S. soldier .... Audie Murphy
Japanese general who ordered attack on Pearl Harbor .... Tojo
Japanese admiral who planned attack on Pearl Harbor .... Yamamoto
Largest Japanese battle ship .... Yamato
Pearl Harbor day .... December 7, 1941
U.S. Pacific fleet commander .... Chester Nimitz
U.S. Third Fleet commander .... William "Bull" Halsey
"The Napoleon of Luzon" .... Douglas MacArthur
Island in Manila Bay lost to Japanese in 1942 .... Corregidor
Island site of first major U.S. offensive against the Japanese ..... Guadalcanal
Five brothers killed in battle of Guadalcanal .... (Fighting) Sullivans
Naval battle off coast of Australia, 1942 .... Battle of Coral Sea
Naval battle in central Pacific, 1942 .... Battle of Midway
Largest sea battle in history of the coast off the Philippines ..... Battle of Leyte Gulf
Island where the U.S. flag was raised on Mt. Suribachi .... Iwo Jima
Leader of 1942 air raid on Tokyo .... Jimmy Doolittle
Code name for U.S. atomic bomb project .... Manhattan Project
Man who headed the Manhattan Project .... Robert Oppenheimer
Plane that dropped atomic bomb on Hiroshima .... *Enola Gay*
Enola Gay commander .... Paul W. Tibbetts
Name for Hiroshima bomb .... Little Boy
Plane that dropped atomic bomb on Nagasaki .... Bockscar
Name for Nagasaki bomb .... Fat Man
First conference site of Roosevelt, Stalin and Churchill .... Teheran, Iran
Asian site of Roosevelt, Stalin and Churchill's 1943 conference
.... Yalta (in the Crimea)
African site of Roosevelt and Churchill's 1943 conference .... Casablanca, Morocco
Postwar conference site of Truman, Stalin and Churchill .... Potsdam, Germany
Site where De Gaulle directed Free French government .... Algiers
Term for a female U.S. factory worker .... Rosie the Riveter
U.S. journalist killed in the Pacific, 1945 .... Ernie Pyle
Native American language used as code .... Navajo
Battleship where Japanese signed surrender .... *Missouri*
V-E (victory in Europe) Day .... May 8, 1945
V-J (victory over Japan) Day .... September 2, 1945
Plan to rebuild Europe after the war .... Marshall Plan
Army deserter executed in 1945 .... Eddie Slovak
Post-war prison where Rudolph Hess was held .... Spandau

63 *Zodiac*

Aries the Ram .... Mar 21-Apr 20

Taurus the Bull .... April 21-May 21

Gemini the Twins .... May 22-June 22

Cancer the Crab .... June 22-July 22

Leo the Lion .... Jul 23-Aug 23

Virgo the Virgin .... Aug 24-Sept 22

Libra the Scales .... Sept 23-Oct 23

Scorpio the Scorpion .... Oct 24-Nov 23

Sagittarius the Archer .... Nov 24-Dec 21

Capricorn the Goat .... Dec 22-Jan 20

Aquarius the Water Bearer .... Jan 21-Feb 18

Pisces the Fish .... Feb 19-Mar 20

CHINESE ZODIAC

Born in:

1952, 1964, 1976, 1988, 2000 .... Year of the Dragon

1953, 1965, 1977, 1989. 2001 .... Year of the Snake

1942, 1954, 1966, 1978, 1990 .... Year of the Horse

1943, 1955, 1967, 1979, 1991 .... Year of the Sheep

1944, 1956, 1968, 1980, 1992 .... Year of the Monkey

1945, 1957, 1969, 1981, 1993 .... Year of the Cock

1946, 1958, 1970, 1982, 1994 .... Year of the Dog

1947, 1959, 1971, 1983, 1995 .... Year of the Boar

1948, 1960, 1972, 1984, 1996 .... Year of the Rat

1949, 1961, 1973, 1985, 1997 .... Year of the Ox

1950, 1962, 1974, 1986, 1998 .... Year of the Tiger

1951, 1963, 1975, 1987, 1999 .... Year of the Rabbit